The Conduct
of the Christian Schools

CONDUITE

DES

ECOLES CHRETIENNES

DIVISE'E EN DEUX PARTIES.

prenez-garde à vous, & ayez foin d'en-
feigner les autres ; Perfeverez dans ces
hexercices, car par ce moyen vous vous
fauverez vous-mefme, & vous fau-
verez ceux qui vous ecoutent 1. Epit.
à Timoth. 4. 16.

A AVIGNON,!

Chez JOSEPH CHARLES CHASTANIER, Im-
primeur & Libraire , proche le College des
R. R. P. P. Jefuittes.

M. D.CC, XX.

AVEC PERMISSION DES SUPERIEURS

Frontispiece: A reproduction of the first page of the printed edition of 1720.

The Conduct
of the Christian Schools
by John Baptist de La Salle

Translated by F. de La Fontainerie
and
Richard Arnandez, FSC

Edited with notes by William Mann, FSC

1996
Lasallian Publications
Landover, Maryland 20785

This volume is a translation of *Conduite des Ecoles chrétiennes* by
John Baptist de La Salle

Lasallian Publications

Sponsored by the Regional Conference of Christian Brothers
of the United States and Toronto

The Conduct of the Christian Schools
is volume 6 of Lasallian Sources:
The Complete Works of John Baptist de La Salle.
Copyright © 1996 by Christian Brothers Conference,
Landover, Maryland, 20785
All rights reserved

Printed in the United States of America

Library of Congress card catalog number 95-069329
ISBN 0-944808-13-1 (hardbound)
ISBN 0-944808-14-x (paperback)

Cover: "Brothers' pupils leaving church after Mass." Painting by Jean-Joseph
Lacroix. Supplied from Emile Rousset, FSC. *John Baptist de La Salle Icono-
graphie*. Slide 178. Boulogne, 1979.

Lasallian Publications

Sponsored by the Regional Conference of Christian Brothers of the United States and Toronto, Lasallian Publications will produce 30 volumes on the life, writings, and work of John Baptist de La Salle (1651–1719), founder of the Brothers of the Christian Schools, and on the early history of the Brothers. These volumes will be presented in two series.

✦ Lasallian Sources, in 13 volumes, consists of new English translations and editions of all the writings of John Baptist de La Salle.
✦ Lasallian Resources consists of the three early biographies of John Baptist de La Salle, four thematic studies based on the documents contemporary with the foundation of the Brothers of the Christian Schools, and translations and editions of current Lasallian studies.

Volumes Already Published in This Series

Lasallian Sources

The Letters of John Baptist de La Salle. Translated and edited by Colman Molloy, FSC, and Augustine Loes, FSC (1988).

The Rules of Christian Decorum and Civility. Translated by Richard Arnandez, FSC, and edited by Gregory Wright, FSC (1990).

Collection of Various Short Treatises. Translated by William J. Battersby, FSC, and edited by Daniel Burke, FSC (1993).

Meditations by John Baptist de La Salle. Translated by Richard Arnandez, FSC, and Augustine Loes, FSC. Edited by Augustine Loes, FSC, and Francis Huether, FSC (1994).

Explanation of the Method of Interior Prayer. Original translation by Richard Arnandez, FSC. Revised and edited by Donald Mouton, FSC (1995).

Lasallian Resources

Early Biographies

The Life of John Baptist de La Salle. Canon John Baptist Blain. Translated by Richard Arnandez, FSC (1985).

Early Documents

John Baptist de La Salle: The Formative Years. Luke Salm, FSC (1989).

Current Lasallian Studies

John Baptist de La Salle and Special Education: A Study of Saint Yon. Othmar Würth, FSC. Translated by Augustine Loes, FSC. Adapted by Francis Huether, FSC. Edited by Bonaventure Miner, FSC (1988).

So Favored by Grace: Education in the Time of John Baptist de La Salle. Edited by Lawrence J. Colhocker, FSC (1991).

Contents

Part Two
Means of Establishing and Maintaining Order in the Schools

APPENDIXES
Appendix A
Part Three: Duties of the Inspector of Schools

Appendix B
Extracts from the 1706 Manuscript of *Conduite*

Appendix C
The Training of New Teachers

Foreword

It is a great pleasure to present to the English-speaking world a new and expanded translation of John Baptist de La Salle's monumental contribution to the history of pedagogy, *Conduite des Ecoles chrétiennes.* The *Conduite* originally appeared in manuscript form in 1706; and De La Salle revised it constantly, in consultation with the Brothers. The first printed edition was published posthumously in 1720.

The present publication is an expansion and modification of the 1935 translation by F. de La Fontainerie of that 1720 edition. That translation has been revised here and is supplemented in the appendices with translations by Richard Arnandez of material heretofore unavailable in English. All of this material is introduced in a new, clear, and insightful Introduction by Brother Edward Everett.

The main body of the text is the translation of the 1720 Edition of the *Conduite* as it appears in *Cahiers lasalliens*[1] 24 (CL 24). It includes the cover letter by Brother Timothée, the Second Superior General of the Brothers of the Christian Schools, the Preface, Part One of the *Conduite,* "School Practices and the Manner in Which They Are to Be Carried Out," and Part Two, "Means of Establishing and Maintaining Order in the Schools."

Appendix A is Part Three, "Duties of the Inspector of Schools." This is a translation of the 1706 Manuscript of the *Conduite* and can be found in CL 24:249–290. Appendix B is a compilation of passages from the 1706 Manuscript which were included neither in the 1720 printed edition nor in the 1935 de La Fontainerie edition. Most of Appendix B can be found in CL 24:231–248. Throughout Appendix B the reader is provided with the page references in CL 24 on which the passages can be found.

This material is provided here to show the reader the more significant changes in the text made between 1706 and 1720 by De La Salle and the first Brothers. What is provided here is only a flavor. Someone would have to compare the two French texts to make a more thorough analysis.

Appendix C was not written by De La Salle. Unfortunately we no longer have an original copy of "The Training of New Teachers," which was originally included in the Third Part of the *Conduite.*

Appendix C presents the translation of a document which is found in the Departmental Archives of Vaucluse (Avignon). It is classified under the heading, "Brothers of the Christian Schools of Avignon" (H.1.2.3). It is a simple copybook with no cover, measures about 46 by 36 centimeters and contains 24 pages and a few additional lines. The first page carries the title "The Training of New Teachers." The entire manuscript is in good eighteenth-century calligraphy.

A copy of this document was made in Avignon in August–September of 1931 by Brother Donat-Charles, Archivist of the Institute of the Brothers of the Christian Schools. In addition to the method of "Training New Teachers," this document includes the "Manual of the Prefect of the Boarding Students," and a listing of the "Various Types of Community Houses in This Institute." Neither is found in the original *Conduite.* This is a translation of the document as found on pages 305–319 of the 1951 French *édition critique* of the *Conduite* by Brother Anselme D'Haese.

At points, the editing of the present text proved to be a rather complicated process. A serious attempt was made to provide a clean, clear, and simplified text. While the Editor has adhered faithfully to the original document, it was occasionally necessary to recast whole sentences. In some places, the cross-references of the text were made much more explicit. Where possible, every effort was made to use inclusive language. Unfortunately, this sometimes led to some additional awkwardness and some necessary repetition; but, hopefully, readers will keep in mind that this is an eighteenth-century text.

The English title of the work has been the subject of much controversy among editors and readers. Some argued in favor of retaining "The Conduct of Schools." Others thought that "The Management of Schools" was a more appropriate and timely title. However, a study of the uses of the word *conduire,* a word so important and rich in the writings of De La Salle, led this Editor to favor *The Conduct of the Christian Schools* as the title for this edition.

My fervent wish is that this new edition of *Conduite des Ecoles chrétiennes* might help sustain the enthusiasm so obvious these days in recapturing the great vision of the Christian school and teacher in the Christian school embodied in the writings of John Baptist de La Salle.

WILLIAM MANN, FSC
Rome, Casa Generalizia
December 1995

Acknowledgments

Very special thanks are owed to Brothers Richard Arnandez and Edward Everett for their assistance with this project. Brother Leonard Marsh spent hours assisting the Editor to clarify phrasings and to make decisions concerning various word choices throughout the text. Many others also contributed to bringing this work to completion. Brothers Erminus Joseph Melofchik and Jules Chambert read the manuscript to guarantee the accuracy of the translation. In addition to assisting in guaranteeing the accuracy of the translation, Brothers Oswald Murdoch, Edward Everett, Paul Grass, and Robert Daszkiewicz contributed numerous excellent suggestions and alternative wordings for an improved and clearer text. Brothers Paul and Oswald were especially helpful in bringing the "Duties of the Inspector of Schools" (Appendix A) to its present form. At various stages, Brothers Joseph Dougherty, Kevin Junk, Robert Romano, Joseph Schmidt, and Francis Huether also provided helpful suggestions and criticism.

Brother Bernard Richard provided invaluable computer technical assistance, and Brother Francis Huether was Copy Editor. Saint Mary's Press, Winona, MN, provided excellent professional help. Mrs. Carol Hamm of the Christian Brothers Regional Office demonstrated extraordinary patience in the many hours of typing and retyping that went into the original revisions of the manuscript. A special word of thanks is owed to Mrs. Jane Gabel Dreher, whose generous gift expedited this project. To all of these individuals, a very sincere word of thanks.

Introduction

Background and Influences

The seventeenth century was a time of crisis for traditional elementary education in France. A new kind of primary school teacher appeared, and a new manner of educating developed in which corporal punishment diminished, school attendance increased, and French came into its own as the language of education. John Baptist de La Salle was one of the prime movers of this educational reform, and *Conduite des Ecoles chrétiennes, The Conduct of the Christian Schools,* is the instrument of his success. Hereafter, we shall identify the text simply as the *Conduite*.

Hundreds of treatises on pedagogy were published in the seventeenth century. The grand career of a philosopher or an essayist, such as Montaigne or Fleury, was not complete unless it included a treatise on education. The Protestant Reformation and the Catholic Counter-Reformation converged in agreement upon the importance of primary schooling. Nearly every page of the register of the deliberations of a French town council under the *ancien régime* has to do with questions of education: contracting for a new teacher, levying a municipal tax for education, repairing the roof of the *grande école,* or just setting a date for the distribution of school prizes. The Jesuits had achieved a reputation for excellence in secondary education that was recognized throughout Europe. The convent schools run by nuns of the Ursuline and Visitation orders flourished as finishing schools for wealthy girls. Since the time of Louise de Marillac and Alix LeClerc many women had opted for the innovative non-cloistered, religious community lifestyle emerging in the Catholic Church. Many of these women were committed to the education of poor girls in parish schools, and at the time of De La Salle there were thousands of these teaching "Sisters" throughout France. In general, there was no lack of primary schooling in France when John Baptist de La Salle came on the educational scene.

The weakest element in French primary education, however, was the preparation of its male teachers. Teaching the poor in primary schools was an unattractive, often part-time position filled by those unable to do better elsewhere. A seventeenth-century pamphlet lampooned the superintendent of schools in Paris, *le grand chântre,* for employing as teachers a motley collection of "low pot-house keepers, second-hand shop proprietors, silk-weaver flunkies, wig makers, and marionette string pullers." Invectives such as these reveal the deep dissatisfaction that the male teachers provoked. Even the clergy involved in education, particularly in rural areas, were neither well-educated nor trained as teachers.

Traditionally, primary school teachers were under the authority of the diocesan superintendent of schools, whose responsibility it was to guarantee that the increase in the number of schools for the poor did not cause financial hardship for the teachers. With Gallican stubbornness, Claude Joly, the superintendent of schools in Paris, carried on a fight in the courts for forty years to resist the enforcement of the decrees of the Council of Trent to decentralize authority over teachers in the reform of the parish schools. De La Salle was caught in this conflict between the problems of primary schooling for the poor and the forces resisting educational reform.

Following upon the path taken by the teaching Sisters, De La Salle struggled his entire life to train male primary teachers for both city and rural schools. The results of De La Salle's efforts at teacher education indicate only partial success. The training institutes for rural schoolteachers that he established in Rethel, Reims, Paris, and Saint Denis during a thirty-year period all closed after a few years, primarily due to opposition from the established educational authorities. However, in forming city schoolteachers, De La Salle enjoyed considerable success. With the intention of forming and animating these schoolteachers with an evangelical spirit and total dedication to the instruction and Christian education of the children of the working class and the poor, De La Salle founded the Institute of the Brothers of the Christian Schools. This community of lay teachers has continued to flourish for over 300 years. The *Conduite* is the result of thirty-five years of collaboration between the educational guidance of De La Salle and the classroom experience of these teachers, who were called Brothers.

De La Salle did not operate in an educational vacuum, and the *Conduite* was not created *ex nihilo.* His own schooling, his association with friends actively involved in teacher-education reform, his study of the works of earlier and contemporary educational innovators, and, above all, his sharing in the classroom experience of his Brothers, all contributed to the writing of the *Conduite*. As good teachers often reflect the good teaching they received, so it was with De La Salle. His own schooling began at the college of the University of Reims, continued at the Seminary of Saint Sulpice in Paris, and concluded with a doctorate in theology from the University of Reims.

Through his association with his close friend Nicolas Roland, De La Salle became familiar with the work of teaching Sisters and worked to obtain legal approval for the Sisters of the Congregation of the Infant Jesus, who taught poor girls and orphans in Reims. At a chance meeting in the Sister's convent with Adrien Nyel, De La Salle unwittingly got caught up in the educational reform movement erupting in northeastern France. Adrien Nyel, a dedicated charity school teacher and administrator from Rouen, introduced De La Salle to the problems of establishing primary schools for the sons of the working class and the poor, and together they formed a six-year partnership for the establishment of these schools. Nyel worked at opening schools; De La Salle worked at forming teachers.

De La Salle's spiritual advisor, Nicolas Barré, founded twin congregations of teaching Sisters and Brothers in Rouen and Paris. Barré's teaching Sisters flourished; but the Brothers who were established by Barré, and who for a while were sometimes mistaken by the public in Paris as De La Salle's teaching Brothers, quickly vanished without a trace. Despite his own failure to establish a permanent foundation of male teachers, Barré encouraged De La Salle in that very task. When De La Salle was discouraged and ready to abandon the project, Barré was among those who inspired him to keep going. Barré's pedagogical writings, a rule for teachers living in community entitled *Statutes and Regulations,* and a book of reflections for teachers, entitled *Maximes,* became inspirational works for De La Salle.

De La Salle was also influenced by Charles Démia, the remarkable educational reformer and superintendent of schools in the diocese of Lyon. It was from Démia that De La Salle purchased his first textbooks and school supplies. Démia outlined his teacher reform in *Règlements,* a book of rules for teachers. De La Salle was deeply moved by Démia's *Remonstrances* (1668), a passionate plea for public support of primary schooling for the poor. De La Salle was to imitate the language of this manifesto, albeit less forcefully, when he would later describe in his own writings the plight of the poor children in Reims and Paris. With the powerful backing of the *Company of the Blessed Sacrament,* a secret association of wealthy clergy and laity, Démia had established a diocesan school board to enact strict teacher-hiring practices and mandatory in-service teacher institutes. Démia also started the Seminary of Saint Charles, where primary school teaching formed an important step in the preparation for ordination. Historians of education still debate whether Démia's seminary, which preceded De La Salle's teacher-training institute by twelve years, qualifies as the first teacher-training school. Recent research into the Seminary's records shows that six out of ten candidates at Saint Charles went on to the priesthood and that three out of ten became schoolteachers. In *Avis Important,* a proposal to King Louis XIV for the establishment of a primary teacher training program in every diocese of France, Démia cited with praise the example of De La Salle's teacher-education program in Reims. Nevertheless, De La Salle's organization for educational reform was very different from Démia's. De La Salle envisioned his community of lay teachers in terms of one autonomous, centralized organization serving all of France and deliberately divorced from clerical identification and diocesan territorial limitations.

Furthermore, De La Salle was directly influenced in writing the *Conduite* by the work of Jacques de Bathencour, a priest who taught for eighteen years in the parish school of Saint Nicholas du Chardonnet in Paris. The wealth of De Bathencour's experience was published in 1654 under the title, *L'Escole paroissiale (The Parish School).* This book became the official manual for the more than 300 primary school teachers in Paris and was popular as well in the other cities of France. *L'Escole paroissiale* was the best that seventeenth-century France could provide for primary education, but it was not adequate to De La Salle's vision of the Christian school. De Bathencour did provide De La Salle with a practical paradigm for the *Conduite,* whose own structure and content are best understood in contrast with that of *L'Escole paroissiale.*

L'Escole paroissiale is divided into four parts. Like a seminary manual, the book begins by deducing the theological and moral virtues needed by the teacher "for such a humble occupation." It then deals with school administration: the physical disposition of the classroom, the admission practices of the school, and the roles of teacher assistants and student monitors. The second part deals with religious instruction: the various catechisms to be used and the method of preparing students for the sacraments. The third part deals with secular instruction: reading in Latin and French, penmanship, Latin grammar, and the daily schedule. The fourth part constitutes a separate student handbook and deals with the rules for writing in French, the four operations in arithmetic, a short form of the catechism, the rules of politeness, and the rules for plain chant.

In general, De La Salle reversed the order of *L'Escole paroissiale* and infused the material with a new vision. He eliminated the deductive and somewhat demeaning approach of De Bathencour's work and established practical school experience as the basis of his approach to teacher training. He emphasized a practical orientation to spelling and arithmetic. He transformed education into a group learning event and curtailed the great amount of time spent by the teacher in supervising the solitary recitation of individual students. He held to what was then understood as small class size, fifty or sixty instead of eighty or a hundred students, and identified a strong teacher-student relationship as the key to learning. He eliminated the practices of discriminating against the poor and of disciplining slow students by ridicule, and tempered and restructured the authority of school monitors.

De La Salle made religious instruction the heart of his school and created a simple, uniform curriculum and method for use in all Lasallian establishments. In a notable change he joined a small, radical movement by teaching reading directly through the French language instead of the almost universal method of using first Latin as the model.

Because of a longstanding misconception on the place of Latin in the Lasallian school, it would be well to clarify this matter.[1] In all upper schools in eighteenth century France, instruction and questions and answers were in Latin; in the primary schools, where the Brothers worked, instruction was in French, except that the instruction in reading was through Latin sounds and words.

Since Latin is something of a phonetic language, students learned the sounds of the letters and their combination into words, on the principle that "What you see is what you say, even if you do not know what it means." De La Salle and others like him simply felt that reading should begin with what the students were hearing already, however difficult: "What you read is what you hear all the time." De La Salle's contribution was his detailed method and especially his French speller, which was in use till the mid-nineteenth century.[2]

De La Salle was not alone in holding this position. The Oratorian Fathers conducted successful secondary schools with a curriculum taught in the vernacular. Claude Fleury, the aristocratic educational historiographer, provided in his learned studies an historical and theoretical basis for the modernist position. The Jansenist Sages taught in the vernacular at the Little Schools of Port-Royal, and the French protestants, using the vernacular, conducted their own academies in the south of France. For reasons of prudence and orthodoxy, De La Salle makes no mention of the modernists in his writing. A concern for student interest, student achievement, social utility, and the needs of practical Christian faith motivated De La Salle's commitment to this position; these reasons are developed in a letter De La Salle wrote to the Bishop of Chartres, who was a traditionalist in this matter.

Finally, the *Conduite* needs to be complemented by De La Salle's vision of teaching as a Christian ministry. This vision is presented in his *Méditations pour le temps de la retraite* (CL 13). In his last years, De La Salle gave expression to the evangelical dimension of a teacher's life in these meditations. They provide a profound and personal synthesis of his own life in teacher education. Perhaps nowhere in the history of education has such an exalted and spiritual conception of the teacher been developed in richer detail. These meditations are sixteen religious reflections on a new kind of teacher-student relationship, which is based on love and mutual respect. De La Salle calls the teacher to a tender, fraternal, and concerned conversion. The teachers are invited to see themselves as called by God to touch and to win the hearts of the students, to be like an older "brother" who guides them, and to act as a guardian angel entrusted with protecting the physical and moral welfare of these young people. The teacher's love, "as gentle as a mother and as firm as a father," is to be understood as the visible sacrament of the love of God for each child.

De La Salle lovingly embraces these children of God; he urges his teachers to assume a loving and tender stance in their ministry. "You ought to have for them the tenderness of a mother in order to receive them and to do for them all the good which depends upon you" (*Méditations sur les principales fêtes de l'année* [CL 12: M 101.3]). "Regard your students as the children of God himself. Have much more care for their education and for their instruction than you would have for the children of a king" (CL 12: M 133.2).

In his meditations, De La Salle further develops his vision of the function of the teacher through other images. The teacher "dresses the students every day with Jesus Christ" and "writes on their hearts"; the teacher is their shepherd, shining light, master builder, and cultivator. Unlike classical French literature, which embraced humanism and rationalism but did not pay much attention to its children, the *Méditations pour le temps de la retraite* uses the noun "child" most frequently, after titles referring to the deity: ninety times.

The *Conduite* prescribes the practices which follow upon the images of the teacher described in the *Méditations pour le temps de la retraite.* The teachers, no longer called "Masters" but "Brothers," apply themselves to acquire an attractive, affable, and approachable appearance. They put themselves within reach of the students and speak to the children on their own level. They do not use clever words; every word is clear and easy to understand. They are sympathetic with the vulnerabilities of the young and the difficulties of growing up; and they are concerned for the mental, physical, social, and moral development of each student.

History

The history of the *Conduite* is the history of a book in process. From its conception, the book has undergone constant change. The evolution of the text is attested to by the 24 printed editions and numerous manuscripts preserved in the archives at the Generalate of the Brothers of the Christian Schools in Rome. This evolution can be traced through four phases: (1) its creation by De La Salle and the first Brothers; (2) its revision, begun around 1718; (3) its restoration begun by Brother Agathon in 1777; and (4) the increasingly radical adaptation sanctioned by Brother Philippe in 1860.

Creation Phase. The *Conduite* is not the creation of De La Salle alone. It is a product of the collective teaching experience of the first Brothers, and it evolved through the interaction of these men with De La Salle. As early as 1705, the *Règles communes des Frères des Ecoles chrétiennes* (CL 25) makes reference to the *Conduite* as the "rules of the school." The oldest extant copy from this period of creation is a manuscript dating from 1706, which is conserved in the National Library in Paris (ms. fr. 11759). Its Preface attests to its creation by collaboration and experimentation:

> This guide has been prepared and put in order ("by the late M. De La Salle" was added in the Preface of the edition of 1720) only after a great number of conferences between him and the oldest Brothers of the Institute and those most capable of running a school well, and after several years of experience. Nothing has been added that has not been thoroughly deliberated and well tested, nothing of which the advantages and disadvantages have not been weighed and, as far as possible, of which the good or bad consequences have not been foreseen (Preface 1706).

De La Salle met frequently with the Brothers in an atmosphere of open discussion and participative decision making to improve upon the running of the schools. The notes from these meetings were compiled into working documents which circulated among the Brothers for many years before the *Conduite* appeared in printed form. Judging from the similarity between the text of the manuscript of 1706 and that of the printed edition of 1720, one would assume that the text was fairly well determined at least fifteen years before its first printing.

As the general practice among the early Brothers was that each beginning teacher made his own copy of the *Conduite*, it is easy to understand how mistakes and inaccuracies entered into the unpublished text. The manuscript of 1706 is without the name of the author and is not in the handwriting of De La Salle or of his secretary. Written possibly by a novice and obviously in haste, it contains several textual and typographical errors. Such mistakes, however, do not account for the complete omission of Chapter 10 of the manuscript, "School Hymns." It is known that songs were sung at the close of the school day and that De La Salle collected and edited nearly one hundred hymns, most of which were set to well-known and popular tunes. However, the page on which the title "School Hymns" appears is otherwise blank.

Fortunately, the peculiarities of twelve sections which are unique to the manuscript of 1706 give a clearer picture of the composition of the first schools. For example, the models of the records of individual students contained in these sections highlight the concern and attention that De La Salle and the Brothers had for each individual student. Two such model records contained in the manuscript of 1706 can be found in Appendix B of this text. They are: (1) the Register of Reception of Jean Mulot, and (2) the Registers of Behavior of François de Terieux and Lambert du Long.

The sections dealing with the causes for frequent absence (See Appendix B) provide an excellent sociological analysis of a major social problem of the time. The sections also suggest the reason why the Register of Home Visitations was dropped: the practice put too much responsibility on the Student Visitors of the Absent Students and did not work. Another section provides a description of the duties of five student officers in the classrooms of the Christian schools (See Appendix B). This glimpse into the functions of the Mass officer, the Almoner, the First Student in the Bench, the Visitors of the Absent Students, and the Distributor and Collector of Books, gives an extended picture of student involvement that would otherwise be missed. In two additional sections, it is revealed that the writing lesson was organized originally into eight levels of instruction and that young people not enrolled in the school were allowed, under certain conditions, to attend the Sunday catechism lesson (See Appendix B).

The most important section unique to the 1706 manuscript, however, is Part Three, on the duties of the "Inspector of Schools" (Appendix A). Contained therein is a detailed description of the responsibilities of this most important position for teacher development.

Revision Phase. The second stage in the history of the evolution of the *Conduite* is the revision phase, which began around 1718 and led to the first printed edition of 1720. In the Foreword to this edition, Brother Timothée, Superior General 1720–1751, speaks of the incorporation of the revisions suggested to De La Salle by the General Assembly of Brothers in 1717 and those made under the direction of Brother Barthélemy, Superior General, 1717–1720, with the approval of the General Assembly of 1720. These revisions were made to meet the increased demand of the Brothers to correct the inaccuracies and errors caused by copyists, to eliminate what is no longer useful, and to give the text a better order. The printed edition of 1720 eliminated the blank tenth chapter on "School Hymns" and 12 other sections. The only models of the records of individual students to survive in the 1720 edition of the *Conduite* were: (1) the Register of Promotions and (2) the Register of Levels in Lessons. The sample names in the models of these student records were prudently dropped from the 1720 edition. Fear of the harm their discovery might bring to the concerned students and parents by outside agents antagonistic to De La Salle's successes seems to have necessitated this decision.

Another matter of note is that the Foreword of the 1720 edition does not explain the discrepancy between the new title page, which indicates that the *Conduite* is divided into two parts, and its Preface, which retains the statement that the book is divided into three parts. Apparently, this third section on the functions of the Inspector of Schools and the Training of New Teachers was omitted in the printing of 1720 on the grounds that its publication would have had only limited usage. Unfortunately, the decision not to print this third section resulted in its subsequent loss. Furthermore, it left the *Conduite* with a rather abrupt and truncated ending.

The Foreword also fails to mention a few additions to the text: (1) a chapter on the construction, uniformity, and furnishings of the school building; (2) a lengthy introduction to Chapter Five on correction in general; and (3) the addition of a list of the twelve virtues of a good teacher at the end of the text. This list of virtues can also be found in De La Salle's *Recueil de differents petits traités à l'usage des Frères des Ecoles chrétiennes* (CL 15).

Restoration Phase. The restoration phase, or the third stage, of the evolution of the *Conduite*, is concerned with the reformulation of the original text as a manual for teacher education.

While demonstrating fidelity to the spirit of the work of De La Salle and the early Brothers, various adaptations to the text were made. For example, two identical eighteenth-century manuscripts, known as *Archive Manuscripts* 39 and 40 and presently at the archives of the Generalate of the Brothers of the Christian Schools in Rome, add two six-page sections: (1) "What a Brother Ought to Think about His Profession" and (2) "The Means He Ought to Take to Teach Well." Another manuscript, numbered 45, was written in 1777 by Brother Agathon, Superior General, who was directed by the General Chapter of 1777 to include a section on the duties of the "Supervisor of the New Teachers." Brother Agathon had fortuitously discovered a partial manuscript dated 1696, which unfortunately has also since been lost. This partial manuscript apparently contained the third or missing section on the duties of the Supervisor of the New Teachers. The manuscript was obviously filled with the pioneering spirit of the Institute, and under its influence Brother Agathon did not hesitate to recreate the section on the education of the new teachers. Furthermore, he moved this section to the beginning of the *Conduite*.

> We see no difficulty that the treatise on the formation of teachers, which had never been printed before, occupies in this "re-founding" its logical place, the First Part. Does it not contain all the pedagogical essentials to be inculcated into the young teacher?
>
> This section is not new. It is as old as the Society of the Brothers of the Christian Schools. It is a collection of the precepts and practices that have always been taught and followed, as is evident by their conformity to the Brothers' rules, constitutions, and practices. It has not been printed sooner because it was for the particular use of the Inspector of Schools and the Supervisor of New Teachers, and the small number of copies needed for them could be supplied by handwritten copies. Unfortunately, however, the manuscripts developed errors due to the inaccuracies of the copyists and to the difficulty of keeping up with the increased number of copies needed. This present edition shall correct these inconveniences and shall produce a better expression of the good which is the goal of the *Conduite*. (Preface of 1787)

A twenty-four page notebook without cover, presently in the departmental archives at Avignon and entitled "The Training of New Teachers, or Part Three of the *Conduite*," has been determined to have been written in the eighteenth century by a hasty young man, very likely a novice copying the essential formulas of the missing 1696 manuscript referred to by Brother Agathon. The Avignon notebook is a treatment of the means of eliminating the qualities harmful in a new teacher and of acquiring the qualities necessary in a good teacher. The present work reproduces the Avignon manuscript in Appendix C. Except for the reformulation work of Brother Agathon, the partial Avignon manuscript is the only indication we have of the original treatment in the third part of the *Conduite*, of the duties of the Supervisor of New Teachers.

In his enthusiastic efforts at restoration, Brother Agathon did not hesitate to add a fourth section to the *Conduite*, one dealing with boarding schools. This addition was justified on the grounds that De La Salle had established the first boarding school as early as 1705 at Saint Yon in Rouen and that the Brothers had subsequently founded boarding schools during the eighteenth century. Brother Agathon also published a separate book, *The Twelve Virtues of a Good Teacher*, elaborating on the simple listing of these virtues supplied in the printed edition of 1720.

The 1811 edition of the *Conduite* restored, for the first time, the duties of the Supervisor of New Teachers and the duties of the Inspector of Schools to their original place at the conclusion of the text. The edition substantially curtailed the use of corporal punishment and further modified the section on correction by the use of a merit-demerit system.

Adaptation Phase. With the approval of the General Chapter, the edition of 1838 added history, geography, and drawing as new branches of study and, in a long note in the Preface, incorporated the mutual (British Lancastrian) method and the simultaneous-mutual method to the list of acceptable teaching methods. After eighteen years of resistance to its imposition on the schools of the Brothers by the French ministry of education, acceptance of the Lancastrian method was justified on the basis of its conformity to the spirit of the student involvement described in the manuscript of 1706. The students who were First in the Bench served as models and helpers (See Appendix B). The 1849 edition replaced the section on the duties of the Supervisor of the New Teachers with a thirty-five-page chapter, "The

Virtues and Qualities of the Teacher," inspired by Brother Agathon's "The Twelve Virtues of a Good Teacher."

This phase of adaptation is the fourth stage in the evolution of the *Conduite*. In 1860, Brother Philippe sanctioned this development when he officially recognized the *Conduite* as a book in process.

> We understand that a book of this nature is not able to receive a final form. New experiences, progress in methodology, legal prescriptions, and new needs demand that from time to time it undergo modification. The *Conduite* has already had several very different editions (Foreword of 1860).

Henceforth, the history of the text of the *Conduite* was characterized by updating and adaptation. Evolving school needs and improved pedagogical practices required change. Brother Philippe changed the title *Conduite des Ecoles chrétiennes* to *L'essai de conduite à l'usage des écoles chrétiennes (An Essay on School Management for Use in the Christian Schools)*. He suppressed all mention of corporal punishment; he expanded the curriculum to emphasize exercises of judgment over memory and ideas over words; and he published the duties of the Inspector of Schools and the Supervisor New Teachers in a separate book. In 1870, Brother Philippe's revision, with two additional sections, "The Twelve Virtues of a Good Teacher" and "The Supervisor of New Teachers," was translated into English under the title *School Management*. In 1887, De La Salle Institute in New York City published a 364-page edition of *The Management of the Christian Schools*, complete with programs for elementary, intermediate, and advanced classes, charts and forms, and a thirteen-page index; an updating appeared in 1907.

By the twentieth century, the *Conduite* had lost all resemblance to the tripartite structure of the manuscript of 1706. The edition of 1906 was divided into five sections: Education, School Regulations, Teaching Organization, Specialties of the Program, and Discipline. The 1916 edition, entitled *Management of the Christian Schools*, acknowledged the inspiration of De La Salle but also took into account progress in modern pedagogy and psychology.

The Brothers of the Christian Schools throughout the world regarded this process of continuous adaptation as the ongoing work of De La Salle. In 1960, the Brothers of the United States began an ambitious eleven-volume project, *The High School Management Series*, "to revise the Founder's manual, to bring it into line with the requirements of the modern era, to serve in the training program of the Brothers, and to integrate the ever increasing number of lay teachers into our school system" (Preface). After five years, the project was discontinued as "a vain attempt to impose an unwanted uniformity upon the rich diversity of teaching methods in American high schools." The interest in and usefulness of adapting the *Conduite* to meet present classroom management and teacher education needs had apparently run its course.

Fortunately, increased awareness of the importance of one's origins and of the unique charism of De La Salle as Founder have brought the evolution of editions of the *Conduite* around full circle. In 1935, F. de la Fontainerie translated the 1720 edition of the *Conduite* into English for the McGraw-Hill series of educational classics. In 1951, Brother Anselme D'Haese published the French critical edition of the manuscript of 1706. The introduction and notes from that edition provided the basis of much of this history of the text of the *Conduite*. In 1965, Brother Maurice-Auguste Hermans provided a French edition of the *Conduite*, in which the manuscript of 1706 and the first printed edition of 1720 are presented in parallel fashion (CL 24).

Brother Jean Pungier provided a brief commentary on the *Conduite* as "a spiritual book" in his *Comment est née la Conduite des Ecoles* (1980). Translated, this appeared in English as *If We Were to Rewrite How to Run the Christian Schools Today?* Brother Edward Everett's *John Baptist de La Salle's The Conduct of Schools: A Guide to Teacher Education* (Loyola University of Chicago, 1984), the Regional Education Committee of the Christian Brothers' *Characteristics of Lasallian Schools* (Romeoville, 1986), Brother William Mann's *The Lasallian School: Where Teachers Assist Parents in the Education and Formation of Children* (Colgate Rochester Divinity School, 1990), the International Secretariat of Education's *Characteristics of a Lasallian School Today* (Rome, 1987), Brother Frederick Mueller's *The Perceived and Preferred Goals of Principals, De La Salle Christian Brothers, and Lay Teachers in Lasallian Schools* (Boston College, 1994), and Brother George Van Grieken's *"To Touch Hearts": The Pedagogical Spirituality of John Baptist de La Salle* (Boston College, 1995) are further examples of the resurgence of interest in the English-speaking world of the unique contribution of Lasallian pedagogy as articulated by De La Salle and presented in the *Conduite*.

As already noted in the Foreword, this present publication has modified and supplemented the 1935 de La Fontainerie edition. Consequently, this edition provides a good glimpse into the *Conduite* as De La Salle and the first Brothers composed it.

Structure and Analysis of the Book

In *Democracy and Education,* John Dewey designates the trinity of topics in the educational enterprise as subject matter, teaching methods, and school administration. Two hundred fifty years before, De La Salle had given the same tripartite structure to the *Conduite*.

Part One of the book deals with subject matter. It includes classroom management, daily lessons, and religious activities, and is designed to help the apprentice teacher successfully "make it through the day." Part Two focuses on ways of creating a sense of community in the classroom. In addressing the issue of problem children, a somewhat "psychological" approach to obtaining order and discipline is enunciated. This section is designed to help the new teacher "make it through the year." In Part Three the manner of teaching presented in Part One and Part Two is solidified, supported, and reinforced by the offices of the Inspector of Schools and the Supervisor of New Teachers. This third section is designed to help launch the practicing teacher on the course of a successful career.

The following is a brief analysis of the significant topics presented in each of these three divisions.

Part One of *Conduite*

Subject Matter

With an eye to practical needs, De La Salle leads the apprentice teacher step-by-step through the school day. The ten chapters of Part One sequentially parallel the times and activities of the daily schedule. The time and activity of each lesson can be coordinated with an appropriate chapter in the *Conduite* (See Figure 1).

In Part One, the beginning teacher is introduced to the elements of classroom management. The teacher is responsible for establishing the psychological, social, and moral atmosphere which is capable of transforming the classroom into an environment which is both pleasant and conducive to learning. The beginning teacher learns to organize and manage the appropriate allocation of time, space, and motion in the classroom. Between the opening of school in the morning and the closing of school in the afternoon, nothing is left to chance. Students are to be kept focused on the task at hand. Individual student placement, learning activities, and promotion are carefully coordinated. A terminology (Place, Level, Lesson, Class, and School) is developed to identify the units of learning and make possible the aforementioned coordination.

- *Place in the classroom:* the seat or desk assigned to the student according to personal background, merit, or need in order to facilitate the student's learning of a designated portion or level of the lesson. For example, a light-headed student might be assigned a place between two serious students or a slow student might be assigned to sit next to a bright student.
- *Level of the lesson:* the ordinary teaching sub-units of a lesson according to the degree of difficulty determined by the number and kind of mistakes made by the students. Three levels are designated: beginning, intermediate, and advanced. The number of students studying the same level of the lesson ranges from five to

Hourly Schedule	School Activity	Chapter of Conduite
7:30-8:30	open school building; preparation for lessons, alone or in student-directed groups	One
8:00-8:30	morning prayer and breakfast; lesson review	Two
8:30-10:30	lessons in reading	Three
	lessons in writing	Four
	lessons in arithmetic	Five
	lessons in spelling	Six
10:30-11:30	reflection; prayer	Seven
	Mass in parish church	Eight
1:00-1:30	preparation for lessons, alone or in student-directed groups	
1:30-2:00	prayer and snack; lesson review	
2:00-3:30	continue lessons in reading writing, arithmetic, spelling	
3:30-4:00	lesson in catechism	Nine
4:00-4:30	examination of conscience; evening prayer; singing, dismissal, close building	Ten

Figure 1: Coordination of time and activity of each lesson in the school with the appropriate chapter in the *Conduite*.

fifteen. The level is the ordinary teaching unit. The teacher first teaches the students in the advanced level while those in the other two levels follow along quietly. The teacher then teaches the next lower level; the students previously taught supply the corrections. Students studying a different lesson work independently and quietly in their respective level groups.

- *Lesson:* the teaching unit of the material to be mastered by the same students. The word lesson underwent an evolution between 1706 and 1720. Initially, it meant a teaching unit in reading; it evolved to mean a teaching unit in any material. The number of students studying the same lesson ranged from twenty to forty.
- *Class:* the administrative unit of fifty to sixty students in the same room under the same teacher. Not all of the students necessarily studied the same lesson. The room became known as the classroom.
- *School:* the hierarchy of classes in the same building. There were usually four.

There is a logical and hierarchical relationship among these Lasallian teaching units.

De La Salle uses his most emphatic language in the *Conduite* when he speaks of the great care that must be given to the assignment of each student to the right place, level, and lesson. Unless serious attention is given to this matter, "the student will learn nothing." It is the principal duty of the Inspector of Schools to assign each new student a place according to information obtained both in the parent registration interview and in the placement examination. No assignment of place is left to chance. Places are grouped according to the levels of the lesson: the advanced level students in the rear, the intermediate level students in the middle, and the beginning level students in front. New places are assigned each month according to individual student needs and the results of the monthly examinations. There is no automatic promotion to the next level of the lesson.

To help clarify this matter of Lasallian teaching units further, an example should help. The reading program illustrates how small groups, incremental learning, and time management form the basis of instruction in the *Conduite*. The nine lessons of the reading program are broken down into twenty-one levels, which are spread over a three year period. The art of the master teacher consists in adjusting the length of the daily recitation to the time allowed in the daily schedule and to the number of students in the various levels. Figure 2 provides a schema which aligns (1) each of the nine reading lessons;

(2) the length of time in months it ordinarily took to master the lesson; (3) the number of levels of each particular lesson; (4) the nature of the typical daily assignment; and (5) the average amount of material to be covered in the recitation that was made at least once every day by each student and upon which each was questioned daily.

Lessons	Months	Levels	Assignment	Daily Recitation
Alphabet chart	2	1	identify	1 line
syllable chart	1	1	spell-pronounce	3 lines
Syllabaire francais	5	3	identify-pronounce	2-4 lines
local choice	3	3	spell-read	3 lines
Les Devoirs . . .	3	3	syllabicate-read	3-5 lines
local choice	6	3	read one section	8-16 lines
Psalter (Latin)	6	3	read two pages	6-10 lines
Les Règles . . .	2+	2	read one section	4-10 lines
manuscripts	2+	2	read in pairs	30-50 words

Figure 2: Reading Program

Each lesson has its own reading book (reader), and every student in the same lesson is required to have the same reader. A Paris printer's list of books approved for printing in 1705 indicates that De La Salle authored a total of 13 readers, prayer books, and catechisms for use in the classroom.

A second chapter of interest in Part One of the *Conduite* is the chapter on writing. This is the most detailed chapter in this part. The teaching of writing is viewed as a type of apprenticeship for the student. The writing program focuses upon the corrective role of the teacher, emphasizes proper care for the tools of writing by the student, and highlights the necessity of good working conditions.

There are two lessons in writing, round hand style writing and Italian script style writing; each lesson is divided into six levels. The spatial relation between the teacher and the writing student differs dramatically from that between the teacher and the reading student. Whereas the reading teachers do not leave their place in the front of the classroom, the writing teacher passes among the students and gives direct help and encouragement. The teacher's movement eliminates the disturbing coming and going of students to the teacher.

The chapter in Part One on the catechism is a pedagogical gem. Traditional recitation is transformed into a fine art of questioning. Sensitivity and concern are to be shown for the slow learner. De La Salle is more concerned in the teaching of catechism with teacher-student interaction than with a body of doctrine.

The teaching of catechism is the only time when all of the students of a class follow the same lesson. There are no levels in the catechism lesson, and the catechism lesson concludes with a personal application or resolution, and not with the usual review. This practice illustrates how the catechism classroom is also, for De La Salle, a place of apprenticeship in Christian living. The student's socialization is fostered through practices of good manners and politeness, and these are presented as marks of the "Christian virtues" of modesty and respect. De La Salle's pedagogical perspective distinguishes this chapter on catechism from the catechetical writings of his predecessors.

Spelling and arithmetic are also taught with an emphasis on practical application. In learning to spell, students are involved in five activities: copying, keeping a notebook, doing homework, taking dictation, and making self-correction. The students make copies of receipts, legal documents, leases, deeds, and official reports. The materials they are to copy are the kinds of documents with which they would later have to be familiar in their adult lives. Advanced students are encouraged to create their own documents.

The teaching of arithmetic, likewise, is approached by the application of the mechanics of calculation, another skill useful in adult life. A four-step process is used in the teaching of arithmetic. First, a model example is presented on the blackboard and copied into the student's notebook. (Spelling and arithmetic are kept in the same notebook; these notebooks are corrected weekly by the teacher.) Second, the students follow the solution of each example presented on the blackboard. Numbers are changed to make the examples progressively more difficult. Third, the teacher is responsible for keeping a record of the students who work on problems at the blackboard; this guarantees that all students have a turn at blackboard work. Fourth, students are assigned to create and solve new problems for homework.

It is appropriate to note that De La Salle did not use the term *simultaneous* in describing the method of teaching presented in the *Conduite*. It is unfortunate that the emphasis given by nineteenth-century educators on the simultaneous aspect of De La Salle's methodology, that is, that the correction of one student served for the correction of all, has overshadowed the features of small group instruction and individual attention which really were hallmarks of the Lasallian school.

Part Two of *Conduite*

Sense of School Community

Part Two of the *Conduite* focuses on the practical means of building the sense of community within the school. The major obstacles to the sense of community in the school in seventeenth-century France were teacher inefficiency, neglect, cruelty, student disorder, and absenteeism. To counter these obstacles De La Salle identified four general means to help the beginning teacher obtain good order and discipline: (1) vigilance; (2) instruction; (3) prayer; and (4) nine practical ways, good example among them, of overcoming the obstacles to school community.

For De La Salle, vigilance is the art of attending to detail. Vigilance is preeminently a pedagogical and pastoral act involving foresight and prevention. Vigilance constitutes the consummate pedagogical art of dealing simultaneously with the individual student and the rest of the class. Classroom discipline depends on it. Unfortunately, vigilance has been reduced by historians of education to a more or less repressive surveillance. De La Salle was an educational realist who optimistically insists that vigilance allows the teacher accessibility to the street-wise city youth of seventeenth-century France. Vigilance allows the teacher to invite the students to live filial and fraternal lives.

De La Salle and the early Brothers were among the first educators to regard silence as both sound pedagogical methodology and an imperative for teacher health. De La Salle's concern for the atmosphere of quiet, which can save the teacher from wear and tear under normal classroom conditions, must be understood in relation to the crowded and chaotic conditions characteristic of seventeenth-century schools. Unfortunately, historians of education have targeted the practice of silence as "creating a tomb-like atmosphere" in the school. De La Salle intended an atmosphere of quiet which would be helpful for study, attention, and learning.

The chapter on student records attests to the attention the Brothers are to give to each student's personal and academic life. In this regard, historians of education are correct when they conclude that "De La Salle did for the primary school what the Jesuits did for the secondary school." Their mutual contribution was the continued concern for the personal and academic life of each individual student. An example of this individual attention is the system of records to be kept on each student. Six registers of information are kept on each student by the Inspector of Schools and the classroom teacher; these registers were used in determining the student's placement, progress, and promotion.

- *Admissions Register:* Gathered during the registration interview and used in student placement were family background, personal and academic information, and the parents' expectations of the school.
- *Register of the Good and Bad Qualities of Students:* teacher evaluation of the student's character and behavior to be made out at the end of the school year and passed on to the next teacher.
- *Register of Promotions in Lessons:* the list of the names of students in each level of the lesson, with dates of entry and promotion, to indicate the student's progress through the curriculum.
- *Register of the First Student in the Bench:* the small wall chart kept by the First Student in the Bench (a student officer), indicating the presence, absence, or tardiness of those in the bench.
- *Register of Levels in Lessons:* the list of the names of the students in each level of the lesson, with the monthly accumulation of absences, tardiness, poor catechism recitations, and illnesses recorded by a series of dots.
- *Register of Home Visitations:* the reports given to the teacher by the two students assigned to visit the absent students of their neighborhood.

The longest chapter in Part Two of the *Conduite* is a collection of three short treatises which set forth precautions against the use of punishment as a means of establishing classroom order and discipline. The use of corporal punishment was deeply ingrained in the culture, but De La Salle cautioned the Brothers to be infrequent, controlled, and moderate in its use.

The first of these treatises enumerates teacher faults which aggravate children, and describes the alternative art of joining gentleness and firmness in dealing with problem children. The second treatise lays down ten restrictions on administering correction, seven of which are concerned with the teacher. De La Salle's message is clear: if teachers have problems with discipline, let them begin by examining their role in the difficulty. The third treatise is a study of problem children and slow children. De La Salle is at his best in this chapter when he analyzes the reasons for the misbehavior of slow children and develops strategies for getting these students to like school.

A brief commentary on the five final chapters of Part Two of the *Conduite* concludes the presentation of the practical means suggested by De La Salle for building school community. The most significant chapter of these four deals with the causes and remedies of student absenteeism: the teacher is identified as the major cause for a child not wanting to come to school. De La Salle declares that only a pleasant, concerned, and competent teacher keeps students interested in school and prevents student drop-out. A short chapter deals with the school calendar of holidays and special events which give stability to the school year.

A long chapter on student involvement encourages the use of student officers who do "various functions which the teacher cannot or ought not do." The use of student officers was common during the seventeenth century in both primary and secondary schools. Unlike the common practice, however, De La Salle does not involve the student officers in any direct teaching responsibilities; he spells out strict limitations on their authority.

The final chapter specifies the appropriate physical location and suitable design necessary to make the school building, furnishings, and materials conducive to the development of the sense of school community. De La Salle invites the teachers to contribute to the improvement of both. At this point the 1720 edition of the *Conduite* ends abruptly with a listing of the twelve virtues of the good teacher. These twelve virtues are at the heart of the matter in creating a sense of community within the school.

Part Three of *Conduite*

Teacher Support System

Part Three of the *Conduite* portrays school administration as the nurturing of both the initial formation and the in-service development of teachers.

In the history of the Brothers of the Christian Schools four administrative positions constituted the teacher support system. They were the *Community Director,* the *Director of Novices,* the *Supervisor of the New Teachers,* and the *Inspector of Schools.* The functions and duties of the Community Director and the Director of Novices are described in *Règles communes des Frères des Ecoles chrétiennes* (CL 25). The *Conduite* describes the duties of the Inspector of Schools and the Supervisor the New Teachers. The first Supervisor was Brother Jean Jacques (1672–1759). Since he had previously been an Inspector of Schools, De La Salle appointed him to this important position.

According to the ordinary pattern of school administration set up by De La Salle, all of the Brothers living in one house constituted a Community. A Community of Brothers might, however, teach in two to four schools of the same city. The Community Director was given the responsibility for all the schools dependent upon the Community House; he delegated his authority for the schools, in total or in part, to an Inspector of Schools (a member of the same Community House). The Inspector of Schools would, on a rotating basis among these schools, serve as the on-site school administrator and teacher Supervisor. In the absence of the Inspector of Schools, a Brother designated the head or principal teacher at the school would handle emergencies. The Inspector of Schools did not teach, but he was a master teacher. Experienced in every level of the curriculum, he was well respected by the other members of the Community. In the early days of the Institute, the Writing Masters and the Masters of the Little Schools spied upon De La Salle's schools in an attempt to discredit them; raids were made upon the schools to close them down; some local pastors attempted to control the schools and the Brothers. Thus the Inspector of Schools held a sensitive position.

Part Three of the book delineates the duties of the Inspector of Schools in three areas:

> The office of Inspector of Schools consists mainly in two [sic] things: (1) to be vigilant over the schools, the teachers, and the students; (2) to place the students in their classrooms and assign the lessons they are to be taught; and (3) to promote the students from one lesson to another when they are capable of doing more advanced work.

The present volume makes available for the first time in English the job description of the Inspector of Schools. Four chapters spell out in detail his responsibilities with regard to the teachers, parents, students, and school building. The Inspector of Schools interviews parents at registration; he verifies the new student's background in reading, writing, and arithmetic; he makes the initial student placement. In a close working relationship with the classroom teacher, the Inspector of Schools examines the students' monthly progress and approves their monthly promotion. De La Salle describes how the Inspector of Schools and the classroom teacher, with great sensitivity for the feelings of the student, should speak with the student who does not make the monthly promotion. The Inspector of Schools has the responsibility for maintaining the school building and supplying the classroom teacher with instructional supplies, materials, and classroom furnishings. In effect, the job description of the Inspector of Schools requires a mastery of the instructional methods and educational practices described in the first two parts of the *Conduite*.

The job description of the Supervisor of New Teachers sets forth the ethical and professional standards which govern the teacher's behavior in relation to students, parents, clergy, fellow teachers, and the public in general. Unlike the description of the duties of the Inspector of Schools, the description of the Supervisor of New Teachers is deceptively simple: "To remove the bad qualities which new teachers may have but which they ought not to have, and to instill the good qualities which new teachers may not have but which it is very necessary that they acquire." Fourteen bad and ten good qualities are identified.

Conclusion

The *Conduite* is a classic work in seventeenth-century French school reform. It can be read as an historical curiosity, or it can be read for pedagogical principles that are as true, beautiful, and good today as they were in the seventeenth century. In this sense, the *Conduite* is both a product of its time and a beacon for all time.

The *Conduite* is a practical teacher-training manual which grew out of classroom experience and, as such, is based upon the principle that one learns to teach by teaching. A unique example of how seventeenth-century school reform was carried out through the reform of teacher education, the *Conduite* has something to say that is still significant to those involved in teaching and teacher education.

Both neglect and misunderstanding have robbed the *Conduite* of its rightful place in the literature on the history of education. Hopefully, the recent resurgence of Lasallian research, the publication of the monumental *Cahiers lasalliens,* and the translations into English of sources heretofore available only in French will provide scholars, teachers, and historians with an appreciation of the significant contribution De La Salle and the *Conduite* have made to the history of education.

EDWARD EVERETT, FSC
December 1995

Ad Majorem Dei Gloriam

To the Brothers of the Christian Schools

My very dear Brothers,

The ardent zeal which you have hitherto manifested in the exercise of the ministry with which God has honored you impels me to exhort you to continue to perfect yourselves in an occupation so holy and useful to the Church as yours. There is nothing greater, my dear Brothers, than to dedicate yourselves to giving to children a Christian education and to inspiring them with the fear and love of God. It is for this purpose that you have consecrated yourselves to God's service—a blessed consecration which will make you great in the Kingdom of Heaven, according to the promise of Our Lord Jesus Christ.

This is what our venerable Founder never ceased to bring to your attention during his lifetime. Ah! what did he not do to this end? With what care and solicitude did he not seek to provide you with the means of fulfilling your duties with as much prudence as charity? You can bear witness, and God knows it, with what attention and what charity he sought, together with the principal and most experienced Brothers of the Institute, suitable means of maintaining among you a holy uniformity in your manner of educating youth. He drew up in writing all that he believed to be expedient for this purpose, and he prepared this *Conduite des Ecoles chrétiennes*. He exhorted you to read it again and again, in order to learn from it what would be most useful to you. Your conformity with his desire and the care which you still take to put into practice what he taught you show clearly enough your zeal and your veneration of so worthy a father.

This guide, my very dear Brothers, was soon introduced into all of the Community Houses of the Institute and everyone gloried in conforming to it. However, as there were several things in it that could not be put into practice, the Brothers of the Assembly which was held for the purpose of electing the first Brother Superior represented to M. De La Salle that it would be expedient to make some corrections. He approved their proposition, and thus it was put into better order than before.

You indicated clearly, my very dear Brothers, by the eagerness with which you requested that this corrected work should be sent to all of your Community Houses, the extent of your approval of what the Brothers of this Assembly had done, and repeated demands which you still make for copies of this work prove sufficiently your desire for uniformity of method. Lack of leisure has always prevented the preparation of a sufficient number of copies to satisfy your just desires. Furthermore, because of the lack of accuracy on the part of copyists, there are numerous errors which often change the sense.

At length, some of the most zealous Brothers, sympathizing with the difficulty which you experience in being thus deprived of something so necessary, have entreated our very honored Brother Superior to allow the work to be printed. He has consented, all the more willingly because he himself has desired for a long time to afford you this satisfaction. He has read the work again with great attention and has had it carefully examined in order to eliminate all that might be useless.

Accept, then, my very dear Brothers, the offer which I make to you of a book to which you are already entitled. Seek therein the prudence and wisdom that are so necessary if you are to establish the reign of God in the souls which are confided to you. Be sure that, if you persevere in so holy a work, you will save yourselves and you will save many others as well. Amen.

(BROTHER TIMOTHÉE, 1720)

Preface

It has been necessary to prepare this guide for Christian Schools so that all may be done uniformly in all the schools and in all the places where there are Brothers of this Institute, and that the practices there will always be the same. People are so subject to laxity, and even to change, that they must have written rules to keep them within the limits of their duties and to prevent them from introducing something new or destroying what has been wisely established. This guide has been prepared and put in order (by the late M. De La Salle) only after a great number of conferences between him and the oldest Brothers of the Institute and those most capable of running a school well, and after several years of experience. Nothing has been added that has not been thoroughly deliberated and well tested, nothing of which the advantages and disadvantages have not been weighed and, as far as possible, of which the good or bad consequences have not been foreseen. The Brothers will, therefore, take great care to observe faithfully all that is therein prescribed, being persuaded that there will be order in the schools only to the extent that they are careful to omit nothing; and they will receive this guide as though it were given them by God through the instrumentality of their Superiors and the first Brothers of the Institute.

This book is divided into three parts. The first part treats of all the practices and everything else that is done in school from the opening until the closing hour. The second section sets forth the necessary and useful means of which the teachers should avail themselves in order to bring about and maintain order in the schools. The third part treats first, of the duties of the Inspector of Schools; second, of the care and diligence to be observed by the person training new teachers; third, of the qualities which the teachers should have or should acquire and of the conduct which they should maintain in order to acquit themselves well of their duties in the schools; and, fourth, of those things to be observed by the students. The third part will be only for the use of the Directors and those who are charged with the training of new teachers.[1]

The Directors of the Community Houses of the Institute and the Inspectors of Schools will apply themselves to learning well and knowing perfectly all that is contained in this book and will proceed in such a way that teachers observe exactly all the practices that are prescribed for them, even the least in order to procure by this means great order in the schools, a well regulated and uniform conduct on the part of the teachers who will be in charge of them, and a very considerable benefit for the children who will be taught there. The teachers who will be working in the schools will read and often reread what in it is suitable for them, so that they will be ignorant of nothing contained in it and will become faithful to it in their practices.

PART ONE

School Practices
and the Manner in Which
They Are to Be Carried Out

1

Entering School
and Beginning School

Article 1:
Entrance of Students

The doors of the schools will always be opened at 7:30 in the morning and at 1:00 in the afternoon. In the morning as well as in the afternoon, the students will always have half an hour in which to assemble.

Care will be taken that they do not assemble in a crowd in the street before the door is opened and that they do not make noise by shouting or singing.

They will not be permitted to amuse themselves by playing and running in the vicinity of the school during this time nor to disturb the neighbors in any manner whatsoever. Care will be taken that they walk with decorum into the street in which the school is situated and that while waiting for the door to be opened they stop there in such good order that those who pass will be edified. The Head Teacher or the Inspector of Schools will assign one of the more reliable students to observe those who make noise while assembling. This student will merely observe without commenting at the time and will afterward tell the teacher what has happened without the others' being aware of it.

When the door is opened, care will be taken that the students do not rush forward and enter in a crowd but that they enter in an orderly fashion, one after the other.

Teachers will be attentive and take care that all the students walk so quietly and so calmly while entering the school that their steps will not be heard, that they remove their hats before taking holy water, that they make the sign of the cross, and that they go at once directly to their classroom.

They will be inspired to enter the classroom with profound respect, out of consideration for the presence of God. When they have reached the center of the room, they will make a low bow before the crucifix and will bow to the teacher if one is present. Then they will kneel to adore God and to say a short prayer to the Blessed Virgin. After this, they will arise, again bow before the crucifix in the same manner, bow to the teacher, and go quietly and silently to their regular places.

While students are assembling and entering the classroom, they will all maintain such complete silence that not the least noise will be heard, not even of the feet. In this manner, it will not be possible to distinguish those who are entering from those who are studying.

Having reached their places, they will remain quietly seated without leaving for any reason whatsoever until the teacher enters.

Teachers will take care to give warning that those who have talked or made any noise in the classroom during their absence will be punished and that they will not forgive offenses against silence and good order committed during this time.

From the time of entering the school until the arrival of the teachers, those who know how to read will study the catechism, and will do this so quietly that they cannot be heard by the others and that not the least sound is heard in the classroom.

During this time, a student in the first class will be charged by the teacher to point out on the two charts of the alphabet and of the syllables first one letter or syllable and then another, in different sequences. In this manner, the students who are learning them may thus study their lessons. Those who are studying all the lessons of each chart will recite in turn in the order in which they are seated. All the others will pay attention to the letter or syllable being pointed out on the chart. While the one who is reciting speaks out loudly, the others will speak quietly, so that they can be heard only by the two on either side. Students chosen to point out the contents of the charts will do so without correcting and without saying a single word. A teacher will take care above all to be faithful in this.

Teachers will take great care that all the students are in the classroom before their own arrival and that none come late except rarely for good reasons and through necessity. They will be very exact in requiring that this point be observed, and the Inspector of Schools will pay special attention to it and even warn the parents when receiving students that the children must come every day at the exact hour and that they will be accepted only on this condition.

Article 2:
Entrance of Teachers
and the Beginning of School

Teachers will go to their classrooms as soon as the rosary has been said in the morning, and likewise in the afternoon immediately after the litany of Saint Joseph without stopping anywhere.

They will walk with great decorum and in silence not hastily, but modestly, keeping their eyes and their entire demeanor in great reserve.

On entering the school, they will take off their hats and take holy water with deep respect. Having reached their own classroom, they will bow before the crucifix, kneel, and make the sign of the cross. After a short prayer and again bowing before the crucifix, they will go to their places.

When the teachers enter the school, all the students of each class will rise and remain standing as their teacher enters. Those before whom the teacher passes will bow as the teacher kneels to say the prayer, and will not sit down until the teacher is seated.

If the Director or anyone else visits the school, students will act in the same manner but only the first time the visitors enter. In case the visitors remain and go from one class to another, the students will remain with their hats off until the teacher gives them a sign to be seated and to put on their hats.

From the time the teachers take their seats until school begins, they will apply themselves to reading the New Testament and will remain silent in order to give an example to the students. They will observe, however, all that takes place in the school in order to maintain good order.

School will always begin punctually at 8:00 in the morning and at 1:30 in the afternoon. At the last stroke of 8:00 and the last stroke of 1:30, a student will ring the school bell. At the first sound of the bell, all the students will kneel in a very modest posture and manner, with their arms crossed and their eyes lowered.

As soon as the bell has ceased ringing, the prayer leader will begin the prayers in a loud voice distinctly and calmly. After making the sign of the cross, and after all the students have also made it, the prayer leader will begin the *Veni Sancte Spiritus*. The other students will recite the prayer with the leader, but in a lower tone. They will, in the same manner, say with the leader the other prayers prescribed in *Le Livre des Prières des Ecoles chrétiennes* (CL 18). In the morning, the prayer leader will say the blessing before the meal in Latin, *Benedicite*. After breakfast, the leader will say the Act of Thanksgiving, *Agimus tibi Gratias*, and so on. In the afternoon, the prayers will be said in French, as is indicated in *Le Livre des Prières des Ecoles chrétiennes* (CL 18).

When the prayers are finished, the teacher will signal by a hand clap. The students will rise and eat breakfast in silence.

2
Breakfast and Afternoon Snack

Article 1:
Teacher Attention During Breakfast
and Afternoon Snack

Teachers should take care that the students bring their breakfast and afternoon snack with them every day. A little basket will be set in an appointed place in the classroom, into which the children when they are so piously inclined may put what bread they have left over, to be distributed among those of them who are poor. Teachers will see that they do not give away any of their bread unless they have enough left for themselves. Those who have bread to give will raise their hands, showing at the same time the piece of bread which they have to give, and a student who has been appointed to receive these alms will collect them. At the end of the meal, the teacher will distribute the bread to the poorest and will exhort them to pray to God for their benefactors.

Teachers will also take care that students do not throw either nuts or shells on the floor, but will have them put them into their pockets or into their bags.

Students must be made to understand that it is desirable that they eat in school in order to teach them to eat with propriety, with decorum, and in a polite manner, and to invoke God before and after eating.

Teachers will see that the students do not play during breakfast and the afternoon snack but that they be very attentive to what is being done in school during this time. In order to discover whether they are exact in this, teachers will from time to time make one of them repeat what has been said, with the exception of those who are occupied in writing.

Students will not be permitted either to give anything whatsoever to one another not even any part of their breakfast, or to exchange it.

Teachers will see to it that the students finish breakfast by 8:30, or as near as possible.

Article 2:
What Is Done During Breakfast and Afternoon Snack

On the first two days of the week upon which school is held all day, the students who read but do not spell will recite the morning prayers during breakfast and the evening prayers during the afternoon snack. For those who are in the writing classes, on Mondays and Tuesdays one student will occupy an appointed place and say all the prayers in an audible tone: during breakfast, the morning prayers; in the afternoon, the evening ones, the commandments of God and of the church, and the confiteor. Students will recite in turn, one after the other. They must learn these prayers by heart and will recite them during breakfast and the afternoon snack on these two days. The Inspector will reprove them when they fail. On the last two days of the week upon which school is held throughout the whole day, they will recite during breakfast and the afternoon snack what they have learned in the diocesan catechism during the week. The teacher will see that they recite everything on these two days without a single exception. What they are to learn in each class during the week will be indicated by the Director or the Head Teacher.

On Wednesdays when there is a whole holiday on Thursday or on those days when there is a half holiday because of a holy day of obligation during the week, those who read Latin will recite the responses of holy Mass during breakfast. This will likewise be done during the first half hour of the catechism in the afternoon.

If there are in the class in which the responses of holy Mass are recited any students who already know them or are capable of learning them even though they are not yet able to read Latin, the teacher will take care that they know them well and will make them recite them also.

The students who recite all the above-mentioned items should have learned them by heart at home or during the time that they assemble for school. They do not recite them in order to learn, but only to show that they do know them, and, as for the prayers and responses of holy Mass, to learn how to say them properly. Those who do not know them, although they have already been a long time in the writing class, will also be made to learn them and to recite them.

All students who recite the prayers and responses of holy Mass will recite them in turn, one after the other, in an order different from that of the other prayers.

In the lower classes, the prayers will be recited in the following manner. One of two students will announce the titles of the prayers, and the other will recite the acts or the articles all in order and in succession from the beginning of the prayers to the end. All students will take turns in doing each of these things in turn.

The student who announces the titles of the prayers and the questions of the catechism will correct the other in case a mistake is made in anything. In case the first one does not do this, the teacher will give the signal for a correction. If the student does not know what has been said incorrectly, the teacher whose duty at the time is to attend both to those who are reciting and to the order of the whole class, will signal another student to make the correction in the same manner as in the lessons.

In the writing class, while the teacher is occupied with writing, a student who has been appointed Inspector will do what the teacher should do but only for this recitation. Teachers shall in no way exempt themselves from watching over the general order of the class during this time.

The responses of holy Mass will be recited in the following manner. Throughout the whole recitation, one student will do what the priest does and will say what the priest says as is indicated in the liturgy. Another student, who will be at his side, will reply as the server should reply and do what the server should do.

The server will do accurately all that is indicated in *Le Livre des Prières des Ecoles chrétiennes*. Those who are reciting the prayers and responses of holy Mass will maintain throughout this time a very decorous and pious attitude. They should hold their hands and their exterior demeanor in the greatest control. They should be obliged to recite these prayers and responses with the same decorum, with the same respect, with the same demeanor, and in the same manner that would be expected if they were serving holy Mass or saying their prayers at home.

Teachers will take care that those who are reciting the prayers and the responses of holy Mass or the catechism speak during this time very distinctly and in a moderately loud tone in order that all may hear them. Nevertheless, they should speak low enough so that the other students must keep silent, listen, and be attentive to those who are reciting.

During this time, teachers will observe very carefully everything that happens in their classes, and make sure that all are attentive. From time to time, a teacher will stop those who are reciting in order to question those who appear to be not sufficiently attentive. If the latter are unable to answer, the teacher will impose some penance upon them or will punish them as may be judged necessary.

During this recitation, the teacher will hold either *Le Livre des Prières* or the catechism; and will take care that the students repeat very exactly and very well.

On the first two days of the week and on the two days upon which the catechism is to be recited, those who are learning their letters from the alphabet chart will learn and repeat only the *Pater Noster,* the *Ave Maria,* the *Credo,* and the *Confiteor* in Latin and in French as they are in *Le Livre des Prières des Ecoles chrétiennes.*

Those who are studying the chart of syllables will learn and repeat the acts of the presence of God, of invocation of the Holy Spirit, of adoration, and of thanksgiving which come in sequence at the beginning of the morning prayers as well as of the evening prayers.

Those who are spelling from the syllable chart will learn and repeat in turn, in the following order, the acts of offering and of petition, which are in the morning prayers; the act of presenting ourselves to God; the confession of sins; the act of contrition and the act of offering of sleep, which are in the evening prayers; the prayer to the Guardian Angel; and those which follow in the morning as well as in the evening prayers.

If any of those who are studying the last two of these three lessons do not know any of the prayers that they should have learned in this lesson or in the preceding ones, the teacher will make them learn and practice these prayers which they do not know with those students who are studying the lesson in which such prayers should be learned. For instance, with those who are studying the alphabet, the *Pater Noster,* the *Ave Maria,* the *Credo,* and the *Confiteor,* if they do not yet know them. When they know them well or assuming they know them well, they will learn with those who are studying the chart of syllables those acts that should be memorized by the students who are studying this lesson.

Those who are spelling or reading in the second book will learn and recite all the prayers, the morning prayers as well as the evening prayers. If the teacher notices that anyone who is reciting these prayers does not know them well, that student will be obliged to learn them privately from *Le Livre des Prières des Ecoles chrétiennes.* The teacher will fix a time for the student to recite them either entirely or in part as will seem fit.

If there are in the same class any students who should recite the catechism, they will do so on Saturday or only on the last school day of the week. If during breakfast and the afternoon snack on this day there is more time than is needed to have all of them recite it, the time that remains will be employed in having the prayers recited.

On the days of the week on which the others are reciting the responses of holy Mass, those learning the catechism will learn to say the rosary and also will repeat it, two together, in the following manner.

They will stand facing each other and will both make simultaneously the sign of the cross. After this, one will say the versicle, *Dignare me laudare te, Virgo Sacrata,* and the other will say the response, *Da mihi virtutem contra hostes tuos.*

Then, the first will say while holding the cross, *Credo in unum Deum,* and so forth. On the large bead which comes immediately after, the student will say the *Pater Noster;* and on each of the three little beads which follow, an *Ave Maria,* at the end of which the student will say, *Gloria Patri,* and so forth, and *sicut erat in principio.* The student will continue in the same manner to say the decade that follows. When it is completed, the student will again say the *Gloria Patri.* When the first student has finished, the other will repeat aloud and intelligibly all that the first has just recited. They will recite thus in turn only this decade of the rosary. The teacher will explain to them that in order to say the chaplet they must say six decades, just as they have said this one.[1]

After this decade they will be made to say *Maria, Mater gratiae, Mater Misericordiae, tu nos ab hostes protectae et in hora mortis suscipe;* and they will be taught that this is to be said at the end of the chaplet.

Those who do not know how to say the rosary will be taught to say it in this manner.

There will be only one group for all the students in these four lessons in memorizing the prayer. They will all repeat one after another what they are to learn, beginning with those who are learning the alphabet, and ending with those who are spelling and reading in the second book.[2]

3
Studies

Article 1:
Lessons in General

Section 1: What Concerns All Lessons

There will be nine different kinds of lessons in the Christian Schools. First, the alphabet chart. Second, the syllable chart. Third, the book of syllabication. Fourth, the second book for learning to spell and read by syllables. Fifth, the same second book, in which those who know how to spell perfectly will begin to read. Sixth, the third book which will be used to teach how to read with pauses. Seventh, the Psalter. Eighth, *Les Règles de la Civilité chrétienne* (CL 19). Ninth, letters written by hand.

All students of all these lessons, with the exception of those who are reading the alphabet and the syllables, will be grouped in three levels: the first composed of the beginners, the second of the intermediate, and the third of the advanced and those who are perfect in the work of the lesson.

The beginners are not called thus because they are only beginning the lesson. A number of them might remain a long time in this level because they did not advance sufficiently to be placed in a higher one.

The beginners' level for each lesson will consist of those who still make many mistakes in reading. The intermediate level will consist of those who make few mistakes in this reading, that is to say, one or two mistakes at most each time. The section of the advanced and perfect will consist of those who ordinarily make no mistakes in reading their lessons.

There will, however, be only two levels of readers of *Les Règles de la Civilité chrétiennes*. The first level will be composed of those who make mistakes in reading it and the second, of those who make almost none.

Each of these levels for the various lessons will have its assigned place in the classroom. In this manner, the students of one level will not be mixed with those of another level of the same lesson. For instance, the beginners will not be mixed with the intermediate. They may be easily distinguished from one another by means of their locations.

All the students of the same lesson will, however, follow the lessons together without distinction or difference as the teacher shall determine.

It is not possible in this *Conduite* to set the duration of the lessons of each class, because the number of students in each lesson is not always the same. For this reason, it will be the duty of the Director or of the Inspector of Schools to prescribe the time allotted to each lesson in each class.

All students of each lesson will have the same book and will have their lessons together. The least advanced will always read first, beginning with the simplest lesson and ending with the most difficult one.

In the highest class in the afternoon, however, when there are some students who are not writing, those who write will read first. The others will read after the writers have read, even during the time for writing, and until half past three.

Section 2: Teachers and Students During Lessons

Teachers should always be seated or should stand in front of their seats during all lessons, those on the alphabet and syllables as well as those in books or letters written by hand.

They should not leave their places except in cases of grave necessity. They will find that such necessity is very rare, if they are attentive.

They will be careful to maintain a very modest demeanor and to act with great seriousness. They will never allow themselves to descend to anything unbecoming or to act in a childish fashion, such as to laugh or to do anything that might excite the students.

The seriousness demanded of teachers does not consist in having a severe or austere aspect, in getting angry, or in saying harsh words.

It consists of great reserve in their gestures, in their actions, and in their words.

Teachers will above all be cautious not to become too familiar with the students, not to speak to them in an easy manner, and not to allow the students to speak to them other than with great respect.

In order to acquit themselves well of their duty, teachers must be trained to do the following three things. First, they must watch over all the students in order to motivate them to do their duty, to keep them in order, and to maintain silence. Second, they must keep in hand during all the lessons the book which is actually being read, and must follow the reader exactly. Third, they must pay attention to the one who is reading and to the manner in which this student reads, so that they may give correction when a mistake is made.

The students should always be seated during the lessons, even while reading from the charts of the alphabet and the syllables. They should hold their bodies erect and keep their feet on the floor in good order. Those who are reading the alphabet and the syllables should have their arms crossed. Those who are reading in books should hold their books in both hands, resting them neither upon their knees nor upon the table. They should also look straight before them with their faces turned slightly in the direction of the teacher. The teacher must take care that the students do not turn their heads so much that they may be able to speak with their companions and that they do not turn first to one side and then to the other.

While one of the students is reading, all the others in the same lesson will follow in their books, which they should always have in hand.

The teacher will take great care to see that all read quietly what the reader is reading aloud. From time to time, the teacher will make some of them read a few words in passing, surprising them and finding out if they are following attentively. If they are not following, the teacher will impose upon them some penance or punishment. If the teacher notices that some of them do not like to follow, or more easily or more frequently neglect to do so, the teacher will be careful to make them read last, and even several different times, a little each time, so that the others may also have the time to read.

All who are studying the same lesson will remove their hats at the beginning of the lesson, and they will not replace them until they have read. If the teacher makes them read several times, at the second, the third, and following times they will take off their hats when they begin to read, and they will replace them as soon as they have finished.

Section 3: Preparing Students for Promotions

Teachers will not promote from a lesson or from any level any students in their class. They will merely present to the Director or the Inspector of Schools those whom they believe ready for promotion.

They will be particularly careful not to present for promotion any student who is not very capable. Students easily become discouraged when they have been recommended by the teacher and then are not promoted by the Director or the Inspector.

In order that there be no mistake in regard to the readiness of the students for promotion, the teachers will examine toward the end of each month and on a day fixed by the Director or the Inspector of Schools, those students in all lessons and in all levels who should be ready for promotion at the end of that month.

After this examination, teachers will mark on their class lists by a pin mark next to the beginning of each name those whom they consider capable of being promoted. If there are any whose ability may seem doubtful or may not appear to be sufficient for promotion to a more advanced lesson or to a higher level of the same lesson, they will mark them in the same place by two pin marks, indicating that the Director examine them more carefully. For those in the writing class, the teacher will mark on the class lists, on the left, close to the name, those judged capable of being promoted in writing. Those whom the teacher judges capable of being promoted to a higher level in writing or in reading manuscripts will also be marked, on the right, close to the name. Those whom the teacher judges capable of being promoted in arithmetic will be marked farther away, close to the line on the left of the column in which are marked those who were tardy.

For promotions in *Les Règles de la Civilité chrétienne* or in reading documents, a pinprick will be placed after the surname of the student. For promotions in arithmetic, a mark will be placed farther away, before the column used to mark the late-comers. Doubtful cases will be indicated by two pinpricks.

The teachers will agree with the Director upon those whom it might be right to promote, but whom it will not be opportune to promote at the time, either because they are too young or because it is necessary to leave some in each lesson or each level who know how to read well enough to stimulate the others and serve them as models, to train them to express themselves well, to pronounce distinctly the letters, syllables, and words, and to make the pauses well.

Teachers will take care, some time before the day upon which the promotions are to be made, to forewarn those students whom the Director or the Inspector has agreed not to promote, either for their own good, because they are too young, or for the good of the class and the lesson, in order that there be some who can support the others.

They will do this in such a manner that these students will be content to remain in the lesson or in the level where they are. They will persuade them by means of some reward, by assigning to them an office such as that of the first student in the bench, making them understand that it is better to be the first, or among the first, in a lower grade than the last in a more advanced one.

Article 2:
Letters and Syllables

Section 1: Use of and Seating at Alphabet and Syllable Charts

Those students who have not yet learned anything will not use a reader until they begin to be able to spell syllables of two and of three letters well.

In the lowest class, for this purpose there will be two large charts attached to the wall, the tops of the charts being about six or seven feet above the floor. One of these charts will be composed of single letters, both capitals and small letters, diphthongs, and letters joined together. The other chart will be composed of syllables of two and of three letters.[1]

The benches of the students who are reading from the Alphabet Chart and the Syllable Chart should be neither too near nor too far away for the readers to be able to see and read the letters and syllables easily. For this reason, care must be taken that the front of the first bench should be at least four feet distant from the wall to which the charts are attached.

For the same reason, students who are studying these charts will be seated facing them, so that if, for instance, twenty-four students are learning the alphabet and twelve are learning to read syllables and each bench seats twelve students, they will be seated upon three benches placed one behind the other, upon each bench eight of those who are learning the alphabet and four of those who are learning to read syllables. They shall be placed so that they all face the charts. The same proportions will be maintained in case the benches seat fewer or more students or a larger or smaller number are studying one or the other of these two charts.

Section 2: Reading the Alphabet

All students who are reading the alphabet will have for each lesson only one line of the small or of the capital letters. They will read the following line only when they know well the one that they have to learn. However, in order that they do not forget the preceding lines that they have learned, they will follow attentively and repeat in a low voice the letters that are being pronounced by the student who is reading aloud. Each student of this class will read over alone and privately at least three times all the small and all the capital letters of the line assigned for this lesson. Each will read them once in the regular order and twice out of order, so that they will not be learned only by rote.

When a student does not know the name of a small letter the teacher will show the student the capital letter of the same name. If the student does not know either of them, some other student who knows it well will be asked to name it. Sometimes, the teacher may even call upon a student who is not in the same lesson. A student will never be allowed to call one letter by the name of another more than once for instance, to say b for q, and p for d, or other similar mistakes.

The student who finds it difficult to remember a letter will be required to repeat it several times in succession, and will not proceed to the next line until this and all the other letters are known perfectly.

When all the lines of the alphabet chart have been learned, but before beginning syllables, students will continue to study the entire alphabet, until the end of the month. During all of this time, students will be called on to read all the letters at random in order to ascertain whether they are all known. Students will not advance in the lesson until they know all the letters perfectly.

It must be noted that it is of very great importance that students should study the alphabet until it is known perfectly. Otherwise, they will never be able to read well and the teachers who will later be in charge of them will have great difficulty.

The students who are learning to read the alphabet will follow and pay attention to those who have the lesson on syllables during all the time the latter are reading their lesson. Likewise, those who are reading the syllables will pay attention to the alphabet during the time of that lesson.

Throughout all the lessons on the alphabet and the syllables, the teacher will always indicate with the pointer the letters and syllables to be pronounced.

Care must be taken that the students when reading pronounce all the letters well, especially those that are at times difficult to pronounce well, such as the following: *b, c, d, e, f, g, h, m, n, o, p, r, t, x,* and *z*. Teachers should apply themselves particularly to the correction of bad accents that are peculiar to the locality, for example, making them say *be* for *b, ce* for *c, de* for *d,* and thus with similar mistakes.

The *m* and *n* should be pronounced like *eme* and *ene, x* like *icce,* and *y* like *i; z* is pronounced *zede; ae* and *oe* should be pronounced like *e* and not as though these letters were separated: *a, e* and *o, e.*

The letters *i* and *u* can be consonants as well as vowels. When they stand alone before one or two other vowels without consonants, they are pronounced otherwise than when they are vowels. The consonant *i* is written with a tail like *j;* the consonant *u* is pointed at the bottom, like a *v.*

The consonant *i* is pronounced like *gi,* and the consonant *u* is pronounced like *vé;* this is done in order to distinguish them in pronunciation as well as in writing from the vowels *i* and *u.*

All the letters of the alphabet should be pronounced very distinctly and separately, with a distinct pause after each one.

Teachers will take care that readers open their mouths well and not pronounce the letters between the teeth; this is a very great fault. They should not read too rapidly, too slowly, or with any tone or manner that savors of affectation, but should speak with a very natural tone. Teachers will also take care that no student's voice is raised too much when reciting the lesson. It suffices that the one who is reading should be heard by all those of the same lesson.

Letters which are joined together must also be pronounced very distinctly, each one separately as though in fact each one were separated from the others. To pronounce *ct* for instance, *c* must first be pronounced alone; then, after a little pause, *t* is pronounced. The same should be done with the other groups.

Section 3: Reading the Chart of Syllables

Students will read from the chart of syllables one after another in turn, just as they would read a lesson in a book. The teacher will always indicate the syllable with the pointer.

Each student will read at least three lines. All that has been said in reference to the alphabet on the subject of pronouncing well and very distinctly all the letters must also be carefully observed in reading syllables.

Teachers will see that the students do not read the syllables in too rapid a sequence, but that while making a short pause between the letters of a syllable, they make a longer one after each syllable. The teacher will take care not to allow them to speak the syllables too quickly and run them together.

There are three letters which present special difficulties in respect to pronunciation; these are *c, g,* and *t.* When *c* comes before *a, o, u,* it is pronounced like *q.* When there is a cedilla (or comma) under the *c* as in *ç,* or when *c* comes before *e* or *i,* then it is pronounced like *s.*

In the same manner, when *g* occurs before *a, o,* or *u,* it must be sounded as though there were a *u* between them. The three syllables *ga, go,* and *gu* are pronounced *gua, guo, gue* in French. When *g* is placed before *e* or *i,* it is called soft *g* and it is pronounced like the consonant *j;* for instance, the syllables *ge* and *gi* are sounded like *je* and *ji.* When *t* is found before *i* and this *i* is followed by another vowel, the *t* is pronounced like *c;* for example, the word *pronontiation* is pronounced as though it were written *prononciacion* and likewise in similar cases.

Article 3:
The Book of Syllables

The first book which the students of the Christian Schools will learn to read will be composed of all sorts of French syllables of two, three, four, five, six, and seven letters and of some words to facilitate the pronunciation of the syllables. Ordinarily, two pages will be assigned for each lesson.

The beginners should not read less than two lines, and the others should not read less than three lines. This is determined according to the number of students and the time that the teacher has in which to make them read. As soon as any students begin this lesson and in order that they may accustom themselves to read their own book while the others are reading, the teacher will take care to assign to each one, for as many days as assistance may be needed, a companion who, when the others are reading, will teach the new student how to follow the lesson and they will follow together in the same book: both will hold the book one on one side and the other on the other. In the Book of Syllables students will only spell the syllables and will not read them. It will be necessary to make them understand first the difficulties which are to be met in the pronunciation of syllables, which are not slight in French. For this reason, each teacher must know perfectly the little treatise on pronunciation.

In order to teach spelling well, it is necessary to have all the letters pronounced in the same tone and very distinctly. In this way, the sound of each one can be fully heard separately from the others. The syllables should be pronounced in the same manner. Thus, the one who is spelling should make each syllable completely and distinctly heard before beginning to spell the following one. The student should pronounce them almost as separately as if there were commas between them. For instance, to spell well the syllable *quo,* each letter must be named separately and distinctly *q, u, o.* This is the same for *c, a,* and *r,* or *t, a,* and *r.* They must not be named quickly and together: *quo, car, tar.* This practice is of very great importance. There is even more to be feared from spelling and reading too rapidly than reciting too slowly, and much more harm can be done.

Article 4:
The First Reader

The first reader to be used in the Christian Schools will be in continuous sentences. Those who read in it will only spell, and they will always be given one page for each lesson.

Each student will spell about three lines at least, depending upon the time that the teacher has available and upon the number of the students. The teacher will insist that those who are in this lesson distinguish and separate the syllables of the words from one another and that they do not put into the first syllable a letter which should be in the second, or the reverse. For instance, in spelling the word *déclare,* they should not say *déc-la-re.* They should say *dé-cla-re;* and the same with other words.

The teacher will insist that they pronounce all the syllables of a word as they should be pronounced in this word and not as they would be pronounced if they were separated one from another and in different words. For example, the syllable *son* is not pronounced in the word *personne* by sounding the *n* as it is always sounded in the word *son* when this syllable alone forms the word which signifies sound, for in that case so much stress is not placed upon the *n*. In the same way, in the word *louppe* the first syllable is pronounced otherwise than is *loup* when it forms the word which signifies the animal. For in the first example, *louppe,* the *p* is sounded in the first syllable; whereas in the second, *loup,* the *p* is not sounded, and the word is pronounced as if there were only *lou*. The teacher will take care that students in this lesson pronounce the words as though they were standing alone, paying no attention either to the preceding word or to the following one. For instance, in the sentence *"Ne pensez point à ce que vous aurez à dire,"* they will pronounce the word *point* as they would pronounce it when alone and not followed by a vowel. Thus they will not pronounce the *t* but will pronounce the word as though it were only *poin,* naming, however, all the letters as follows: *p, o, i, n, t.*

Likewise in the word *vous,* they will name all the letters: *v, o , u, s*. They will pronounce it as though there were no *s* and will say *v, o, u, s, vou*. They will do the same in the word a*urez,* not pronouncing the *z,* but, after naming all the letters of the second syllable, *r, e, z,* they will say, as though there were no *z, ré,* with an accent on the *e,* paying no attention in case of either of these words to the vowels which follow them.

Article 5:
The Second Reader

The second reader to be used in the Christian Schools will be a book of Christian instruction. The students will not study this book unless they can spell perfectly without hesitating.

There will be two kinds of readers of this book: those who spell and read by syllables and those who do not spell but only read by syllables.

All will have the same lesson. While one is spelling or reading, all the others will follow, both those who spell and read and those who only read. Those who both spell and read will do nothing but spell in the morning. In the afternoon, they will spell first. After all of them have spelled, they will read without distinction together with those who read only. If those who only read are in the same class with those who both spell and read, they will only follow while the latter are spelling. The teacher will take care from time to time to surprise some of them and have them spell some words, in order to ascertain whether they are following attentively.

All those who read in this book will read only by syllables. That is to say, they will read with a pause of equal length between each syllable, without paying any attention to the words which they compose: for instance, *Con-stan-tin, Em-pe-reur, as-sis-ta, au, con-ci-le, de, Ni-cé-e,* and so on. If these two kinds of readers are in different classes, those who only read will each day in the afternoon, before any one of them begins to read, spell about one line, at most.

Those who spell will spell about three lines and will read afterward as much as they have spelled. Those who only read will read five or six lines, according to the number of students and the time which the teacher may have.

Article 6:
The Third Reader

The third reader which will be used to teach reading in the Christian Schools will be one upon which the Directors in each place and the Superior of the Institute will agree.

All who read from this book will do so by sentences and in sequence, stopping only at periods and at commas. Only those who know how to read by syllables perfectly and without fail will be in this lesson. Two or three pages will be given for a lesson each time, from one complete idea to another, a chapter, an article, or a section.

The beginners will read about eight lines. The more advanced will read about twelve or fifteen lines, according to the time that the teacher has and the number of the students.

Those who are reading the third book will also be taught all the rules of French pronunciation, both how to pronounce syllables and words perfectly correctly and how to sound the consonants at the end of words when the following word begins with a vowel. The teacher will teach the students all these things while they are reading, calling their attention to all the mistakes in pronunciation which they make. The teacher will correct them carefully without overlooking any.

Article 7:
Vowels, Consonants, Punctuation, Accents, Numerals

Students who are studying the third book will be taught to recognize the vowels and the consonants and to distinguish them from one another. They will be taught the reason why some letters are called vowels and others are called consonants. They will also be instructed concerning the pauses that must be made at a period, a colon, a semicolon, and a comma. They will be taught the reasons for and the differences among these signs.

They will be taught the significance of an interrogation mark, of an exclamation mark, of parentheses, of a hyphen, of the two dots over an *ë*, an *ï*, or *ü*, and the reason why all of these are used. They will be taught the different abbreviations and their meanings and the three different accents, the reasons for which they are used and what they signify. They will likewise be taught to read the numerals both French and Roman at least up to 100,000, and in various combinations.

There must be for this purpose in each classroom two charts. One will contain separately the vowels and consonants; above each consonant will be the syllable which is pronounced in naming this consonant. On this chart will also be the different punctuation marks for words and sentences, that is to say, the apostrophe, parentheses, the hyphen, the two dots over *ë*, *ï*, or *ü*, the three different accents, and the abbreviations of words in all the forms in which they may be found. The other chart will contain separately and in columns the French and Roman numerals, at least up to 100,000.

To teach these things at the beginning of the lesson in the third book, one half hour in the afternoon twice each week will be taken.

On the first day of the week, during this half hour all that is on the first chart will be taught. It will be done in the following manner.

The teacher will have several students one after another explain different difficulties and the reasons for each as the teacher points them out on the chart.

While one student is explaining, the others will look at the chart and pay attention. In this way, they will better understand and retain what is being said.

The teacher will take care from time to time to question some other students on the same subject, in this way ascertaining both whether they are paying attention to what their companion is saying and whether they understand it.

In the afternoon of the day following a holiday or on the third school day of each week when there is no holiday, the numerals will be taught in the same way. In places where there are only two classes, the charts will be recited by the students of the writing class on Fridays instead of arithmetic.[2]

Article 8:
The Reading of Latin

The book in which the reading of Latin will be taught is the Psalter. Only those who know perfectly how to read French will be taken in this lesson. There will be three sections of readers of Latin: the beginners, who will read only by syllables; the intermediate, who will begin to read with pauses; and the advanced, who will read with pauses and without making any mistakes whatsoever.

Only those who are able to read perfectly by syllables will be made to read with pauses. Although both those who read by syllables and those who read with pauses will have the same lesson, they will read separately. However, the one group will follow along while the other group is reading.

Those who are learning to read Latin will study both in the morning and in the afternoon except on the days when they learn the vowels and numerals. On those days, they will not read in the afternoon after having read in the third book.

Those who are learning to write will read only Latin in the morning and French in the afternoon. Only about two pages will be assigned as a lesson each day. The readers by syllables will read about six lines; those who read with pauses will read about ten lines. The teacher will take care to teach the students who are beginning to read

Latin the manner of pronouncing it correctly, since the pronunciation of Latin differs in several respects from the pronunciation of French. The teacher will make them understand above all that all the letters are pronounced in Latin and that all the syllables which begin with *q* or *g* are pronounced otherwise than in French, as is indicated at the end of the treatise on pronunciation.

The teacher will explain to the students those things which concern Latin pronunciation while they are reading, as has been indicated in respect to French.

Article 9:
The Rules of Christian Civility

When the students both know how to read French perfectly and are in the third level of Latin reading, they will be taught to write and they will also be taught to read the book, *Les Règles de la Civilité chrétienne.*

This book contains all the duties of children both toward God and toward their parents and the rules of civil and Christian decorum. It is printed in Gothic characters, which are more difficult to read than French characters.

They will not spell, and they will not read by syllables in this book; but all those to whom it is given will always read with continuity and with pauses.

This book will be read only in the morning. One chapter or as far as the first division or asterisk will be assigned for each lesson. The beginners will read at least four lines; the more advanced will read at least ten lines.

Article 10:
Documents

When the students are in the fourth section of round hand writing or are beginning the third section of inclined hand writing, they will be taught to read papers or parchments written by hand and called documents, or records, or something similar. At first, they will be given the easiest to read. Then they will be given the less easy ones. Afterward, they will be given the more difficult ones as they advance and so on until they are capable of reading the most difficult writing that they may encounter.

No student will be permitted to bring from home any document to read in school without the order of the Director. Each teacher of the writing class should know perfectly how to read all kinds of papers written by hand. Above all, the teacher should have read and studied well those which are in the classroom, and the Director should make sure that the teacher knows how to read them perfectly.

Those documents which are of equal difficulty are ordinarily written by the same person using the same type of lettering. This is especially true of those consisting of only one sheet or leaf, such as writs, receipts, and notes of hand. Therefore, it is very useful to have the students learn at once to read all the writings of any one writer. In this way, the form of this writer's characters and abbreviations will have impressed themselves on their imaginations and they will have no further difficulty in reading them. By this means, the most difficult and confused writing will become very easy for them.

Documents will be read twice each week at the beginning of school in the afternoon of the first and fifth school day, if there are no holy days of obligation in the week. If, however, there is a holy day which does not fall on a Wednesday or if there are two holy days in the week, documents will be read on the first and fourth school day.

The students will read one after another. They will come before the teacher in turn two by two and in the order in which they are seated on the benches. In this way, all those of one bench will come in succession and be followed by those of the next bench or the one behind it.

The beginners will read about thirty words. Those of the more advanced levels will read about ten words more than those of the preceding level. Thus the amount read will be increased by ten words for each successive level.

4
Writing

Article 1:
General Considerations

It is necessary that students should know how to read both French and Latin perfectly well before they are taught to write.

If, however, it should happen that there are any who have reached twelve years of age and have not yet begun to write, they may be put in the writing class at the same time that they begin Latin provided that they know how to read French well and correctly and that it seems that they will not be attending school for a time long enough in which to learn to write sufficiently well. This is a matter to which the Director and the Inspector of Schools will attend.

Article 2:
Writing Materials

Section 1: Paper

Teachers will take care that the students always have white paper for school use. For this reason, they will instruct the students to ask their parents for more, at the latest when they have only six white sheets left. They will see that they bring to each writing period at least half a quire of good paper, not too coarse, too gray, or too heavy; white, smooth, well dried, and well glazed; above all, not too easily absorbent of ink, which is very defective and a great hindrance in writing. Teachers will neither permit any student to bring loose paper nor permit any student to fold the paper in quarters. The sheets must be sewed together their entire length.

Finally, teachers must have the students keep their paper always very clean and neither crumpled nor turned down at the corners. There will be in the school a chest or a cupboard in which all paper and other school material will be put.

The officers of the writing class, who will distribute and collect the papers one by one, will carefully do so with order and in silence. They will be careful not to mix the papers.

Section 2: Pens and Penknives

Teachers will instruct the writers to bring to school each day at least two large quills. In this way, they may always be able to write with one of them while the other is being trimmed.

Teachers will see that the quills are neither too slender nor too thick; they should be round, strong, clear, dry, and of the second growth. Care must be taken that the pens are clean and not full of ink, that they are neither bitten at the end nor trimmed too short, and that the students do not put the pen tips in their mouths or leave them lying about. Writers of the third level should also have penknives, so that they may learn to trim their pens.

All the writers will also have writing cases in which to put their pens and penknives. The teacher will require that they be the longest that can be found in order that the students will not be obliged to cut their pens too short. This would prevent them from writing well.

Section 3: Ink

Students will be supplied with ink. For this purpose, there will be as many inkwells as possible. They will be made of lead, so that they cannot be overturned. One will be placed between each two students. The teacher will have ink put into them when needed and have the students who are appointed to collect the papers clean the inkwells once a week, on the last school day. There will be only ink and no cotton in these inkwells. The ink will be supplied gratuitously.

The teacher will see that the students ink their pens carefully, dipping only the pen tip and then shaking it gently in the inkwell and not on the floor.

Section 4: Models

There will be two kinds of models given to the students. The first will consist of two alphabets, one of letters not joined and one of letters joined together. The second will consist of sentences, each one of which will contain five or six lines.

The models which are given to the students will be written on loose sheets. Teachers will not write any examples on the papers of the students, or any large capital letters or strokes at the beginning of their pages. This is a matter of importance.

All lined models will consist of sentences from holy scripture, of Christian maxims taken from the works of the Fathers, or from devotional books.

For this purpose, there will be in each school two collections: one of sentences from holy scripture, both the Old and the New Testament, and the other, of maxims of piety taken from some good books.

Teachers will give no models that are not taken from one of these two collections. They will make special use of those taken from holy scripture, which, as it is the word of God, should make a greater impression and more easily touch the heart.

All the alphabet models shall be in a large business hand. The models used by those who write in lines should be of three different characters: large business characters, financial numbers, and small characters.

Section 5: Transparencies and Blotting Paper

Transparencies will be given only to such students as are unable to write straight without lines. The Inspector of Schools and the teacher will examine those who may need them, and they will make the least possible use of them.

A transparency is a sheet of paper with lines drawn across it at proper intervals. It is called a transparency because when it is placed beneath the sheet upon which writing is to be done, the lines are visible through the paper and serve to guide the lines of writing.

Each one of the writers will have a sheet or two of coarse paper, which easily absorbs ink. In order to dry what they have written without blotting it, they will place the coarse paper over the page on which they have written. This coarse paper is, on account of the use made of it, called blotting paper.

Article 3:
Time for and Amount of Writing in School

Students will spend, both in the morning and in the afternoon, one hour in writing, from eight o'clock until nine and from three o'clock until four. From the beginning of November until the end of January, however, they will begin to write at half past two and will finish at half past three. Should it happen that some students will not be continuing in school much longer, and that they need to write for a longer period than the others in order to learn to write sufficiently well, they may be permitted to write at other times during school hours. However, they may not write during the time devoted to the reading of manuscripts, to prayers, and to catechism. They should know how to read French, Latin, and *Les Règles de la Civilité chrétienne* so well that they would derive no further benefit from reading them. They should read in their turn during all lessons. They should also take their turn in reciting the catechism, the responses of holy Mass, and the prayers during breakfast and the afternoon snack. They should have been writing in lines for at least six months. This will, however, be granted to none without the order of the Director. Each student will write at least two pages a day, one in the morning and the other in the afternoon.

Article 4:
Different Levels of Writing Round Hand

There will be six levels of writers of round hand, distinguished one from another by the different skills which are taught the students in each of them.

The first level will consist of those who are learning to hold the pen and the body correctly and to make with ease the straight and circular movements. The teacher will attend to them only to see that they hold their pens, their bodies, and their hands correctly and that they make these two movements well. It is very important that students should not begin to write until they have learned to hold their pens correctly and have acquired a free movement of the fingers.

The second level of writers will consist of those who are learning to form the five letters, *c, o, i, f,* and *m*. For this purpose, they will write one page of each of these letters one after another. With the students of these two levels, the teacher will take care only and often to see that the students form the letters properly, that they join them together neatly and as they should be joined, and that they place them correctly. Before advancing in the third level, students will be taught the letters which are based upon *o, i,* and *f* and the manner of forming the derivatives based on these three letters.

The third level will consist of those who are learning to form correctly all the letters of the alphabet. For this purpose, they should write one page of each letter one after another. When the teacher considers it appropriate, the students will write a line composed of each letter.

The fourth level will consist of those who, in addition to perfecting themselves in those things which the two preceding levels should learn, are learning to place the letters properly and evenly, as they should be when on the same line and to extend the long letters above or below the body of the writing as much as they should be according to the rules of writing. To achieve this the students of this level will write all the letters of the alphabet joined together on each line. They will be required to apply the same rules that should be observed for a long word which would fill an entire line.

The fifth level will consist of all who are writing sentences in large commercial characters, such as are used in accounts. As long as they continue to write in these characters they should first write one page of each line of their models, one line after another. When the teacher, in agreement with the Director, considers it appropriate, they will copy the entire model. Their models will be changed every month. They will also write on the reverse side of their papers the entire alphabet joined together on each line. They will do this until they know how to write it perfectly. They will then be required to copy their models of a connected sentence on all the pages of their paper.

The sixth level will consist of those who are writing sentences in these same large business characters on the front side of their paper and in financial characters on the reverse side.[1]

Article 5:
Different Levels in Writing Italian Script

When the students begin to learn to write Italian script, they will be required to observe all that is indicated above in connection with the first and the following levels in round hand.

There will also be six levels of writers of Italian script.

The first level will consist of those who are learning how to hold the pen and the entire body in a proper position. They will not be permitted to write until they have acquired a complete movement of the thumb and the fingers.

The second level will consist of those who are learning to form the five letters *c, o, i, f,* and *m* and who should write one page of each letter as has been indicated for the second section in round hand.

The third level will consist of those who are being taught the manner of correctly forming the letters of the alphabet and their proper position and slant. To achieve this purpose, they will write one page of each letter joined together, over and over. Thereafter, the teacher in agreement with the Director will have them write one line of each letter, provided they have made progress in this level.

The fourth level in Italian script will consist of those who are being taught the relative proportions of the letters, the distance that should separate them, and the space that there should be between the lines.

They must also be trained in this level to write with firmness and to pass easily from one letter to another. The students in this level will write the entire alphabet in proper order on each line.

In the fifth level, the students will write sentences formed of large characters, in the same manner as has been indicated for the fifth level in round hand.

Those of the sixth level will write sentences formed of large characters on the front side of their paper. On the reverse, they will write in small characters. In these last two levels, the teacher and the students will apply the same rules as in the fifth and sixth levels of the writers of round hand.

A student who is beginning to learn to write Italian script and has one year, that is to say eleven months, in which to learn it, will be taught during the first month how to hold the pen and the body and to make with ease the straight and circular movements as is indicated above. For the next two months the student will practice writing one page of each letter, the letters connected. The two following months, the student will practice writing one line of each letter joined together. During the next two months, the student will practice the entire alphabet in order on each line. During the last four months, the student will write sentences in medium-sized characters.

The time of these students who will have little time to learn to write, will be distributed as indicated above in proportion to the time which they have at their disposal for this purpose. They will, of necessity, be advanced at the end of the assigned period whether they do or do not know what they should know in order to be advanced.

The teacher will, however, take pains to review during the advanced lessons what pertains to the preceding ones, in case they do not know completely what they need to know.

Article 6:
Correct Position of the Body

The writing teacher will take care that the students always hold their bodies as erect as possible, only slightly inclined but without touching the table. In this manner and with the elbow placed on the table, the chin can be rested upon the hand. The body must be somewhat turned and free on the same side. The teacher will require them to observe all the rules of writing concerning the position of the body.

Teachers will, above all, take care that students do not hold their right arms too far from their bodies and that they do not press their stomachs against the table. Besides being very ungraceful, this posture might make them very uncomfortable. In order to make students hold their bodies correctly, teachers will themselves place them in the posture which the students should maintain, with each limb where it should be. Whenever teachers notice students changing this position, they will take care to put them back into it.

Article 7:
Correctly Holding Pen and Positioning Paper

The second thing of which the teacher should be careful in regard to writing is to teach how to hold the pen and how to place the paper. This is of great importance, because students who have not been trained in the beginning to hold their pens correctly will never write well.

In order to teach the manner of holding the pen properly, it is necessary to arrange the hand of the student and to put the pen between the student's fingers.

When the students begin to write, it will be useful and appropriate to give them a stick of the thickness of a pen to hold. On the sticks, there will be three grooves, two on the right and one on the left. These grooves indicate the places where the three fingers should be placed. This teaches the students to hold the pen properly in their fingers and makes them hold these three fingers in a good position.

Care must be taken that the students place the three fingers on these three grooves and that for a fortnight at least during writing time they practice rendering their fingers supple by means of this stick or of an unpointed pen. The teacher will urge them to practice this, as often as possible, at home and everywhere else. The two other fingers should be under the pen, and it would be well to have the students tie them for as long a time as is necessary in the position in which they should be held.

The position of the paper should be straight and the teacher will pay great attention to this. If the paper is slanting, the lines will be slanting, the body cannot be held in a good position, and the letters cannot be so well formed.

Article 8:
Training to Write Well

As soon as students begin to write and are in the second or third level, they will be taught how to form the letters, where to begin them, when to ease the pressure on the pen, and when to raise it; the teachers must do this several times. Next, they will make the students understand the manner of doing all these things correctly.

In order that the students observe carefully and learn well the form of the letters, the teacher will guide their hands from time to time and for as long a time as judged needful. However, this will be done only with those who are in the first and the second level of writing.

The teacher will let them write alone for some time after having guided their hands and shown them how to form the letters. However, from time to time, what they have written should be examined.

The teacher will then both have them practice making the connections between letters in an easy manner, and help them to do so. This is done by lessening the pressure on the pen slightly on the side next to the thumb. It is important that they always do this in the same way.

Care must also be taken that when the students are writing the alphabet they do not crowd or space either the letters or the lines too much. As soon as they are in the second lesson of writing, they will be given transparencies to accustom them to writing their lines straight. The teacher will see that they place the bottom of the body of the letters on the line of the transparency.

Students must not, however, make use of the transparencies continually. From time to time, the teacher will have them write five or six lines without using the transparency. In this manner, they will imperceptibly accustom themselves to writing straight of their own accord and without this aid. Those who are writing in lines will use transparencies as little as possible.

It is important not to have the students write in lines until they know how to form all the letters properly and to write the entire alphabet in all the manners which are indicated for the different levels in writing. One may be sure that by keeping to this practice the students will make more progress in one month than they would otherwise make in six.

Teachers will not permit the students to write anything other than what is on their models.

Article 9:
Teaching Students to Trim Pens

The teacher will trim the pens of the students when necessary, but only during the writing periods.

To effect this, the students whose pens need to be trimmed will carefully place their pens in front of them, so that the teacher may perceive them when coming around to correct the writing. The students will remain with their hats off until the teacher has returned their pen. When they get the trimmed pens back, they will kiss the teacher's hand and bow low. The students will not cease writing while the teacher is trimming their pens.

After the students have been writing at the most for one month in the third or fourth level, the teacher will require them to trim their pens themselves and will teach them individually how to do this. For this, the teacher will have them individually come to the teacher and will show them in the following manner all that is necessary to do this properly.

The teacher will take a new quill and teach the students these steps. First, both how to strip the quill of feathers without tearing it and how to straighten it if it is bent. Second, how to hold it in their fingers. Third, how to open the stem both at the top and at the bottom. Fourth, how to hold the quill to slit it. Fifth, with what and how to slit it. Sixth, how it should be slit both for round hand and for Italian and rapid script. Seventh, how to hollow it, explaining that to do this the point of the penknife must be used.

Eighth, demonstrating that for the rapid script style of writing the two angles of the pen tip must be equal, while for other styles of writing one of the angles of the pen tip should be thicker and longer and the other should be finer and shorter. Ninth and tenth, showing which side should be thicker and longer, and which side should be finer and shorter. Eleventh, how to open the quill, how long and deep the opening should be, and with what part of the blade of the penknife the opening should be made.

Twelfth, how to clear the pen tip and to cut it with the middle of the blade. Thirteenth, how to hold the penknife upright or flat. And finally, fourteenth, both that the quill should not be cut against the nail of the left thumb, on the table, or on wood, but that it should be cut on the stem of another quill pushed into the one which is being cut. The teacher will then explain to the students all the terms used in pens, the angle, the pen tip, and so on, and will make them repeat these terms.

In order to make the students understand, retain, and practice all that pertains to the proper way of trimming pens, teachers will themselves demonstrate trimming on three successive days. They will make students understand all that they do in trimming and why. Immediately afterward, teachers will have the students trim a pen, telling them all that they must do and how to do it well, and correcting them when they fail in anything. This lesson will continue for about a week.

Article 10:
Inspecting Writers and Correcting Writing

It is necessary that teachers inspect all the writers every day and, in the case of beginners, even two or three times a day. The teachers must observe whether the pens of those who trim their own are well trimmed; whether their bodies are in a correct position; whether their paper is straight and clean; whether they hold their pens properly; whether they have models; whether they are practicing as much as they should; whether they are trying to do well; whether they are writing too fast; whether they are making their lines straight; whether they are placing all their letters in the same position and at a proper distance; whether the body of all the letters is of the same height and in the same type, and the letters are distinct and well formed; and whether the words and the lines are too close together or too far apart.

At each inspection, the teacher will correct the writing of one-half of the writers. In this manner, the teacher will daily and without fail correct all of them, half in the morning and half in the afternoon.

Teachers will walk behind the writers, observing each one. For this reason, there will be some space between the benches. Teachers will place themselves at the right of the one whom they are to correct, and will show the student all the mistakes being made, in the writing, in the posture of the body, in the manner of holding the pen and forming the letters, and in all the other things which are explained above and which the teacher should examine when inspecting the writers.

When speaking of hangers, feet, heads, tails, members, and bodies of letters, of divisions, distances, and separations, of height, width, curve, semicurve, thick and fine, small character, large character, and so forth, the teacher will explain all these terms, each one precisely, and will afterward ask the explanation, saying, for instance, "What is meant by hangers?"

Teachers will insist that the students be attentive when their writing in being corrected. The teacher will mark with a slight stroke of the pen the principal mistakes made. However, in the beginning care should be taken not to call attention to more than three or four mistakes. If teachers mark a greater number, they might confuse the students and make them forget what they have been taught. Correction for a greater number of mistakes would create confusion in their minds.

When examining these exercises, teachers will show the students how to write the syllables or the letters which they are correcting. In order that the students may afterward practice forming them in the same manner, the teacher will, after having written the syllables or letters at the top or on the margin of their papers make the students write a line of each letter or syllable which has been corrected and two lines of each word. If they have not the time to do all this on that day, they will be directed to finish the work the next day before beginning to copy the model.

If they do not succeed even after that, the teacher will have them practice during all the time they have for writing only the letters, syllables, or words which they have written incorrectly. They will do this two or three times in succession.

When correcting the writing, the teacher will not write on the papers of the students any lines or words of several syllables. It will suffice that the teacher write the letter which the student has written badly, and, if the latter has failed in connecting some letters, the teacher will write the two letters joined together or the syllable at the very most.

While inspecting and correcting the writing of some of the students, the teacher will be careful both to keep all the other students always in sight and to observe all that takes place in the class. If anyone is at fault, the teacher will warn that student by making a sign. The teacher will watch particularly over those who most need watching, that is, the beginners and the negligent. The teachers will take care above all during this time that nothing escape their eye.

The teacher will also pay very particular attention to the students who are making the two movements, the straight and the circular, and will watch that their pens are not slipping out of their fingers. If the pens are slipping out of their fingers, the teacher will place them as they should be and explain what should be done to keep them so. The teacher will also see to it that in making the movements, the students do not move the arm instead of extending and bending only the fingers; that they move their fingers instead of their arms; that the thumb always moves first; that they do not rest the hand when making these movements; and that they do not press down when making the strokes instead of making them lightly.

The teacher will indicate the mistakes that they may have made in these things and the means of correcting them. The teacher will show them how they must bend and extend their fingers; how they should rest the arm without pressing it too much on the table; and how they should write from one side of their paper to the other touching the paper only slightly with the pen tip and lightly gliding the arm from the left side to the right side.

In regard to the straight movement, teachers will insist that the students draw straight from top to bottom; that they do not hold their fingers too stiffly but bend them as much as is necessary to make the movement well; and that they keep the pen always level without varying either in the ascending or in the descending stroke. For the circular movement, teachers will notice both whether they begin it at the bottom and at the top with the same smoothness as well from left to right as from right to left and whether they hold their fingers too stiffly and keep their arms fixed on the table. From time to time, teachers will watch the students of the first level make these two movements in order to see for themselves the mistakes which the students make in respect of all the above-mentioned things. At the same time, the teacher will indicate to them the means of correcting these mistakes, and will have them correct them at once.

Teachers will call the attention of the students of the second and third levels, and even of the higher ones, to mistakes in the way they are forming their letters. For instance, a teacher will ask them whether a *B* which a student has made in round hand is too much inclined to one side or to the other; whether it is curved or humped; whether all its dimensions are correct: its height should be twice that of the body of the letter or eight pen tips; whether it is too high; whether it has the width that it should at the top and at the bottom; whether it lacks some of its parts; and whether the thick strokes or the fine ones are where they should be. The teacher will do the same with all the other letters. The teacher will mark with a stroke of the pen at each place all the mistakes that the students have made in forming these letters. For example, if the *b* is too much inclined to the right, the teacher will mark it in this manner ↘. If the *b* is too much inclined to the left, the teacher will mark it thus ↙

The teacher will call the attention of those of the third and of the following levels to all the mistakes which they may have made in the connecting strokes: failure to make any where they should have been made, or making any where they should not have been made; beginning a connection at a point of the letter other than at the one where they should start; making the connecting stroke too high or not high enough, or too fine or too thick; making the strokes wavy when they should be circular, or straight when they should be circular; holding the pen as it should be held to make the strokes, and turning the pen instead of easing the pressure.

To make the students understand easily and very well the defects of the letters and their connecting strokes after having shown them, the teacher will ask the students what is wrong with the letter or the connection. The teacher will ask why the one or the other is not good, and will then correct the letter or the connection which the student has formed badly. The teacher will do this by writing the one or the other over the letter or the connection which the student has formed badly, and will ask why the one which they have retraced is good and what there is in it that was not in the letter made by the student. After this, the teacher will write a letter or two joined letters between the lines. The teacher will have the students practice this, and will observe how they form it.

When a student in the first three levels has been taught something or has had something corrected, the teacher will not immediately leave. Instead, in the teacher's presence the student will practice what has been taught or corrected. The teacher will watch to see whether the pen is being held in the way that has been shown, whether the letters are begun properly, and whether all is done well that has been taught. The teacher does this so that the students may be told in what they fail. If the teacher were to leave the student at once, all that had been said or taught would be forgotten. Furthermore, this manner of instruction will please the parents. The children will not fail to tell their parents that the teacher has taught them by making them write while supervised, that the teacher has personally guided their hand, and so on.

If a student fails to place the letters properly, that is to say, when they are not in line with each other, the teacher will draw two straight pen lines at the entire place in the line where the student has erred, one line from the base of the last letter which is properly placed and the other from the top of the body of that letter. The teacher will then explain the mistake in position and which letters are not well aligned. The teacher will do the same when the hangers are not of equal height or uniformly situated. To correct a defect in distance between letters, the teacher will point out the space that should be between the preceding letter and the following one, and make a downward stroke with the pen at the point where the first member should be placed of the letter which is too close to or too far from the preceding one.

To correct a defect in distance between two words that are either too close together or too far apart, the teacher will make an *m* of the width of seven times that of the pen tip, the space that should be between two words. If there is a period between the words, the teacher will make five hangers of an *m* joined together. This is the width of thirteen pen tips and is the space that should be between two words separated by a period. If there is a comma, a colon, or a semicolon, the teacher will make between the two words two *n*'s of ten times the width of the pen tip, which is the distance at which they should be from each other.

To correct a defect in distance between lines the teacher will make a set of four letters joined together on the margin of the paper, between the lines which are either too close together or too far apart. The teacher will make, for instance, four *o*'s joined together of the width of sixteen times that of the pen tip. This will help the student note what distance there should be between the two lines. To make them acquire lightness and avoid lack of boldness in writing, the teacher will instruct the students not to press on their paper, but just touch it with the pen tip and almost without feeling it and not to write too slowly. The teacher will point out that this defect comes from holding the arm as though fixed on the table, from not bending the fingers to impart to them the movement that they should have, or from leaning the body too much or even bending it over the table.

To make the students correct these faults themselves, they must, if they are slow, be urged to write fast, without resting the arm on the table, resting only the tips of the two sustaining fingers on the table. The teacher must do this without paying any attention to whether the students form their letters well or badly, taking pains only to make them acquire boldness and ease of movement.

If a student is naturally quick, it will be necessary only to arrange correctly the student's hand, arm, and body. After having been taught what to do, the students should be allowed to practice by themselves. Restrain them, however, and moderate the students who are too active.

To make all sorts of students acquire freedom and ease of movement, teachers will show them how to pass properly from one letter to another, such as from an i to an f, from a c to an l, and from an o to an i, without interruption and without raising the pen. To correct the mistakes which the students may have made in all things pertaining both to boldness and to ease of movement, a teacher will demonstrate what the students must do in order to correct themselves. Then, the students are to imitate what the teacher has just done and correct what they had previously done badly.

5

Arithmetic

In the study of arithmetic students will have different lessons according to how advanced they may be. Some of them will be learning addition, others will be learning subtraction, multiplication, or division. Teachers will take care to write on the board a problem for each operation every Saturday or on the last school day if Saturday is a holy day. They will see that all who are learning arithmetic copy their examples on Monday morning at the beginning of the writing lesson or on the first school day if there is a holy day on Monday. For this, each must have a notebook of white paper folded in quarters.

Arithmetic will be taught only to those who are entering the fourth level in writing, and it is the duty of the Director or of the Inspector of Schools to promote to this lesson as well as to the others. Arithmetic will be taught on Tuesday and Friday afternoon from one thirty to two o'clock. If there is a holy day on Tuesday, it will be taught on Wednesday, unless there is a holy day on Monday as well as on Tuesday. If there is a holy day on Friday, it will be taught on Saturday.

To teach arithmetic, the teacher will either remain seated or will stand before the teacher's chair. A student of each lesson will stand in front of the class and solve the problem for the lesson. The student will indicate the steps and, with the pointer, the figures, adding, subtracting, multiplying, or dividing the numbers aloud.

Thus, to make an addition properly, the students will always begin by adding *deniers,*[1] and speaking out loud, saying for example: "Ten and six make sixteen," and so on.

While the example of the lesson is being done, the teacher will ask the student several questions concerning it, in order to make the student better understand and retain the lesson. If terms pertaining to the subject are used which the student does not understand, the teacher will explain them and make the student repeat them before going further. From time to time, the teacher will also question some other students who have the same lesson, to ascertain if they are attentive and if they understand. If the one who is doing the example fails in any respect, the teacher will make a sign to another student who is learning the same lesson or one who is learning a more advanced lesson to make the correction. The latter will do this by correcting aloud what the other one had said wrongly. If there are no lessons more advanced than this one and if no student is able to correct the mistake properly, the teacher will make the correction.

The student who is doing the example on the board should, as part of doing the example, write at the bottom both the result of the addition, subtraction, multiplication, or division and the proof of the problem which has just been done. After this, the students will erase all that they themselves have written but nothing more. In this way, another student may do the same example.

In arithmetic, as well as in the other subjects, it is with the most elementary examples that the lesson will begin and with the most advanced that it will end.

When a student is doing an example in arithmetic whatever the grade, all the others who have the same lesson will remain seated facing the board and will pay attention to the figures that the student writes and to what the student says when doing the example. The students who are reading and who are not yet learning arithmetic will also pay attention. The teacher will have a register of all the students who are learning arithmetic, divided according to the lesson that they are studying, and will have each of them, one after another and without any exception, do an example from their lessons on the board in school.

On Tuesday of each week or the first day upon which arithmetic is taught, all the students who are learning it and who are among the advanced students will bring already done on their paper the example for their lesson which the teacher has written on the board for that week. They will also bring some other examples which they have invented for themselves. On Friday, they will bring a certain number of examples from their own lessons as well as from the work of more elementary lessons which they have done by themselves and which the teacher has, according to their capacity, assigned for them to do.

During the writing time on Tuesday and Thursday afternoons, instead of correcting the writing, the teacher will correct the examples which the students of arithmetic have done by themselves on their papers. The teacher will explain why anything is incorrect. Concerning addition, the teacher will, for example, ask them: "Why do we begin with *deniers?*" "Why do we reduce the *deniers* to *sols* and the *sols* to *livres?*" The teacher will ask other similar questions, as needed, and will give the students a full explanation.

6

Spelling

Teachers will take care to teach spelling to the students who are in the sixth level of round hand writing and of Italian script. The Director will see to this. The manner of teaching them spelling will be to have them copy letters written by hand. They will copy especially such things as it may be useful for them to know how to write and of which they might later have need, such as notes of hand, receipts, agreements with workers, legal contracts, bonds, powers of attorney, leases, deeds, and official reports. This is done so that they may impress these things on their memories and learn to write similar ones.

After they have copied these kinds of writings for some time, teachers will have them make and write by themselves some notes of hand, receipts, agreements with workers, some bills for different kinds of work done by the hour, bills for goods delivered, estimates by workers, and the like.

Teachers will also oblige them at the same time to write what they remember of the catechism which had been taught them during the week. They will be obliged to write especially what has been taught them on Sundays and holy days, or on Wednesdays just before a holiday, if there has been no holy day in the week. If it appears some of them are unable to do this, the teacher will have them write the lesson of the diocesan catechism which they learned by heart in the past week. They will be obliged to write this lesson from memory and without looking at the book. For this purpose, they must have a notebook, which they will bring to be corrected Tuesday and Friday or any other day on which arithmetic is taught. The students must do this so that teachers may correct the examples of arithmetic and the mistakes in spelling in what they have written. Teachers will, in their own writing, add the letters which students have omitted or correct the errors after having drawn a line through the latter.

Teachers will require that the students whose writing has been corrected for spelling rewrite it at home. They will be obliged to make a fair copy, just as the teacher had corrected it. The next time that their spelling is corrected the teacher will carefully check if they have acquitted themselves of this duty.

Spelling will be taught in the following manner also. The teacher will dictate, for example, *Dieu tout puissant et miséricordieux*. All will write; one student alone, while writing, will spell the syllables aloud: *Di-eu tout puis-sant et mi-sé-re-cor-di-eux*. If the student has said anything wrong in spelling, for instance, saying *mis* instead of *mi-sé*, the teacher or whoever is dictating will correctly repeat the letter or the syllable that this student has said incorrectly. The one dictating will be careful to indicate where periods and commas are to be placed.

After what has been dictated has been written, the teacher will make one student spell aloud what the others have written. All the others will spell along with the reader in a low voice.

The teacher will take care that this student who is spelling aloud state when there are acute or grave accents, and name the letters upon which these accents are to be placed; and also state when there is a period, a colon, a semicolon, a comma, an exclamation point, or an interrogation mark. Those who have made mistakes on their papers will correct the mistakes for themselves.

The students will write their spelling on the back of their paper. They will write the fair or corrected copy on the paper folded in squares.

7

Prayers

Article 1:
Prayers Said in School Daily

At the opening of school at eight in the morning and as soon as the bell has ceased ringing, all will make the sign of the cross and then say *Veni Sancte Spiritus* and what follows. In the afternoon, the *Venez Saint Esprit* will be said.[1] This is as indicated in the *Le Livre des Exercices de Piété des Ecoles chrétiennes*. Before and after breakfast and the afternoon snack and during the entire school time from 8:30 until 10:00 in the morning and from 2:00 until 3:30 in the afternoon, the prayers which are indicated in this same book will be said.

There will always be two or three students, one from each class, kneeling and reciting the rosary in some place in the school which has been chosen by the Director or the Inspector and arranged for this purpose. At each hour of the day, some short prayers will be said. These will help the teachers to recollect themselves and recall the presence of God; it will serve to accustom the students to think of God from time to time and to offer God all their actions, and to draw upon themselves God's blessing. At the beginning of each lesson, a few short Acts [prayers] will be said to ask of God the grace of studying well and learning well.

The morning prayers will be said at 10:45, if the students assist at holy Mass during school. If they do not assist at holy Mass before the end of school in the morning, the morning prayers will be said at ten o'clock.

In the afternoon, the evening prayers will be said at the end of school at 4:30. During the winter, from the first school day in November until the end of January, these prayers will be said at four o'clock.

Article 2:
Morning Meditation and
Evening Examen of Conscience

There are five meditations in the morning prayers for the five school days of the week. All of them will be read each day, a short pause being made after each one. The student who is leading the prayers, after having read all of these meditations, will repeat the one to which special attention is to be given that day. Then a pause of the duration of a *Miserere*² will be made. During this time, the teacher will make a little exhortation suited to the capacity of the students and on the subject of this meditation.

All of these five meditations will be repeated in the order indicated and each in turn will serve as the subject of an exhortation on each of the five school days in the week. An examination of conscience is part of the evening prayers. This examination contains those sins which children most ordinarily commit. The examination is divided into four articles, and each article is subdivided into five points. Only one of these articles will be read each day, and this same article will be read every day during that week. Thus, the four articles will be read in four weeks.

Each teacher will explain to the class one of the points of the article which is being read during that week. Teachers will make known in detail to the students the sins which they are liable to commit, without ever deciding whether the sin is mortal or venial. Teachers will, at the same time, seek to inspire horror of these sins and suggest the means of avoiding them.

Article 3:
Prayers Said in School on Special Occasions

On all Saturdays and on the eves of the feasts of the Blessed Virgin, the litany of the Blessed Virgin will be recited after evening prayers.

On the eve of Christmas, of the Epiphany, and of the Purification, the litany of the Holy Child Jesus will be recited at the end of evening prayers.

On the eve of the feast of the Circumcision, the litany of the Holy Name of Jesus will be recited. On the eve of the feast of Saint Joseph, the litany of that saint will be recited.

All of these prayers will be recited in the manner that is indicated in the *Le Livre des Exercices de Piété des Ecoles chrétiennes.*

During the octave of Corpus Christi and on the Monday and Tuesday before Lent, the following is to be done. Instead of the rosary which is usually said in school, students from each class will be sent two by two, to adore the Blessed Sacrament in the nearest church where it is exposed. If there are three classes they will go by three, and in greater number according to the number of classes. They will remain there kneeling for a half hour. However, care will be taken that there always be one student capable of insuring the good conduct of any of these groups.

On the three Ember Days, on the feast of Saint Mark, and on the Rogation Days, the litany of the Saints will be recited in the morning after the prayer which is said on entering school and immediately before the prayer which is said before breakfast. This litany is recited for the needs of the Church, the special intention on these days, and for the priests and other ministers of the Church who are to be ordained on that Ember Saturday.

Whenever in the school the sound is heard of the little bell which warns that the Blessed Sacrament is being carried to some ill person, all the students will kneel down. Each student will use this time to adore the Blessed Sacrament, until the teacher makes a sign to rise.

When one of the teachers in the town dies, the psalm which begins, *De profundis*, will be said for the repose of the teacher's soul. This prayer will be said on the first three school days after the teacher's death. It is to be said at the end of prayers, both in the morning and in the evening before the Benediction. The leader of prayers will say one versicle, and the other students will say the next. When the psalm is finished, the leader will say the collect which begins, *Inclina Domine.* In all the other houses of the Institute, on one day a *De Profundis* with the collect which begins, *Inclina Domine* will be said in school.

When a student of one of the classes in a school dies, the psalm which begins, *De profundis*, and the collect which begins, *Inclina Domine*, will be said at the end of the evening prayer on the first school day after the death, provided the student be at least seven years old.

No other prayers will be said in school; there will be prayers on no other occasions than those which are indicated in the present

Article. Nothing will be added to the prayers indicated in the present Article without the orders of the Superior of the Institute. In case of some public necessity or for some other occasion which concerns the needs of the Institute, the Superior may add the litany of the Blessed Virgin or some other short prayer at the end of prayers, and for a specified time only.

Article 4:
Posture, Manner of Praying, and Order During Prayers

Teachers will act during prayers, as well as on all other occasions, as they wish the students to act. To effect this, during the prayers on entering school, the morning prayers, the night prayers, the prayers said at the end of school, and the Acts which are said before going to holy Mass, teachers will always remain standing before the teacher's chair with a very serious demeanor, very restrained and thoroughly composed, with arms crossed, and maintaining great decorum. In this way, teachers will give an example to the students of what they should do during this time.

The students will always kneel in orderly rows. They will keep their bodies erect, their arms crossed, and their eyes lowered. The teacher will watch that they do not move, that they do not change their position, that they lean neither on the bench before them nor on the one behind them, that they do not touch the benches nor seat themselves on their heels, that they do not turn their heads to look around them, and, above all, that they do not touch one another, something they will not do if the teacher sees that they always keep their arms crossed.

During the other prayers which are said at various times in school, teachers and students will remain seated at their places, with their arms crossed, and with the same decorum that they should maintain at morning and evening prayers, as described above.

There will be in each school one student of the principal class who will be appointed to begin all the prayers which are said in that school. For this reason, this student will be called the "Reciter of Prayers."

This student alone will announce all of the titles of the Acts, the meditations, and the examination, all according to the usage established in the schools.

The Reciter of Prayers will be especially careful to say the prayers in a loud voice and in a manner intelligible to all, saying the prayers very slowly, so that the others can hear very distinctly all that is said, even to the least syllable, and observing all of the pauses. Meanwhile, teachers will see that the students do not shout out and that they do not speak too loudly. Students should recite their prayers so that they can barely be heard.

All of the students will follow the Reciter of Prayers in such a manner that they will not say a single word either before or after the Reciter of Prayers does. They will stop at all the pauses and pause as long as the Reciter does. In this way, there will be no confusion. Students will prepare to say the prayers as soon as the bell begins to ring, and the Reciter of Prayers will begin as soon as it has stopped ringing.

All will make the sign of the cross every time that the words *In nomine Patris*, etc. or *Au nom du Pére, du Fils*, etc. are said, and in the Benediction, at the words "Father, Son, and Holy Spirit."

Teachers will speak neither to any particular student nor to them all in general during prayers, either to reprimand them or for any other reason. Teachers will not correct any student during this time for any reason whatsoever. If a teacher notices someone who is doing something reprehensible and who deserves chastisement, the teacher will defer it to another time. Teachers will likewise abstain from everything that could distract the attention which the students owe to the prayers, and from everything that might cause distraction, such as making a student move from one place to another, and the like.

The principal duty of teachers during prayers will be to watch with very great attention over all that takes place in the school. Teachers will also watch over themselves, and much more during this time than at any other. In this way, they will not do anything inappropriate and, above all, they will not be guilty of any frivolity.

8

Holy Mass

It will be so arranged everywhere that the students assist at holy Mass in the nearest church and at the most convenient hour.

The most convenient time to go to holy Mass is at the end of school [in the morning]. In order to go at this time, it will be necessary that the Mass should not begin much before 10:30. In this way, there may be time to say the morning prayers before going to holy Mass, beginning them at ten o'clock.

If it is not possible to go to holy Mass at the end of morning school, it will be arranged to go at or around 9:00 o'clock.

Article 1:
Leaving for Mass; Deportment on the Way

When the students are to attend holy Mass after morning school they will prepare to leave the school in the same manner they follow in the afternoon as they prepare to leave school at the end of the day. The manner to be followed is indicated in Chapter 9,[1] which treats the topic of leaving the school.

When the students are to assist at holy Mass during school time, they will leave school in the order of the benches. The first on a bench will take the second one as companion, the third one will take the fourth one, and so on with the others. Teachers will see to it that all leave the school in silence, with great decorum and reserve, and that, while on the street on their way to the church, they walk two by two in a line. They are not to leave their companion or walk apart from the time they leave the school until they are kneeling in the church.

Teachers will take care that the students do not go too near the walls, the shops, or the gutter, and that they walk immediately behind the ones who precede them, only two paces apart. Teachers will also take care that the students walk sedately and without making any noise, and will urge each pair to say the rosary or some other prayers in a low voice. In this way, they will be more attentive to themselves, more restrained, and more modest.

Teachers will watch very carefully over the students at this time. It would, however, be best if the students are not aware of the extent of the vigilance over them.

By their modesty and restraint, teachers will give an example of the manner in which the students should walk. In order that the teachers may more easily see the students and observe how they behave themselves on the way to holy Mass, teachers will walk on the opposite side of the street from them, ahead of the line, with their faces sufficiently turned toward their students to be able to see them all. While on the street, teachers will not admonish students for any faults of which they may be guilty, but will wait until the next day, just before going to holy Mass, to correct them.

Finally, teachers will take care from time to time to warn the students in the school, while they are preparing to leave or while the students of the other classes are going out, concerning the manner in which they should walk on the street and behave in the church, and of the edification which they are obliged to give their neighbor. Teachers will urge the students to good conduct through Christian motives. They will also make the students understand that they will be more exact to punish lack of restraint and the faults that are committed on the street and in the church than those which are committed in school. The reason for this is the scandal which students would give those who might see them there.

Article 2:
Manner of Entering the Church

Teachers will take the greatest care to have the students enter the church in silence and in a particularly respectful manner. It would be well that teachers always enter the church before their students. Those who follow a teacher should, while watching over their own students, be careful to watch over those students who remain in the street. It is important that teachers should watch carefully over the conduct of students, especially when they are entering the church. Teachers should prevent them from making any noise either with the tongue or with the feet, and should require them to walk very modestly, with their eyes lowered. In this way, students will behave on the street in the manner indicated above and without the least confusion.

There will be one student, called the "Holy Water Bearer," who will have the duty of offering holy water to all the students. This will be offered to them one after another as they enter or leave the church.

This student will enter church first, and from time to time will take holy water from the font with the aspergillum. The Bearer will hold the aspergillum in such a manner that all the students can easily touch it.

Teachers will not permit students to take holy water directly from the font, but will have them take it properly from the aspergillum in a manner which manifests the piety with which one should do this act. When the students reach the place in the church assigned to them, they will all kneel, one after another.

Teachers will have the students seated in proper order in the church, and placed two by two one pair behind another. Ordinarily, they will be placed in several ranks of two each depending upon the width and length of the place that they occupy. They will be seated in such a manner that those in a same row and rank, both lengthwise and crosswise, will be exactly beside or behind one another in a straight line. If there are pillars in the middle of the section which they occupy, the students will be seated in such a manner that those of a same class will be between the pillars and the wall. In this way, each teacher may be able to see all of the students easily and watch over them. The students will be trained to take their respective places without the teacher's being obliged to attend to them.

Article 3:
Conduct During Holy Mass

The teacher of the lowest class in each school will make sure that the student who has charge of rosaries always brings them to church and that one be given to each student who does not know how to read.

There will be as many of the best behaved students appointed to distribute the rosaries as there are ranks of two in the church. As soon as the students are kneeling, the "Rosary Carrier" and the Carrier's assistants will distribute the rosaries to each one in the assigned rank, going from the top of the rank to the bottom. They will collect the rosaries in the same manner at the end of holy Mass. They will take care to collect them all and to lose none of them.

Teachers will take great care that all those who have rosaries use them to pray continuously. When students are being taught in school how to say the rosary, teachers will show them how to hold it. Teachers will require them to hold it in such a way that it may be easily seen.

Each of those who know how to read will have *Le Livre des Prières de la Sainte Messe à l'usage des Ecoles chrétiennes* and will use it during this time.

In order to avoid the noise and confusion which it might occasion, students who assist all together at holy Mass on school days will not rise when the priest reads the gospels. Teachers will, however, recommend that they make the sign of the cross three times at the beginning of each gospel and at the response, *Gloria tibi Domine*, the first on the forehead, the second on the mouth, and the third on the breast.

When the bell is rung to warn the faithful to prepare for the consecration, all who have books will place them under their arms and all of those who have rosaries will put them on their arms. Then all including teachers will clasp their hands until after the elevation of the chalice. When the bell is rung for the elevation both of the host and of the chalice, all the students will bow their heads and bend slightly forward to adore Our Lord in the host and in the precious blood in the chalice.

Article 4:
Duties of Teachers During Holy Mass

Teachers will keep a continuous watch over their students during holy Mass, observing the manner in which the students behave and the faults that they may commit. They will prevent students from speaking with each other, from passing anything to one another, from exchanging books, from pushing each other, or from doing any other of those foolish things which are only too common among children.

To prevent the students from falling into all these faults and into all the others which they could commit during holy Mass, the three following means will be used. First, teachers will oblige the students to hold their books with both hands and not cease reading them. Second, the teachers will be sure to position themselves so that the faces of the students can be easily seen. Third, teachers will always separate the students as much as possible from each other as far as space and the arrangement of the place will permit.

Except in the case of great necessity, teachers will not leave their places to reprimand students when they commit a fault. Neither will they threaten students in church. Teachers should be persuaded that it is not for their own benefit that they assist at holy Mass when they take their students. They are there only in order to watch over the students. This is, therefore, the only thing of which they will think, and they will do it with attention. They will not have any books at this time, and they will be content with a simple attention to the sacrifice.

They will take care that students bring nothing into the church that is improper or that might be a subject of distraction, as their papers could be when they have finished writing them. If they bring a brazier during winter, they should put it near to themselves in some place where it cannot be seen. They should not make use of it when in the church.

Article 5:
Entering Church After Mass Has Begun

If holy Mass has begun and is already advanced when the students reach the church, they will still be made to assist at it unless there is another Mass beginning a little later. If there is another Mass which begins immediately after the one at which they arrived late, they will remain until the end of the second Mass. If, however, there is no other Mass following, they will remain in the church for as long a time altogether as it would take for an entire Mass, including the time of the Mass at which they assisted in part.

Great care will be taken that all the students get to church and are in their places and kneeling before Mass begins. All necessary steps to effect this will be taken, even if it is necessary to send a student to the church to give notice of their coming or to request that the bell be rung a little sooner or that Mass begin a little later. This point is of very great importance. In case of necessity, it is better to omit the prayers in the school rather than to fail to assist at holy Mass.

When it is not possible to have the students assist at holy Mass on account of sleet or extraordinary rain, they will say the rosary in school. The students will stand for the rosary. Part of them will begin *Ave Maria*, and so forth, and the others will continue *Sancta Maria*, and so forth.

Article 6:
Leaving Church

When holy Mass has ended, students will leave church for school after a pause about as long as it takes to say a *Pater Noster*. The teacher or whosoever is in charge of the class that should be the first to leave will give the usual signal. Once the signal is given, all of the students of one rank will rise, make a genuflection, and at once leave their places to go out as they came, two by two. The same procedure will be followed for all the other rows. All teachers will do the same with their own class.

When the students go home after Mass, they shall be dismissed two by two. This is the same as the way in which they went from the school to the church. The Director, the Inspector of Schools, or one of the teachers who has been charged with this duty will stand at the door of the church and see that the students do not play or make any noise in the street. This teacher will take note of those who do or who stop on the way. All the students will always walk two by two in the streets and in the church, the pairs always being at least four paces away from each other. This will avoid noise and confusion. The teachers will take care to instruct the students concerning the manner of entering and of leaving the church.

Article 7:
Assistance at the Parish Mass and at Vespers

Students will be taken to the parish Mass when this can be easily done. They will also be taken to the nearest and most convenient church for vespers after catechism on Sundays and holy days of obligation. It is the duty of the Superior of the Institute to decide what should be done about this.

Teachers will explain to their students the purpose of the parish Mass and the manner of assisting at it. If there is a sermon, they will take care that the students listen to it very attentively and respectfully. Teachers will inspire the students with a great respect and affection for the offices of the church, especially for those which are celebrated in their own parishes. Students will, therefore, assemble in the church on Sundays and holy days of obligation. They will be required to be there before the *Asperges*, or blessing with holy water, and to remain until the end of the Mass. If there are benches for them in the church, they will sit there. Teachers will see that they do so in proper order. They will sit, stand, or kneel according to the practice of the diocese or the parish.

The students will, however, all kneel during the offertory, and until the preface if there is no offering. They will kneel until the offering, if there is one and it is made immediately after the offertory. This will help them unite themselves during this action with the intention of the priest and also to offer themselves to be consecrated entirely to God. They will stand throughout the preface and will all kneel when the *Sanctus* is sung. They will remain kneeling until the end of the Mass.

If there are no benches for the students, they will stand all the time that the others are seated except during the offertory. Teachers who are present to watch over them will see that they are always well lined up and in good order.

During the parish Mass and during vespers, teachers will always keep the students in sight and will take care that those who do not know how to read say the rosary as on other days. They will take care that those who know how to read have *Le Livre des Prières de la Sainte Messe* in their hands all the time at Mass and a *Livre d'office* throughout vespers, and they will see to it that they read them continuously. When the students leave the church after Mass and after vespers, the same order will be observed as after holy Mass on school days. When the "blessed bread" is given for the students, the one who has charge of the rosaries will bring a basket in which to put it. At the end of the Mass, this student will distribute the bread to them all in turn.[2]

9
The Catechism

Article 1:
Teaching Catechism and the Parts to Be Taught

Catechism will be taught every day for a half hour from 4:00 until 4:30 in the afternoon.

From the first day of November until the last of January inclusive, catechism will be taught from 3:30 until 4:00 o'clock.

On the Wednesdays preceding holidays, it will be taught for one hour from 3:30 until 4:30 in the afternoon. In the winter, it will be taught from 3:00 until 4:00 o'clock. It will also be taught for one hour on the eve of the feast of Saint Joseph, of the Presentation of the Blessed Virgin, of the Transfiguration of Our Lord, and of the Exaltation of the Holy Cross. When there is a holy day in the week, there will be only a half holiday in the afternoon, on Tuesday or Thursday. On that day in the morning, the lessons will be shortened, and the catechism will be taught for a half hour at the end of school. On Wednesday afternoon in Holy Week the students will have neither reading nor writing. Only the catechism will be taught, from 1:30 until 3:00 o'clock as is done on Sundays and holy days. The same will be done on the eves of the feast of the Most Holy Trinity and of Christmas. At 3:00 o'clock at the end of catechism, the prayers will be said, and the students will be dismissed in the regular manner.

On Wednesdays before full holidays and on Sundays and ordinary holy days, catechism will be taught in all the classes. The first half hour will be spent on a summary of the principal mysteries. The rest of the time will be spent on the subject indicated for the week.

On solemn feasts for which there is a particular subject in the catechism, the subject of the feast or of the mystery will be taught, as it is indicated in the catechism.

Catechism will be taught on the afternoon of Wednesday in Holy Week. From 1:30 until 2:00 o'clock, the teacher will explain the principal mysteries. From 2:00 until 3:00, the teacher will explain the manner in which the ensuing days until Easter Sunday should be spent. On the eves of the Most Holy Trinity and of Christmas, the same will be done. On Mondays, the subject that will be treated throughout the week will be begun. On Sunday, the last day on which this subject is treated, a summary will be made of all that has been propounded during the five days of the week. In those classes in which only the abridgment of Christian Doctrine is taught, the teacher will also examine the students on all of the questions contained in the lessons for the preceding five days. On Sundays and holy days and on Wednesdays before a whole holiday, the catechism lesson will be on the particular subject assigned for the week.

Article 2:
How to Ask Questions During Catechism

Teachers will not speak to the students during catechism as though they were preaching, but will ask the students questions and subquestions almost continuously. In order to make them understand what is being taught, a teacher will ask several students, one after another, the same question. Sometimes the teacher will ask it of seven or eight, or even of ten or twelve, sometimes of even a greater number.

The teacher will question the students in the order of the benches. If, however, the teacher notes that several in succession cannot answer a question or do not do it well, the teacher may call upon one or several out of the regular order and in different parts of the class. Then, after having given the signal once, the teacher will make a sign to another to answer. After one or several have answered, the one upon whom the teacher had called before in the regular order will be called on.

The teacher will question all of the students each day, several times, if possible. However, the teacher will interrupt the regular order and the sequence from time to time to question those observed to be inattentive or worse, ignorant. A special effort will be made to question, much more often than the others, those whose minds are slow and dull and who have difficulty in remembering. This is particularly necessary with the abridgment of Christian Doctrine, especially more so on those questions in it which every Christian must know.

On the two days of the week upon which the catechism lesson is given for half an hour on the summary of the principal mysteries, that is, on Wednesdays or on Sundays and holy days, teachers will not question students on the summary in succession in the order in which they are seated on the benches, as done for the lessons on the subject assigned for the week. Neither will they ask the questions in succession in the order in which they are in the catechism.

A teacher may sometimes question one or more students in different places around the room. Similarly, a teacher might ask sometimes one or more questions on the mysteries, sometimes one or more questions on the sacrament of Penance, sometimes one or more questions on the holy Eucharist or some other subject. These questions will be asked in the above manner and without regular order. The teacher will continue to ask questions on the summary in this manner throughout the first half hour.

In the questions, the teacher will make use of only the simplest expressions and words which are very easily understood and need no explanation, if this is possible, making the questions and answers as short as possible.

No answers are to be given in a single word or two. It will be required that complete answers are to be given in complete sentences. If a little child or some ignorant one is unable to give an entire answer, the teacher will divide the question in such a way that the child may give in three answers what could not be given in one.

If it happens that a student slow in mind cannot repeat properly an answer even after several others have already given it one after another, the teacher will, in order to help the student to remember the answer, have it repeated four or five times alternately by a student who knows it well and by the one who does not know it. This is done to make it much easier for the slower student to learn.

Article 3:
Duties of Teachers During Catechism

One of the principal tasks of the teacher during catechism is to conduct the lessons in such a manner that all the students will be very attentive and may easily retain all that is said to them. To effect this, teachers will always keep all of the students in sight and will observe everything they do. Teachers will be careful to talk very little and to ask a great many questions.

Teachers will speak only on the subject assigned for the day and will guard against departing from it. Teachers will always speak in a serious manner, which will inspire the students with respect and restraint. They will never say anything vulgar or anything that might cause laughter, and will be careful not to speak in a dull way which could produce weariness.

In every lesson teachers will be sure to indicate some practices to the students, and to instruct them as thoroughly as is possible concerning those things which pertain to morals and to the conduct which should be observed in order to live as a true Christian. They will reduce these practices and these matters of morals to questions and answers. This will make the students very much more attentive and make them retain the answers more easily.

Care must be taken not to disturb the catechism lesson by untimely reprimands and corrections. If it happens that some students deserve punishment, it should ordinarily be postponed until the next day, without letting them notice it. The punishment will then be given just before catechism. The teacher may, however, sometimes, but rarely and when considered unavoidable give a few strokes of the ferule during this time.

On Sundays and holy days, when catechism lasts three times as long as on the other days, teachers will always choose some story that the students will enjoy, and will tell it in a way that will please them and renew their attention, with details that will prevent the students from being bored. Teachers will not say anything during the catechism lessons unless they have read it in some well-approved book and of which they are very certain.

Teachers will never decide whether a sin is venial or mortal. They may only say, when they judge this to be the case, "That will offend God very much." "It is a sin very much to be feared." "It is a sin that has evil consequences." "It is a grievous sin." Although sins should not be considered more grievous than they are, it is, however, more dangerous to make them appear slight and trifling. A great horror of sins, however slight they may appear, must always be inspired. An offense against God cannot be slight, and nothing that concerns God can be trifling.

Teachers will plan that the questions, the subquestions, and the answers to the subquestions fulfill the following four conditions: (1) they must be short; (2) they must make complete sense; (3) they must be accurate; and (4) the answers must be suited to the capacity of the average and not of the most able and most intelligent students, so that the majority may be able to answer the questions that are asked of them.

Teachers must be so careful in the instruction of all their students that they will not leave a single one in ignorance, at least of those things which a Christian is obliged to know in reference both to doctrine and to practice. In order not to neglect a matter of such great importance, teachers should often consider seriously that they will render an account to God and that they will be guilty in God's sight for the ignorance of the children who have been under their care. They will be held accountable for the sins into which this ignorance has led the students, if they have been in charge of them but have not applied themselves with sufficient care to deliver the students of their ignorance. Teachers should often consider that there will be nothing on which God will examine them and by which God will judge them more severely than on this point.

Teachers will help students to apply themselves perfectly to the catechism. This is not naturally easy for them and ordinarily does not last long. For this purpose, teachers will employ the following means: (1) they will take care not to rebuff or to confuse students, either by words or in any other manner, when they are unable to answer properly the question which has been asked them; (2) they will encourage and even help them to say what they have difficulty in recalling; and (3) they will offer rewards, which they will give from time to time to those who have been the best behaved and the most attentive, or sometimes even to the more ignorant who have made the greatest effort to learn well. They will employ various other similar means, which prudence and charity will enable them to find, to encourage students to learn the catechism more readily and to retain it more easily.

Article 4:
Duties of Students During Catechism

During the time when catechism is being taught, students will be seated, their bodies erect, their faces and eyes turned toward the teacher, their arms crossed, and their feet on the floor. The teacher will indicate with the signal the first who is to be questioned. Before answering, those questioned will rise, take off their hats, make the sign of the cross, remove their gloves if they are wearing them, and cross their arms. Students will answer the question in such a way that, by including the question, the answer will make complete sense.

When the first student has almost finished answering, the one who comes next will rise, make the sign of the cross, saying the words in a tone low enough not to interrupt the one who is reciting and, making sure of having completed the sign of the cross by the time the other one has finished, repeat the same answer, unless the teacher should ask another question. All of the others who follow on the same bench or on the next bench will do the same.

If the teacher should happen to call upon one or several students in succession out of the regular order, the one whose turn it was to answer will remain standing during all of this until notified to speak, or until one of those called out of turn gives the correct explanation. When that student finishes, the one whose regular turn it was will resume answering. When answering during catechism, students will keep their eyes modestly lowered, will not stare fixedly at the teacher, and will not turn their heads slightly from side to side. They will keep their bodies erect and both feet properly placed on the floor. They will speak in a moderate tone, rather low than loud, so that they will not be heard by the other classes and the other students will be more attentive. They will, above all, speak very slowly and distinctly, so that not only the words but also all of the syllables may be heard. Teachers will see to it that a student pronounces all the syllables, particularly the last ones.

All students will be very attentive during the entire catechism lesson. Teachers will allow them neither to cross their legs nor put their hands under their garments, so that they do not do the least thing contrary to purity. A teacher will not permit any student to laugh when another has not answered properly, nor any one of them to prompt another who is unable to answer. The teacher will see to it that the students leave the room as infrequently as possible during catechism, and then only in case of great necessity.

Article 5:
Catechism for Sundays and Holy Days

On all Sundays and holy days, there will be catechism for an hour and a half. The exceptions are Easter Sunday, Pentecost Sunday, Trinity Sunday, and Christmas Day. On these days, there will not be any catechism. The students will assemble during the half hour preceding the time for catechism. While they are assembling, they will question one another in pairs on the diocesan catechism, as in the repetition during breakfast and the afternoon snack. The teacher will indicate those who are to question one another and repeat the catechism at this time.

In places where vespers are sung at 3:00 in the afternoon, catechism will be taught from 1:00 until 2:30 and the students will assemble between 12:30 and 1:00. At 2:30, they will say the prayers which are ordinarily said every day in the afternoon at the end of school. After that, if there remains sufficient time, some verses of a canticle will be sung as usual. The students will then be taken to vespers.

In places where vespers are sung at 2:30 the catechism will begin at 12:30 and will be finished by 2:00. At 2:00, the prayers will be said and the students will be taken to the church as indicated above.

In places where vespers are sung at 2:00, the catechism at 12:30 will be on the summary. From 1:00 to 2:00, the catechism will be on one special subject. The prayers will not be said. At 2:00, the students will be taken to the church for vespers. After vespers, they will be sent home.

During the first half hour, the catechism will be on the Abridgment. Teachers will do nothing but ask questions, without giving any explanations. Teachers will not speak on one subject only, but will ask various questions on the Abridgment without following any regular order. During the next hour, the catechism will be on the entire subject which has been taken in parts on each of the days of the preceding week or on the subject of the feast. During this time, teachers will question all of the students several times. At the end, they will make some practical applications, which should be the fruits that the students ought to obtain from the subject which has been expounded to them. Students who do not regularly attend the school may be admitted to the catechism provided they cause no disorder.[1]

10

Dismissal of School[1]

Article 1:
How Students Should Leave School

Students of the lowest classes will leave the school before those of the higher ones. For example, those of the lowest class will be the first to leave, those of the next to the lowest will follow them, and so on for the other classes up to the highest. When there are three or more classes in the school of a neighborhood, the students of the lowest class will leave while the canticles are being sung. They will leave their classroom and the school two by two, each one with the companion with whom they have been assigned.

Students will leave their classrooms in order and in the following manner. When the teacher makes a sign to the first student on a bench to rise, this student and the one who has been assigned as this student's companion will leave their places with hats off and arms crossed. They will both stand side by side in the middle of the classroom. After having made a deep bow before the crucifix, they will turn and bow to the teacher. If the Director, the Inspector of Schools, or some strangers happen to be in the classroom at this time, they will bow to them before bowing to their teacher. After this, they will leave with decorum, their arms crossed and their hats off until they are outside the classrooms.

When the first two students reach the middle of the room, the next in order on the same bench as the first will rise with the following student. They will likewise go to the middle of the room and will then make their bow as did the other two.

All the students of every class will go out in the same order and in the same manner. Teachers will see that they always walk two by two, the pace a few feet apart, until they reach their homes.

Article 2:
Prayers Said by Students While Leaving Classes

As soon as the singing of the canticles is finished, the *Pater Noster,* the *Ave Maria,* the *Credo,* the *De profundis,* and the *Miserere* will be recited aloud. The leader of prayers will say alone in a loud and distinct tone, "Let us pray that God may preserve our living benefactors in the faith of the holy catholic, apostolic, Roman church and in God's holy love, and let us say *Pater Noster,*" and so forth. The other students will then join in reciting these prayers in a lower tone until the end of the Creed.

After the Creed has been recited, the leader will say, "Let us pray for our benefactors who are dead, and let us say for the repose of their souls the *De profundis, Requiem aeternam, A porta inferi,* and *Domine exaudi,*" and so forth. All of these prayers will be said alternately in the manner usual in the school. Then the same prayer leader will say, "*Oremus, Fidelium Deus,*" and so forth. The others will reply, "Amen."

When these prayers are finished, the leader will continue to say alone in a loud voice, "Let us pray God to forgive us the faults which we have committed in school today, and let us say for that intention the *Miserere mei Deus.*" This psalm will be said alternately, like the psalm *De profundis.* The leader will say one entire versicle, and the students will all say the one following together.

When the students have left the classroom, they will cease to pray aloud to God and will walk in silence, following each other in order. Teachers will, however, exhort their students to walk with much restraint and decorum from the school to their homes and will take measures to compel them to do so. They will also urge each pair to recite the rosary together for the entire way. This will keep them in control and will without doubt be most edifying.

Article 3:
Teachers' Duties as Students Leave School and Later

One of the teachers, if there are more than two, will supervise the departure of the students from the last classroom to the street door, at the same time watching what takes place in that classroom. If there are only two teachers, one of them will watch over both classrooms and make the students go out in order. The other will watch at the street door. The one to whom this duty at the door has been assigned by the Director will make sure that the students leave the school with order and restraint. This teacher will see to it that the companions do not leave each other and that in the street they do not throw stones or shout, that they do not approach too near to each other, and that they disturb no one.

Teachers will especially recommend to their students not to satisfy their natural necessities in the streets, since this is a thing contrary to decency and modesty. They will admonish them to go for that purpose to places where they cannot be seen.

As a teacher cannot see what takes place except in the street where the school is situated, the Director or the Inspector of Schools, with the teachers, will direct some of the students to observe what occurs in the neighboring streets, especially where there are many students, and to report faithfully what they have observed.

However, these students must merely observe and not say a single word. If they do, they should be punished or some penance should be imposed upon them for having spoken.

When all students have left the school, and the last two have reached the street door and greeted the Inspector of Schools or the teacher there, one of them will make a hand sign to this teacher that there are no more students and that the teacher may go in. The teacher will reenter the school immediately. When all of the teachers are assembled in one of the classrooms and are kneeling before the crucifix, if the school is in the Community House where the teachers live, the Inspector of Schools or the Head Teacher will say, "Live Jesus in our hearts." The others will answer, "Forever." They will then all go to the living quarters. If, however, the school is at a distance from the Community House, the teacher will say, *Dignare me laudare te*, and so forth. The others will answer, *Da mihi virtutem*, and so forth. After this, the *Pater Noster* will be said. They will then all leave the school in silence continuing to say the rosary all the way to the Community House. When they have arrived there, they will go to the chapel and say the prayer, *O Domina mea.* After that, they will say, "Live Jesus in our hearts. Forever."

PART TWO

Means of Establishing and Maintaining Order in the Schools

There are nine principal things that can contribute to establishing and maintaining order in the schools: (1) the vigilance of the teachers; (2) the signals; (3) the records or registers; (4) the assiduity of the students and their exactitude in arriving on time; (5) the regulation of holidays; (6) the rewards; (7) the punishments; (8) the appointment of several class officers and their faithfulness in fulfilling their duties; and (9) the structure, quality, and uniformity of school buildings and suitable furniture.

1

The Vigilance Teachers Must Show in School

The vigilance of teachers in school consists particularly of three things: (1) correcting all the words which are mispronounced by a student when reading; (2) making all the other students who have the same lesson follow along when any one of them is reciting; and (3) enforcing a very strict silence. Teachers should constantly pay attention to these three things.

Article 1:
Care in and the Proper Manner of Correcting Words

Teachers must be very exact in correcting all the words, syllables, and letters which a student pronounces badly when reciting the lesson, convinced that the students will advance much more rapidly in reading when the teacher is exact on this point.

The teacher will not say a word or make any movement of the lips when making corrections in reading, but instead will immediately sound the signal twice. At once, the student who is reading will repeat the last word said. If the student again pronounces the word incorrectly or repeats a word other than the one that has been mispronounced, the teacher will continue to strike the signal in the same manner until the student pronounces correctly the word that has been mispronounced. If the student continues to mispronounce the word three times without perceiving the error made or without correcting it, the teacher will signal another student to do so. This student will say only the letter, syllable, or word which the first has said incorrectly, and the latter will now repeat the correction two or three times.

When a student makes a mistake in the lesson, the teacher must be exact in striking the signal at the very moment that the mistake is made. In this way, the student will not be obliged to look for the word that has been mispronounced. If, nevertheless, a student mispronounces a word and continues to read two or three words before being stopped by the signal, for instance, if in reading *Seigneur Dieu Tout puissant et éternel*, the student should make a mistake on the first syllable, care must be taken not to let the student continue without correction. On this occasion and on all other such occasions, the signal must be repeatedly struck twice in quick succession until the student finds the word that has been mispronounced. Or, the teacher will at first strike three times to indicate that the word at which the signal is struck is not the one that has been mispronounced. If a student who is reading by syllables fails to pronounce properly and cannot make the correction without assistance, a sign must be given to some other student to offer the correction. This latter student will not only say the syllable which the other has said incorrectly, but will repeat the entire word, pronouncing each syllable one after another. For example, if the reader, instead of saying *semblable*, should say *semblabe*, the student who offers the correction will say *semblable* and not only the syllable *ble*.

The teacher will take great care that the students who are spelling do not draw out their syllables and that they do not repeat a syllable several times. If they do this, the teacher will impose a penance. In this way, they will not accustom themselves to this manner of reading, a habit very disagreeable and very difficult to correct once it is acquired.

The teacher will likewise take care that the students do not pronounce too rapidly and so clip their syllables, for example, saying *qo*, but will insist that they sound all of the letters distinctly: *q, u, o*. The teacher will also take care that they do not drawl or pronounce their syllables too slowly, which is very disagreeable. They should pronounce their syllables evenly. When they read too rapidly or heedlessly, they are liable to reverse letters; for instance, they might say *mo* for *om* or *su* for *us*. Furthermore, those for whom the lesson is new and those who are backward, are unable to follow students who read too rapidly. Besides, students who read slowly and carefully learn much more readily.

Finally, the teacher should take great care that a student who is reading pronounces all of the syllables so distinctly that all of the others can easily hear what is read; that those who read with pauses read correctly without drawling or acquiring any other unbecoming manner; that they pronounce all of the syllables distinctly so that they can be distinguished from each other; and that readers stop for as long as is required at all of the pauses, a short pause at a comma, a slightly longer one at a semicolon, once again as long at a colon as at a comma, and once again as long at a period as at a colon.

Article 2:
All in the Same Lesson
Must Follow the Same Lesson

During all of the lessons on the alphabet chart, on the syllable chart, in the other books, both French and Latin, and even during the lessons in arithmetic, all the students having the same lesson will follow along while each individual student is reading. That is to say, all will read silently in their own books without making any sound whatsoever with their lips of what is being read aloud.

The teacher will take care that all of the students having the same lesson follow the one who is reading, syllable by syllable or word by word. Another student, when called upon to read, should continue without repeating any of the words that have been said by the preceding one. This will show better than anything else whether the student has been following along exactly.

Teachers will never permit students to suggest to each other any letters, syllables, or words in the lessons, nor to suggest either entire or partial answers, whether during instructions or during the catechism. The teachers will be very attentive to the lessons. They will always keep their own book in hand and do this in such a manner that they do not lose sight of the students and are sure that all are following. In order that nothing may prevent them from being exact in this practice, teachers will hold nothing in their hands throughout the entire school time except the signal and the lesson book, and, if the teacher is in charge of a class of writers, pens, paper, and other things necessary for writing.

If one of the students should play with anything in school, the teacher will order another student from among the most reliable to take it and keep it until the end of the school day. At that time, all of the others having left, the student will return what was taken, unless the teacher considers that it would be harmful.

The same thing will be done with books, printed sheets, or pictures, other than those which they need, which the students might bring to school. Teachers will neither keep them nor read them during school time, even though they might believe it necessary to examine them in order to see if there is anything bad in them. But this will be done for a moment at the end of school, when all of the students have left, by looking at the title of the book.

Teachers will be exact in receiving nothing from the students and in keeping nothing which the students have brought to school. They will keep nothing, under any pretext whatsoever, except bad books. These they will take to the Director who will burn them. This point is of great importance.

A very useful means for obliging the students to follow the recitations is to observe the following practices. First, watch them constantly and very carefully, particularly those who are not exact in following. Second, have each one of them read several times, a little each time. Third, oblige all who are discovered not to be following along to come of their own accord to receive the punishment for their fault. In order to encourage them to do this faithfully, it is necessary to pardon them sometimes, especially, those who usually follow. If they do not then follow the lesson, it is necessary to punish them severely.

Article 3:
Teachers Must Enforce Silence in School

Silence is one of the principal means of establishing and maintaining order in schools. For this reason, every teacher will enforce it rigorously in all of the classrooms and will permit no one to speak without permission.

To effect this, teachers will make students understand that they must keep silent because God sees them and it is God's holy will and not just because the teacher is present.

Teachers will especially keep a strict watch over themselves, speaking only very rarely and in a very low tone when it is necessary that all of the students hear what the teacher has to say. Teachers will always use a moderate tone when they give any instructions, as well as on all other occasions when they need to speak to all of the students together. They will never speak either to any student in particular or to all in general until they have carefully thought about what they have to say and unless they consider it necessary.

When they speak, teachers will do so very seriously and in few words. When a student asks to speak, the teacher will listen to the student only very rarely, only when seated or standing before the teacher's chair, and always in a low voice. Teachers will not permit students to speak or to leave their seats without permission during the time that they are receiving some correction. Teachers will make students understand that they are permitted to speak only three times during the school day: when reciting their lessons, during catechism, and during prayers.

Teachers will themselves observe a similar rule. They will speak on only three occasions: (1) to correct the students during lessons, when necessary and when no student is able to do so; (2) during catechism; and (3) during the meditations and the examination of conscience. Except on these three occasions, teachers will not speak unless it seems necessary, and they will take care that this necessity be rare.

When the students are moving about in the school, teachers will see to it that they have their heads uncovered and their arms crossed, and that they walk very carefully, without dragging their feet or making any noise on the floor. This must be done so that the silence which should be continuous in school be not disturbed.

To make it easy for the students to observe all of these things, the teacher will see that these rules which follow are kept. Students are always seated, facing forward and with their faces turned slightly in the direction of the teacher. Students must always hold their books with both hands and always look at them. They should keep their arms and their hands placed in such a manner that the teacher can always see them well. They are not to touch each other either with their feet or with their hands, nor give anything to each other. They are not to look at each other or make signals to each other. They must always have their feet properly placed and not take off their shoes or sabots.[1] And, finally, students of the writing class must not sprawl on the table or maintain any unseemly posture when reciting their lessons.

2

Signs Which Are Used in the Christian Schools

It would be of little use for teachers to apply themselves to making the students keep silent if teachers did not do so themselves. Teachers will better teach students this practice by example than by words. A teacher's own silence will do more than anything else to produce good order in school, giving teachers the means of watching more easily over both themselves and their students. However, as there are many occasions on which teachers are obliged to speak, a great many signs have been established in the Christian Schools. To make it easier for teachers to keep silence and to reduce these signs to some order, the signs have been classified according to those practices and activities which most ordinarily occur in schools. An iron instrument used by the teachers and called "the signal" is employed to give most of these signs.

All of the signals used in all of the Houses will be of the same form. Nothing is to be changed or added. All teachers will make use of the same signs. The signs in use are explained in the following articles.

Article 1:
Signs Used During Meals

To have the prayers said, teachers will clasp their hands.

To indicate that the responses of holy Mass are to be repeated, teachers will strike their breast.

To indicate that the catechism is to be recited, teachers will either make the sign of the cross or indicate with the signal the place in the classroom where the catechism is usually recited.

To discover whether a student is attentive during recitations, teachers will strike the signal [*See* Figure 3] once to stop the one who is speaking. Teachers will then point the signal to the other student, thus indicating that the student is to repeat what a previous student has just said.

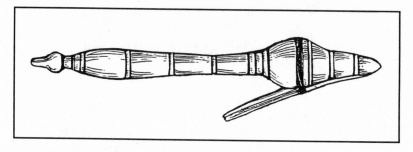

Figure 3: The "signal."

Article 2:
Signs Concerning Lessons

To make the sign to the students to prepare to begin a lesson, teachers will tap their hand once on the closed book in which they are to begin reading.

To stop a student who is reading, teachers will strike the signal once. All students will immediately look at the teacher, who will then point with the signal to another student, thus giving that student the sign to begin.

To make the sign to a student who is reading to repeat something when the student has read badly or has mispronounced a letter, a syllable, or a word, the teacher will strike the signal rapidly twice. If, after having been given the sign two or three times, the student does not correct the mistake, the teacher will strike the signal once, as is done when the reading is to stop. All the students will look at the teacher, who will immediately make a sign to another student to read aloud the letter, the syllable, or the word which the previous student has read badly or mispronounced. If, after the sign has been given two or three times, the reader, having gone several words beyond the mistake before being called to order, does not find and repeat the word which has been badly read or mispronounced, the teacher will strike the signal three times in rapid succession. This is a sign for the reader to begin to read further back. The teacher will continue to make this sign until the reader finds the word which has been said incorrectly.

The sign to speak louder is to point upward with the tip of the signal. The sign to speak lower is to point the tip of the signal down.

To warn one or more students not to speak so loudly when they are following the lesson or studying, the teacher will slightly raise the hand carrying the signal, as though wishing to touch the ear.

Teachers will make the same sign when they hear any noise in the school. If it is on their right that the noise is being made, they will raise their right hand. If it is on their left, they will raise their left hand.

For the sign to read calmly, the signal is struck twice, separately and distinctly.

To make the sign to spell a word which a beginning reader does not pronounce properly, teachers will place the tip of the signal once on the book which they have in their hands.

To indicate to a student spelling or reading by syllables that the pauses are not long enough between two letters or syllables, teachers will slowly touch the tip of the signal several times on the book which they are holding.

To indicate to students reading with pauses that they are not pausing long enough at a comma, a colon, or a period, the teacher will place the tip of the signal on the passage that is being read and hold it there.

To signal that a reader has paused in the wrong place, or too long, the teacher will move the signal over the open book. The same sign will be given to one who drawls while spelling or reading by syllables.

To make the sign to change from one subject to another, teachers will slap the open book. At once, the reader will say aloud, "Blessed be God for ever and ever." All the students must remove their hats at once and make ready their books or lessons. All of this should be done in an instant.

To make the sign to finish the last lesson and to put the books away, teachers will strike their hand twice on the book which is being held and which, at that time, is being read.

Article 3:
Signs Used in the Writing Lesson

To start the lesson after the papers have been distributed, the signal will be sounded once for each of the separate steps. At the first sound, students will take out their writing cases and place them so that they will all be seen. At the second sound, they will open their writing cases, take out their pens and their penknives if they have any, and place them similarly. At the third, they will dip their pens in the ink and begin to write, all at the same time.

When students lean on the table or assume some other unseemly posture when writing, the teacher will raise a hand and move it from the right to the left. This is the sign to the students to place their bodies in a proper posture.

When students do not hold their pens correctly, teachers will demonstrate how to do so. If teachers notice a student who is not writing, they will give a sign by looking steadily at the offender. They will then raise their hand and move their fingers. If they again see that the same student is not writing, they will assign a penance.

Article 4:
Signs Used During Catechism and Prayers

To signal students to cross their arms, teachers will look fixedly at them and at the same time cross their own arms. To remind students to hold their bodies erect, the teacher will look at them and then stand or sit up straight, with feet properly arranged.

When a student has not properly made the sign of the cross, teachers will place their own hand on their forehead in order to make the student begin again. To make a sign to students to lower their eyes, the teachers will look at them fixedly and at the same time lower their own eyes.

For the signal to fold hands, teachers will, while looking at the students, fold their own hands.

In short, on all these occasions and on all other similar ones, the teacher, while looking at the students, will do what the students are to do or observe.

Article 5:
Signs Used in Reference to Corrections

All of the signs referring to corrections will be reduced to five. Teachers will make sure the students understand for which of these five things they are to be punished.

The five things for which corrections will be given in school are: (1) for not having studied; (2) for not having written; (3) for having been absent from school or for having come late; (4) for having been inattentive during catechism; and (5) for not having prayed to God.

These five things will be expressed in written rules which will be hung in various places in each classroom. Each of these rules will be expressed in the following terms:

1. students must never be absent from school or come late without permission;
2. students must apply themselves in school to studying their lessons;
3. students must always write without losing time;
4. students must be attentive during catechism;
5. students must pray to God with piety in church and in school.

When teachers wish to correct a particular student, they will call the student's attention by a signal, and will then indicate with the signal the rule against which the student has offended, at the same time giving the student a sign to approach. If it is to administer the ferule, the teacher will make the student a sign to extend the left hand. If it is to give a correction, the teacher will show the student with the signal the place where it is received.

When a teacher wishes to alert students to possible punishment, the signal shall be sounded once. When all of the students are attentive, the teacher shall point out the rule for the violation of which the teacher is threatening correction.

Article 6:
Signs That Are Used Only on Special Occasions

When students seek permission to speak, they will stand at their place, with arms crossed and eyes lowered. They will make no sign. To permit them to speak, teachers will give a sign to approach by pointing the end of the signal toward themselves. The same sign will be used every time that the teacher has to speak to a student. To refuse permission to speak, the signal will be pointed down, toward the ground in front of the teacher.

A student who seeks permission to attend to the wants of nature will remain seated and will raise a hand. To grant this permission, the teacher will point the signal toward the door. To refuse it, the teacher will give a sign to remain still by pointing the signal toward the ground.

To make a student kneel, the teacher will point with the signal to the middle of the classroom. To make one rise who is kneeling, the teacher will raise a hand slightly while holding the signal.

3
Records or Registers[1]

One thing that can contribute much to the maintenance of order in the schools is that there be well-kept Registers. There should be three kinds of Registers: (1) the Register of Promotion in Lessons; (2) the Register of Levels of Lessons; and (3) a Pocket Register.[2] The first of these will be for the use of the Inspector of Schools. The last two will be used by the teachers.

Article 1:
Registers of Promotions in Lessons

The Inspectors of Schools will each have a record or register upon which the names of the students will be inscribed according to the lessons and levels in which they are. The name of each student will be entered upon this register according to the level of a lesson in which the student is. There will be a separate register for each school associated with the same House. Each register will begin with the first level of the lowest lesson and will continue in this manner to the last level of the highest lesson.[3]

The student Registers of Promotion in Lessons, of writing both round hand writing and Italian script, and of arithmetic will be written one after another in the same book.

Each leaf of this register will be divided into five columns. Each column will be separated by lines from top to bottom. The middle column should be wider than the four others.

In the middle column will be written the names and surnames of the students of the same level in a lesson, one after another in the order in which they have been admitted to the school or promoted to this lesson, as the case may be. In the first column and beside each name, the day of the month on which each of the students was put into this level of the lesson will be written. In the second column, the month will be written. In the third column, the name and the surname will be written. In the fourth column, the day of the month that each student of this level was transferred to another level will be written. In the fifth column, the month in which the student was transferred will be written. All of this will be arranged according to the following model [*See* Figure 4].

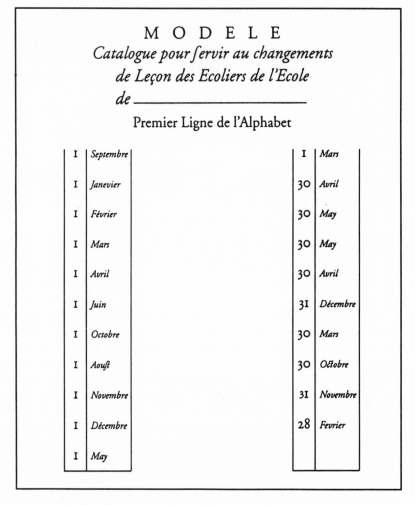

Figure 4: Model of Register to be used for the promotion to lessons of students of the school at . . . (CL 24:135).

Article 2:
Register of Levels in Lessons

Each teacher will have a register in the form of a book containing twenty-four leaves, two for each month, upon which will be inscribed the names of the students of the class, according to the level of each lesson in which they are. The names of all the students of the same level of a lesson will be written one after another under the name of the level of the lesson in which they are.

On each leaf of this register, there will be three columns each marked [identified] by [vertical] lines from top to bottom. In the first column, which will be the narrowest, the month and day of the month on which each of these students has been put into this level of the lesson will be written beside each name. In the middle column, the names and surnames of the students of the same level of a lesson will be written one after another and in the order in which they have been admitted to the school or placed in the level of the lesson in which they are. All of the names will be separated from one another by lines drawn from one side of the sheet to the other. In the third column, there will be four squares beside each name. Each of the squares will be marked by little dots in the following manner: in the first square, how many times a student has come late; in the second square, how many times a student has been absent with permission; in the third square, how many times a student has been absent without permission; and, in the fourth square, how many times a student has failed to know the lesson in the diocesan catechism. At the top of the first column of squares, "late" will be written; at the top of the second column, "absent with permission"; at the top of the third, "absent without permission"; at the top of the fourth column, "did not know catechism."

Toward the end of school, teachers will mark on these registers those who have come late or been absent and those who have not known their diocesan catechism when called to recite it [*See* Figure 5].

M O D E L E *Catalogue de la* ____ *Claſſe la ruë* _____ *pour* *pour le mois de* _____							
1e table 1e ligne			*Tards*	*Ab au p.*	*Abſp.*	*lg. du Cat.*	*Malades*
1. *Décembre*							
1. *May*							
1. *Mars*							
1. *Juin*							
1. *Avril*							
1. *Juillet*							
1. *Aouſt*							
		S					

Figure 5: Model of Register of levels in lessons for the first class in the school at . . . for the month of March 1722 (CL 24:137).

4

Rewards

From time to time, the teachers will give rewards to those of their students who are the most exact in fulfilling their duties. This is done in order to inspire them to fulfill their duties with pleasure and to stimulate other students by the hope of reward to fulfill their duties.

There are three kinds of rewards which will be given in the schools: (1) rewards for piety; (2) rewards for ability; and (3) rewards for assiduity. The rewards for piety will always be more beautiful than the other rewards. The rewards for assiduity will be better than those for ability.

The things which may be given as rewards will be of three different degrees: (1) books; (2) pictures on vellum, and plaster statuettes, such as crucifixes and images of the Blessed Virgin; and (3) pictures on paper, engraved texts, and even rosaries.

Engraved texts will most commonly be given to the students as rewards.

The pictures and texts will always be religious. Pictures of Our Lord on the Cross, of the Mysteries of our Religion, of the Holy Child Jesus, of the Blessed Virgin, and of Saint Joseph will ordinarily be used most.

Rosaries, books, and other valuable objects of piety will be used only for extraordinary rewards. They will be given only by the Director after the Director has examined those whom the teacher considers worthy of receiving them.

The books which may be given as rewards will always be religious books, such as *The Imitation of Christ*, spiritual dialogues, books explaining the truths of religion, and other books containing salutary maxims.

Hymn books, prayer books, diocesan catechisms, and other books that are used in the Christian Schools may be given only to poor children. These will not be given to those who are able to buy them.

Rewards for ability will be given only once every month after the Director has examined the students. There will be but one such reward for the most capable in each lesson. A reward may also be given every month to the student of an entire class who has excelled in everything, that is, to the one who has shown the most piety and decorum in church and during prayers and also the greatest ability and assiduity.

Ten or twelve holy pictures according to the discretion of the Director will be given every month to the teachers of each class, to be distributed by them to their students during the month.

5

Introductory Remarks on Corrections[1]

The correction of the students is one of the most important things to be done in the schools. The greatest care must be taken in order that it may be timely and beneficial both for those who receive it and for those who witness it. For this reason, there are many things to be considered in regard to the use of the corrections which may be administered in the schools and which will be discussed in the following articles. This will be done after the necessity of joining gentleness to firmness in the guidance of children has been explained.

Experience founded on the unvarying teachings of the saints and the examples which they have set us affords sufficient proof that, to perfect those who are committed to our care, we must act toward them in a manner at the same time both gentle and firm. Many, however, are obliged to admit—or they show by their behavior toward those confided to their care—that they do not see how these two things can easily be joined in practice. If, for example, absolute authority and an overbearing attitude are assumed in dealing with children, it is likely that a teacher will find it difficult to keep this way of acting from becoming harsh and unbearable. Although this course may begin as great zeal it is not wise, as Saint Paul says, since it overlooks human weakness.

At the same time, if too much consideration is had for human weakness and if, under the pretext of showing compassion, children are allowed to do as they will, the result will be wayward, idle, and unruly students.

What, then, must be done in order that firmness may not degenerate into harshness and that gentleness may not degenerate into languor and weakness?

To throw some light on this matter, which appears to be of no little importance, it seems opportune to set forth in a few words some principal ways in which teachers express that severity and harshness in guiding and educating children which become unbearable. Then will be described how a contrary weakness by the teacher can lead to all laxness, disorder, and so forth among the students.

The following are examples of a teacher's conduct which becomes unbearable to those in the teacher's charge.

First, the teacher's penances are too rigorous and the yoke which the teacher imposes upon the students is too heavy. This state of affairs is frequently due to lack of discretion and judgment on the part of teachers. It often happens that students do not have enough strength of body or of mind to bear the burdens which many times overwhelm them.

Second, the teacher enjoins, commands, or exacts something of the children with words too harsh and in a manner too domineering. Above all, the teacher's conduct is unbearable when it arises from unrestrained impatience or anger.

Third, the teacher is too insistent in urging upon a child some performance which the child is not disposed to do, and the teacher does not permit the child the leisure or the time to reflect.

Fourth, the teacher exacts little things and big things alike with the same ardor.

Fifth, the teacher immediately rejects the reasons and excuses of children and is not willing to listen to them at all.

Sixth and final, the teacher, not mindful enough of personal faults, does not know how to sympathize with the weaknesses of children, and so exaggerates their faults too much. This is the situation when a teacher reprimands them or punishes them and acts as though dealing with an insensible instrument rather than with a creature capable of reason.

At the other extreme, the following are examples of the teacher's weakness which leads to negligent and lax conduct by the students.

First, care is taken by the teacher only about things that are important and which cause disorder, and other less important matters are imperceptibly neglected.

Second, not enough insistence is placed upon the performance and observance of school practices and those things which constitute the duties of the children.

Third, children are easily permitted to neglect what has been prescribed.

Fourth, in order to preserve the friendship of the children, a teacher shows too much affection and tenderness to them. This involves granting something special or giving too much liberty to the more intimate. This does not edify the others, and it causes disorder.

Fifth, on account of the teacher's natural timidity, the children are addressed or reprimanded so weakly or so coldly that they do not pay any attention or that the correction makes no impression upon them.

Sixth and final, a teacher easily forgets the teacher's own proper deportment, which consists principally in maintaining a gravity which encourages respect and restraint on the part of the children. This lack of deportment manifests itself either in speaking to the students too often and too familiarly or in doing some undignified act.

It is easy to recognize by these examples what constitutes too much harshness and too much gentleness. Both of these extremes must be avoided if one is to be neither too harsh nor too weak, if one is to be firm in attaining a purpose and gentle in the means of attaining it, and in all to show great charity accompanied by zeal. A teacher must be constant in persevering. However, children must not be permitted to expect impunity or to do whatever they wish, and the like; gentleness is not proper in such cases.

We must know that gentleness consists in never allowing any harshness or anything whatsoever that savors of anger or passion to appear in reprimands. Instead, being gentle means showing the gravity of a father, a compassion full of tenderness, and a certain ease, which is, however, lively and effective. The teacher who rebukes or punishes must make it very clear that such punishment arises from necessity and that it is out of zeal for the common good that it is administered.

Article 1:
Different Kinds of Corrections

The faults of children can be corrected by several different methods: (1) by word; (2) by penances; (3) by the ferule; (4) by the rod; and (5) by expulsion from school. As there is something special to remark about penances, these faults will receive special attention after all other matters pertaining to punishments have been discussed.

Section 1: Correction by Words

As one of the principal rules of the Brothers of the Christian Schools is to speak rarely in their schools, the use of corrections by word or reprimands ought to be very rare. It seems even much better not to make use of them at all. Threats, being a sort of reprimand, might be used, but only very rarely and with much circumspection. When a teacher has threatened the students with something, and one of them commits the fault on account of which they have been threatened, the student must invariably be punished and never pardoned.

Unconditional threats must never be made. For example, the teacher should never say, "You will get the ferule," or "You will be corrected." Threats should always be subject to some condition. For example, the teacher might say, "Anyone who fails to pray during holy Mass or whoever is the last to come to school late will be corrected."

Ordinarily, threats must be made by nonverbal signs, as explained in the chapter on the use of signs in making corrections.

A teacher may nevertheless sometimes speak to the students in a firm manner in order to intimidate them. This must be done without affectation, however, and without passion. If it is done with passion, the students will easily recognize this, and it would not receive God's blessing.

Section 2: The Ferule: When and How to Use It

The ferule is an instrument consisting of two pieces of leather sewn together. It should be from ten to twelve inches in length, including the handle, and should end in an oval of two inches in diameter. The inside of this oval should be stuffed. In this way, it will not be completely flat and will be somewhat rounded on the outside.

The ferule may be used for several offenses: (1) for not following a lesson or for playing during a lesson; (2) for coming to school late; (3) for not obeying at the first sign given; and (4) for several other similar reasons. All of this is to say that the ferule is used for faults that are not very important.

Only one slap of the ferule on the hand should be given. If it is sometimes necessary to administer more, it must never be more than two.

The left hand should be struck, especially in the case of students in the writing class. This is done so as not to make the right hand heavy; such would be a great obstacle in writing.

It should not be given to those whose hands have some damage. A different penance should be imposed on them, for it is necessary to foresee the injuries that might arise from this form of correction and to try to avoid them.

The students should not be allowed to cry out when receiving a slap on the hand with the ferule or when receiving any other correction. If they do so, they must be punished again without fail for having cried out. They must then be made to understand that it is for crying out that they are now being corrected.

When the ferule or any other punishment is given to the students for having committed some fault which caused them to neglect their duties, such as for having talked or played in school or in church or for having looked behind them, and the like, it is important that they not be told that it is merely for having talked or played that they are receiving the correction, but for not having studied their lesson, or for not having prayed in church.

Section 3: Correction with the Rod

According to the usage established in the Christian Schools, the rod may be used to correct the student: (1) for not having been willing to obey; (2) when they make a practice of not following the lessons and of not studying; (3) for having scribbled on their paper instead of writing; (4) for having fought in school or on the streets; (5) for not having prayed in church; (6) for not having behaved with decorum at holy Mass or during catechism; and (7) for having been absent through their own fault from school, from Mass, or from catechism on Sundays and holy days.

These corrections should be administered with great moderation and presence of mind. Ordinarily, no more than three blows should be given. If it is sometimes necessary to go beyond this number, never more than five should be given without a special permission from the Director.

Section 4: Expulsion of Students from School

Students may be, and sometimes ought to be, dismissed from the school. However, this should be done only upon the advice of the Director. Those who should be sent away are the dissolute who are capable of ruining others, those who absent themselves easily and often from school, from the parish Mass, or from catechism on Sundays and holy days through the fault of their parents and with whom it is becoming a habit, and the incorrigible, that is to say, those who, after having been corrected a great number of times, do not amend their conduct. It should, however, be an extraordinary occurrence to expel a student from school.

Article 2:
Frequent Corrections and How to Avoid Them

If a school is to be well-regulated and in very good order, correction must be rare.

The ferule must be used only when necessary, and things must be so ordered that this is a rare necessity. It is not possible to determine precisely the number of times that it may be given each day, because of the different circumstances that may render it obligatory to use it more or less frequently. Nevertheless, steps should be taken to guarantee that its use will not exceed three times in a half day. To make use of it more than these three times, the circumstances must be truly extraordinary.

Correction by use of rod should be much rarer than that with the ferule. It should, at most, be inflicted only three or four times in a month.

Extraordinary correction should, consequently and for the same reasons, be very rare.

To avoid frequent correction, which is a source of great disorder in a school, it is necessary to note well that it is silence, restraint, and watchfulness on the part of the teacher that establish and maintain good order in a class. It is not harshness and blows that establish and maintain good order. A constant effort must be made to act with skill and ingenuity to keep students in order while making almost no use of correction.

In order to be effective, the same means of correction must not always be used. Otherwise, the students will grow accustomed to them. Rather, a teacher must sometimes threaten, sometimes correct, sometimes pardon, and sometimes make use of various other means which the ingenuity of a skillful and thoughtful teacher will easily suggest on the appropriate occasion. If, however, a teacher should happen to think of some other particular means and believes these could be adopted to keep the students at their duties and forestall correction, they should be proposed to the Director. The teacher will not make use of them until having received permission.

Teachers will not administer any extraordinary correction without having first consulted with the Director. For this reason, they will postpone them, which is, at the same time, a very proper thing to do, in order to have adequate time for some reflection beforehand and to give more weight to what they intend to do, and leave a greater impression on the minds of the students.

Article 3:
Qualities Which Corrections Should Possess

Correction, in order to be beneficial to the students, should be accompanied by the ten following qualities.

First, it must be pure and disinterested. That is to say, correction must be administered purely for the glory of God and for the fulfillment of God's holy will. It must be administered without any desire for personal vengeance, teachers giving no thought to themselves.

Second, correction must be charitable. That is to say, correction must be administered out of a motive of true charity toward the student who receives it and for the salvation of the student's soul.

Third, correction must be just. For this reason, it is necessary to examine carefully beforehand whether the matter for which the teacher is considering correcting the student is effectively a fault and if this fault deserves correction.

Fourth, correction must be proper and suitable to the fault for which it is administered. That is to say, it must be proportionate to the fault both in nature and in degree. Just as there is a difference between faults committed through malice and obstinacy and those committed through weakness, there should also be a difference between the chastisements with which they are punished.

Fifth, correction must be moderate. That is to say, it should be rather less rigorous than more rigorous. It should be of a just medium. Neither should punishment be administered precipitously.

Sixth, correction must be peaceable. Those who administer it should not be moved to anger and should be totally self-controlled.

Those to whom it is administered should receive it in a peaceable manner with great tranquillity of mind and outward restraint. It is especially necessary that those who inflict a punishment should take great care that nothing appear in their demeanor that might indicate that they are angry. For this reason, it would be more proper to defer a correction until a time when one no longer feels agitated than to do anything that one might later regret.

Seventh, it must be prudent on the part of the teacher. The teacher should pay great attention to what is done, so as to do nothing that is inappropriate or that could have evil consequences.

Eighth, it must be willingly accepted by the students. Every effort must be made to make the students accept it. The seriousness of their fault and the obligation under which the teacher is to remedy it must be made clear to them. They must be helped to understand the great harm that they can do to themselves and, by their bad example, to their companions.

Ninth, those punished must be respectful. They should receive punishment with submission and respect, as they would receive a chastisement with which God would punish them.

Tenth, it must be silent. In the first place, the teacher must be silent and should not speak, at least not aloud, during this time. In the second place, the student must be silent and ought not to say a single word, cry out, or make any noise whatsoever.

Article 4:
Faults Which Must Be Avoided in Corrections

There are many faults that must be avoided in corrections, and it is important that teachers should pay very particular attention to them. The principal ones which must be avoided are described in what follows.

No correction should be administered unless it be considered useful and advantageous. Thus, it is bad to administer correction without having previously considered whether or not it will be of some use either to the student to whom it is to be administered or to the others who are to witness it.

When a correction is considered useful only to give an example to the others and not to the one who is to receive it, it should not be administered unless it be necessary in order to maintain order in a class. When delay is possible, the advice of the Director should be asked. If it is a case concerning a teacher of one of the lower classes, that teacher will ask advice of the Head Teacher. If it is the Head Teacher who has the problem and at the same time must resolve it, action will be taken only with much precaution and under an evident necessity.

No correction that could be harmful to the one who is to receive it must ever be administered. This would be to act directly contrary to the purpose of correction, which has been instituted only to do good.

No correction should be made that could cause any disorder in the class or even in the school. Examples of this would be those that would only serve to make the child cry out, be repelled or embittered, or want to leave the school. Such action would lead the student to hold the school in aversion. The complaints that the child or the child's parents would make would repel others and prevent children from coming to school. The teacher should endeavor to foresee these possible consequences before administering any correction for it is important not to fall into them.

A student should never be corrected because of a feeling of aversion or of annoyance that a teacher may have for that student, because the student causes trouble, or because the teacher has no liking for the student. All these motives, which are either bad or merely worldly are very far from those which should animate people who ought to act and conduct themselves only according to the spirit of faith.

Nor should students be corrected because of some displeasure caused either by themselves or their parents. Students who lack respect for their teachers or commit some fault against them should rather be urged by words to recognize this fault and correct it themselves. This is preferable to punishing them for it. Even if it should be necessary to punish them on account of the bad example which they have given, it would be well to assign some other motive for the correction, such as having caused disorder or having been obstinate.

When administering corrections, familiar forms of address must not be used. Instead of *tu, toi, ton, va, viens,* one should say *vous, votre, vos, allez, venez,* etc.[2]

It is also important never to use insulting words, or words that are even in the slightest degree unseemly, for example, rascal, knave, or sniveler. None of these words should ever be in the mouth of a teacher in the Christian Schools.

No other means of correction should be used than those approved for the Christian Schools. Thus, students should never be slapped or kicked. Neither should they be struck with the pointer. It is altogether contrary to the decorum and seriousness of a teacher to pull the children's noses, ears, or hair. It is even more unseemly for a teacher to strike them, to push them roughly, or to pull them by the arms.

The ferule must not be thrown at a student who is then to bring it back. That is highly unbecoming behavior. A student must not be struck with the handle of the ferule on the head, on the back, or on the back of the hand. Neither must two slaps in succession be given with it on the same hand.

In using the ferule, great care must be taken not to strike either the head or the body. The ferule is used only on the palm of the hand.

In punishing students teachers must be very careful not to strike them on any place where they may have any sore or injury, lest it worsen, and not to strike so hard that marks may appear.

Teachers should not leave their place to administer the ferule or speak while administering it. They should not allow the student who is receiving it to speak, much less to cry aloud, either when being punished or afterward.

Teachers will also be careful not to assume any improper posture when administering correction, such as stretching their arms or contorting their bodies, nor to make any other unseemly motions contrary to modesty.

Teachers will, finally, be very careful not to administer any correction impulsively or when agitated. They will watch so carefully over themselves that neither angry passions nor the least touch of impatience shall have any part when administering correction. Such behavior can prevent the benefit and place an obstacle to the blessing God would give.

Here is the practice to follow concerning who should or should not administer correction.

Every teacher may, in the teacher's own class, use the ferule as often as necessary. Teachers who have not yet reached the age of twenty-one will not administer correction with the rod, unless they have consulted the Director, or the one whom the Director has put in charge of such matters, and have taken their advice upon the subject. The teacher in charge of such matters will also watch very carefully over the punishments which these younger teachers administer, either with the ferule or otherwise, and will report twice each week to the Director on all that has been done in the classes.

The same line of conduct will be followed with respect to teachers who have reached the age of twenty-one, during the six months of trial which they will spend in the schools and during the first year after their novitiate.[3]

Article 5:
Children Who Must or Must Not Be Corrected

There are five vices which must not ordinarily be excused: (1) lying, (2) fighting, (3) theft, (4) impurity, and (5) indecorum in church.

Liars must be punished for their lies, even the least, in order to make students understand that there are no little lies in the sight of God, since the devil is the father of lies, as Our Lord tells us in the holy gospel. Let them rather be pardoned or punished less severely when they frankly acknowledge their faults. They may be led afterward to conceive the horror which they ought to have of lies, and they will be persuaded to ask pardon humbly of God, while kneeling in the middle of the classroom.

Those who have been fighting will be corrected in the same way. If two or more were involved, they will be punished together. If it was a student and another child who is not of the school, the teacher will ascertain exactly who was at fault. The student will not be corrected unless the teacher is very certain that the student was at fault. Teachers will act in exactly the same way with all other faults committed outside of the school. If students have been fighting in the school, they are to be punished as an example, and they must be made to understand that this fault is one of the gravest that they can commit.

Those who have taken and concealed anything, however small its value be, even if it be only a pen, will be similarly punished. If they are found to be subject to this vice, they will be expelled from the school.

Those who have been guilty of any impure act or have used obscene words will be punished by the same correction.

Those who have been playing with persons of the opposite sex or who have been frequently in their company will be seriously warned the first time. If they persist in this fault, they will likewise be severely punished. Teachers will often seek to instill into their students a great disinclination for the company of these persons and will urge them never to mingle with them. Even if they are their relatives and even if they are sometimes obliged to converse with them, however young they may be, let it be very rarely and always in the presence of their parents or of some sensible elderly persons.

Those who have been disorderly in church will be severely punished, and they will be made to understand the great respect that they must have for God in this holy place. Furthermore, they must understand that it is to be lacking in faith to be in church without piety and without both inner and outward self-control.

For this last fault, one must not punish all kinds of students, large and small alike, in the same manner. Unless the little ones are very carefully watched while they are in church and unless the teacher has acquired great authority and control, it will be difficult for the young ones to observe the moderation and control that is required of them. It is necessary, however, to pay great attention to this matter. There is nothing that should be omitted to prevent any student from behaving in a disorderly way in church.

If a teacher is not sufficiently vigilant and does not possess sufficient authority to keep order in church, another teacher must be appointed to do so. The one who is appointed on this occasion will do what the other cannot.

Section 1: Ill-bred, Self-willed, or Delinquent Children

There are some children to whose conduct their parents pay very little attention, sometimes none at all. From morning until evening, they do only what they please. They have no respect for their parents. They are disobedient. They grumble at the least thing. Sometimes these faults do not come from an evil disposition of heart or mind; they come from their having been left to themselves. Unless they are naturally of a bold and haughty temperament, they must be frequently admonished. They must also be corrected for their bad dispositions. When they let some of their faults appear in school, they must be subdued and rendered submissive. If they are of a bold and haughty spirit, they should be given some charge or responsibility in the school, such as Monitor, if they are considered qualified, or Collector of Papers. They should be promoted in something such as writing, arithmetic, or spelling in order to inspire them with a liking for school. But along with this they must be corrected and brought into line, never allowed in anything whatsoever to act as they please. If such students are young, there are fewer measures to be taken. They must be corrected while they are young, in order that they may not continue in their bad conduct.

As for those who are bold and insolent, one must speak with them little and always only seriously. When they have committed some fault, they should be told and corrected if it appears that it would help them to confuse and humble their disposition. They must be held in check and not allowed to reply to anything that is said to them. It would be a good thing to admonish and reprimand them sometimes in private for their faults. Such admonishment must always be administered with great seriousness and in a manner which will keep them respectful.

Those who are heedless and frivolous must be corrected a little. Ordinarily, they do not reflect much, and a short time after having been corrected they sometimes fall again into the same fault or into another fault which deserves the same punishment. Their faults do not come from pure malice but from thoughtlessness. They must be treated in a way which may prevent them from misbehaving. They can be shown affection, but they should not be given any charge or responsibility. They should be seated as near the teacher as possible, under the pretext of helping them, but in reality, in order to watch over them. They should also be placed between two students of a sedate disposition who do not ordinarily commit faults. They should also be given some rewards from time to time to make them assiduous and fond of school, for it is these who are absent most frequently, and to induce them while there to remain in order and silent.

Section 2: Stubborn Students

The stubborn must always be corrected, especially those who resist and are not willing to accept correction. However, two precautions must always be taken in regard to this kind of children. (1) No attempt to correct them is to be made without having thoroughly examined the faults that they have committed, and unless it is clear that they deserve correction. (2) When such children resist, either because they do not want to submit to correction or because they do not want to leave their seats, it will often be much more to the purpose to let their bad attitude pass. In this case, it is best not to let it appear that there is any intention of making the correction. Some time later, the teacher will call them and speak with them gently making them realize and admit their fault, both originally and in resisting. The teacher will then correct the student as an example. In case the student is not yet willing to accept the correction, the student must be forced to do so, for only a single example of resistance would be needed to produce several others afterward. Some time later when it seems that the bad mood has passed, the teacher will gently make the student draw near to reflect on the incident. The teacher will lead the student afterward to admit the fault and ask pardon while kneeling.

However, the school should be so ordered as to forestall this sort of resistance and to make it happen very rarely. Otherwise, it would cause a very bad effect.

There is another kind of stubborn children who mutter after they have been corrected. When they have returned to their seats, they lean their heads on their arms or maintain some other unseemly posture. Such manners must never be permitted. These students should be obliged to study or to follow the lesson. If the teacher cannot prevent a student who has been corrected from grumbling, muttering, weeping, or disturbing the school in some other manner, because of youth, low intelligence, or some other reason, and if it has been observed that punishments not only do not bring a sense of duty but perhaps even render the student more stubborn, it would ordinarily be more to the purpose not to make the correction. It would be better to pretend not to notice it when such a student does not study or fails to do some other duty. It might be better even to send the student home.

In these situations, the teachers will take care to obtain clarification or permission from the Director concerning what they should do. Silence during correction and a proper manner of administering it will ordinarily prevent most of these failures.

One of the most effective means for avoiding many of these problems is not to send students back to their places immediately after administering the ferule or the rod. They should be left kneeling in full view of the teacher.

Section 3: Gentle Children, Newcomers, Special Cases

There are some parents whose manner of bringing up their children is to give them all that they ask. They never contradict or oppose them in anything, and they almost never correct them for their faults.

It seems that they fear to cause them pain, and so they cannot suffer that the least correction be administered to them.

Such children are almost always of a gentle and peaceable nature. For that reason, it is ordinarily better not to correct them. It is ordinarily better to correct their faults by some other means, such as giving them some penance that is easy to perform, preventing their faults in some skillful manner, pretending not to see them, or admonishing them gently in private.

If it is sometimes felt that it is necessary to correct them, it should not be done without consulting the Director or the Head Teacher. In such cases, correction should be light and very rare.

If the means that are used to prevent their faults or to correct them are of no avail, it is often better to send them away than to correct them. An exception to this might be made after speaking with their parents and making them agree that it will be well to correct the child.

Those who have a gentle and timid disposition should not ordinarily be corrected. The example of students who do well, the fear which they naturally have of the chastisements which they see inflicted, and some penances will suffice to make them do their duty. They do not often commit faults, and they easily keep still. Furthermore, their faults are not considerable, and they should sometimes be tolerated. At times, a warning will suffice for them, at other times, a penance. Thus, there will be no need of corrections and chastisements to keep them in good order.

Much the same can be done in the case of slow-witted children who create disturbance only when it becomes necessary to correct them. Ordinarily, this should not be done. If they are troublesome in school, it is better to send them away. If they cause no trouble and create no disturbance, they should be let alone.

The faults children like these commit ordinarily include not following the lesson, not reading well, not remembering or reciting catechism well, and learning nothing or very little. What is beyond their capacity must not be required of them. Neither should teachers let them become discouraged but should manage somehow to advance them, encourage them from time to time, and be satisfied with the little progress that they make.

In respect to those who are sickly, it is important that they should not be corrected. This is especially the case when the correction might increase their ailment. Some other means of correction should be used with them, or a penance be imposed on them.

There are also many little children who likewise must not be corrected or only very rarely. They have not attained the use of reason and are not capable of profiting from correction. Deal with them in much the same manner as with children of a gentle and timid disposition.

Finally, one must abstain from correcting children who are just beginning school. It is necessary, first, to know their minds, their natures, and their inclinations. They should be told from time to time what they are to do. They should be placed near some students who acquit themselves well of their duties. In this way, they may learn by practice and by example. They should ordinarily be in school about two weeks before being corrected, for correcting newcomers can only repel them and alienate them from school. However, if it is important to act thus to new students, it is no less important that a teacher who is new in a class refrain from administering any correction until the students are understood.

Section 4: Accusers and Accused

Teachers must not readily listen to reports and accusations made against students. However, they will not rebuff those who make these reports but will be careful to examine the reports well and not correct hastily without due consideration for reports that have been made to them.

If it is some of the students who report or accuse one of their companions, the teacher will without delay determine privately whether other students have seen the fault committed. The teacher will do what is needed to learn the circumstances that will help to discover the truth. If the matter appears dubious or not altogether certain, the teacher will not correct the accused unless the latter admits the fault. When the fault is admitted, correction will be less severe, assigning only a penance, but making the student understand that this is because the truth was told. If the teacher ascertains that the student has been falsely accused or that it is through revenge or some other passion that it has been done, the accuser will be severely punished.

If it is parents who come to accuse their children and say that they should be corrected, this should not be done just for this reason. Parents often speak thus from anger, and they would not do so at any other time. If, however, the fault deserves correction, the parents must be given to understand that they should correct their children themselves. If it happens that several students commit the same fault and each one knows that the others are guilty, if one is corrected all of them must be; for instance, if several students have been fighting or if two or three have been talking or playing during holy Mass. However, if several have committed the same fault and are unaware of the guilt of the others, or if they believe that the teacher is ignorant of it, it will ordinarily be well to correct only one of them and to pretend to be unaware of the faults of the others.

On such occasions, the student whose correction will be of the greatest benefit both to the offender and to the others must be corrected. At the same time in situations like these, do not correct those whom an example alone suffices to frighten and make attend to their duties, and those who have committed a fault for the first time or who commit it rarely.

Article 6:
Procedures for All Corrections

When the teacher wishes to administer the ferule to a student, the usual signal will be given to attract the attention of the students. The teacher will then indicate with the point of the signal the rule which has been violated and immediately make a sign to the offender to draw near. The offender will go to the teacher, make the sign of the cross, and hold out the left hand. Care must be taken that the student holds the hand well extended and quite steady, and does not withdraw it. If the hand is not held properly, the teacher will personally demonstrate how this is to be done. If the refusal to comply continues, the student must be forced to do so and given two strokes of the ferule instead of one.

When there is a refusal to hold out a hand, the teacher will make a sign to the student to go to the place where correction is administered, and will then administer it. In such instances, teachers will conduct themselves as they have been told to do when correcting with the rod, and so forth.

When the ferule is being administered the students must neither put their thumb in the middle of their hand nor hold their hand half open. After the punishment the teacher will oblige them to cross their arms and kneel, or will have them go modestly to their seats, without permitting them to make any contortions with their arms or their bodies or to do any unseemly thing like grumbling or crying aloud. If any of these things is done the teacher will make the student come back and will again administer the ferule, unless the improper conduct ceases at once.

When correction is to be administered with the rod, the teacher will make the ordinary sign to attract the attention of the students, then indicate with the tip of the signal the rule that has been violated, and immediately point to the place where it is the custom to receive this correction.

The student will at once go there and prepare to receive the correction in such a manner as not to be appear indecently to anyone. This practice of having students prepare themselves to receive the punishment without any assistance from the teacher will be very rigorously observed. If any student fails to do this, the punishment will be severe.

While the student is preparing to receive the correction, the teacher will also prepare inwardly to administer it in a spirit of charity and with thoughts fixed on God. The teacher will then go calmly and sedately to administer the correction.

The teacher may say a few words to dispose the student to receive the correction with humility, submission, and for the proper reason. After this, the teacher will give the usual three strokes.

Teachers will be careful not to lay their hands on the students for any reason whatsoever while they are correcting them. If the student is not yet ready, the teacher will return to the desk without saying anything. When the teacher does come back, the severest ordinary punishment will be administered, that is to say, five blows with the rod.

All the students will be instructed that they must be ready to receive punishment before the teacher comes and that if they are not ready then they will later receive five blows.

After waiting quietly a little while, the teacher will return to the student. If the student is not yet submissive and is not yet prepared, the teacher will proceed in the way described above for stubborn children. It is very important in such encounters to unite moderation with firmness.

When a student has been compelled to receive correction, the teacher will manage in some way at some later time to make the offender recognize and admit the fault. The student should be led to reflect and to make a strong and sincere resolution never to yield again to a similar obstinacy.

After having been corrected, the student will go and kneel modestly in the middle of the classroom in front of the teacher and, with crossed arms, thank the teacher for having been corrected. The student will then turn toward the crucifix to thank God and to promise at the same time not to fall again into the fault for which the correction was administered, and will do this without speaking aloud. After this, the teacher will make a sign for the student to be seated.

Article 7:
The Place and Time for Corrections

Teachers must never leave their places in the classroom to administer the ferule. Should any happen to be elsewhere, they will return there for this purpose.

Ordinary corrections with the rod will be administered in one of the most remote and obscure places in the classroom, where any nudity cannot be perceived by the others. Great care must be taken in regard to this matter. Also, care must be taken to inspire the students with a great horror of the least glance in that direction on these occasions. Extraordinary corrections, inflicted for certain particular faults that are very grave in comparison with others, such as stealing, disobeying, or resisting the teacher, should be publicly administered. That is to say, they should be administered in the presence of the students and in the middle of the classroom. This is done to give an example and to make a greater impression. It would even be useful to correct a student sometimes in all of the classrooms for very considerable and extraordinary faults.

Corrections must not be administered during catechism or during the prayers. During these times the teacher can and should take particular note of those who have committed some fault, and without saying anything to them, should name them in a low tone to a reliable student, who will be instructed to remind the teacher at some other specified time. A teacher may, however, sometimes, but rarely and only if the teacher believes that it cannot be avoided, administer the ferule during catechism. Corrections must not be made on Sundays and holy days.

It is better to give correction only in the afternoon and not in the morning, and never at the end of school.

It is also very important to do nothing in church or on the street that is seen as correction, for example, striking with the hand or pulling the ear or the arm. Such acts indicate impatience and are very contrary to the gravity and wisdom which a teacher should always show, particularly in these places.

Article 8:
Penances: Their Use, Qualities, and Imposition

Penances will be much more ordinarily used in the schools than corrections. They repel the student less, cause less distress to parents, and are much more useful.

Teachers will make use of them to humble their students and to bring them to a state of heart to correct themselves of their faults.

Penances should be remedial and proportioned to the faults committed. They should be administered to help students give satisfaction for their faults in the sight of God, and in the hope that they may be a preserving remedy to prevent repetition of the faults.

Teachers will take great care that the penances that they impose are in no way ridiculous and do not consist only of words, and will see that they be performed only in the classroom of the student who has committed the fault.

No penance will be imposed that might be prejudicial to the silence and good order of the school. Nothing that causes loss of time and that is useless should ever be given as a penance.

Teachers will impose no other penances than those which are approved for use in the schools and which are indicated in the following section. They will not impose extraordinary penances unless they have previously discussed them with the Director, who has given approval.

When a teacher imposes a penance, this will be done while seated at the teacher's own place and with a very grave manner. This is done to inspire respect in the one who receives the penance and to make this student perform it with humility, with simplicity, and for the edification of the others.

When about to impose a penance the teacher will give the student the ordinary sign to kneel in the middle of the classroom, with hands joined as had been signaled. The teacher then will in a serious tone pronounce the penance and name the fault for which it is being imposed, without saying a single word more than required. The teacher will use the following or similar terms, in a loud, calm, and intelligible tone: "For having come to school late today, you are to be among the first to come to school for a week, and, if you fail to do so, you will be corrected." To be effective, this should be done when the student is least expecting it.

After the penance has been imposed, the student will make a bow to thank the teacher, and will then remain some little time longer kneeling, facing the crucifix, to show God that the penance is accepted willingly and to ask of God the grace to perform the penance faithfully and for the love of God. Then, the student will be seated, if permission to do so has been given.

When penances are assigned to be performed at another time than that at which they are imposed, the teacher will delegate some of the students to watch over the one to whom the penance has been given. They are to observe whether the penance is performed or not, and they are to inform the teacher without fail.

Section 1: Penances Which Are in Use

When students come late for a second time and through their own fault, they may instead of receiving a punishment be required as a penance to be at school as soon as the door is opened, for a period of a week or two. The inspector of the class will be instructed to notice whether these students are there or not.

When students are so engrossed in eating that they do not listen as attentively as they should to the prayers, the responses of holy Mass, or the catechism, they will be made to kneel for a certain time.

Students who make several mistakes in reading because they have not studied may be ordered to learn by heart something from the diocesan catechism or even a part of the lesson which has not yet been studied, which would be very appropriate. They may be ordered to read one or two pages according to their ability after all of the others have read. At the same time, students will be threatened with correction if they do not know the lesson better in the future. The amount that such students will be required to read will depend on the level of the lesson in which they are.

Students who do not follow during a lesson may be required as a penance to hold up a book and keep their eyes on it a half hour without looking elsewhere.

Those who have not written all that they should write or who have not applied themselves to doing it well may be required as a penance to write one or two pages at home. What they write will consist of some particular letters, words, or phrases that have been indicated to them and which they must take pains to write well and bring the next time.

Those who have been lacking in decorum during the prayers or who have not prayed to God may be ordered to stand for one or more days in the middle of the classroom during the prayers. Their hands should be joined, their eyes should be lowered, and they should demonstrate great modestly. If they raise their eyes or commit any other breach of decorum, they will be corrected.

The same will be done with those who have been lacking in decorum in church. That is to say, they may be ordered the next day to keep their hands joined throughout all of the holy Mass. They will do this without turning their heads, raising their eyes, or other similar things.

When students who are kneeling seat themselves back on their heels, they will be required to remain about a half hour kneeling in school, or they will be made to remain standing for some time with their hands joined and their eyes lowered or resting on the crucifix.

Those who lean on the table or who maintain lax or unseemly postures will be made to stand.

A student who has not remembered the catechism lesson of the preceding day will be obliged to learn it and repeat it at the end of school without making a mistake or omitting anything. The student might be obliged to listen to the lesson of the day standing and with hands joined. The student might also be made to learn the catechism in one day, or two, according to the student's capacity.

Students who do not know perfectly the catechism lesson which is to be learned during the week will be obliged to learn it and repeat it perfectly on Monday or Tuesday, without making a single mistake under penalty of a double correction and of continuing the same penance the following week.

Class officers who have not properly acquitted themselves of their duties may be punished by being deposed for some days and made to suffer some embarrassment.

The most appropriate penance and the one that is of the greatest utility is to give the students something to learn by heart.

6
Absences[1]

Article 1:
Regular Absences and Absences with Permission

Some students ask permission to be absent regularly on every day in the week for a certain length of time each day. This may be accorded them in moderation and for the following reasons, after they have been carefully investigated.

For example, certain students may sometimes be permitted to absent themselves from school during the week on market days to go to work or on account of their employment. This permission may be given provided that the absence is not in the afternoon and is only for the purpose of going to work and for nothing else.

Some may be allowed, for the same reason, to come to school in the afternoon every day. However, no student will be permitted to come to school only in the morning. It will also not be permitted any student to come only at 9:00 in the morning or at 3:00 in the afternoon. Besides the fact that this disturbs the order of a school, many other students would want to do the same.

Nor must others be allowed to come to school in the afternoon and to go away before the catechism. All students must be present at the catechism as well as at the prayers every day. Nevertheless, for weighty reasons, students who work may be permitted sometimes, and those of the writing class daily, to come in just as school begins in the morning in order to read or to write, and to leave before the end of school. This permission presumes that they come also in the afternoon and are present at the catechism and at the prayers.

Article 2:
Irregular Absences; Permitted or Not Permitted

It sometimes happens that students ask permission to be absent on Sundays and holy days. Some wish to go on trips or to visit their relatives; others wish to go to some village celebration or to some confraternity. None will be permitted to absent themselves from the catechism on Sundays and holy days for any of these reasons except upon rare occasions and only when their parents ask it for them.

On school days, students will be permitted to go on pilgrimages to places which are a distance from the town and at which there is ordinarily a great concourse of people. This absence will be permitted when they go with their parents and when it is evident that it is only devotion and piety which impels them. However, they will not be allowed to absent themselves from school to be present at processions. The exception is the procession of the Blessed Sacrament during the octave of the feast, if it happens to be held in some parish on a day on which school is kept.

Students will be permitted to absent themselves from school on the feast of the Patron Saint of the parish in which they live, provided it be a solemn feast and celebrated by the parishioners.

Students whose fathers follow a trade may be permitted to absent themselves from school on the feast of the Patron Saint of their fathers' trade. However, they will be required to come to school in the afternoon.

Children will be permitted to absent themselves from school in order to buy stockings, shoes, and so forth. They will be permitted to absent themselves even to have their clothes mended. However, these permissions will be given only when it appears absolutely necessary and when the parents cannot choose another time.

No student will be permitted to be absent on Monday and Tuesday before Lent. This prohibition must be considered of very great importance and be very rigorously observed.

Article 3:
Causes of Absences
and Means of Preventing Them

When students are frequently absent from school, it is either through their own fault, through that of their parents, or through the fault of the teachers. The first cause of absences of students proceeds from the students themselves. It is because they are frivolous or undisciplined, because of their wildness, because they have a distaste for school, or because they have little affection for or a dislike of their teacher.

Those who stay away through frivolity are those who follow the first idea that comes into their minds, who go to play with the first child they meet, and who ordinarily act without paying attention to what they do.

It is very difficult for students of this sort not to absent themselves from time to time. All that can be done is to deal with them in such a way that their absences are rare and of short duration.

Such students should be corrected only a little for their absences. This is because they will again absent themselves on the next day or on the first occasion afterward. They will reflect neither upon what has been said to them nor upon the correction that they have received. They will be induced to come to school more by gentleness and by winning them than by correction and harshness.

The teachers will take care, from time to time, to stimulate children with this type of mind and to encourage them by some reward or by some outside employment if they are capable of undertaking it. Above all, they will never threaten them with correction.

The second reason why students absent themselves is lack of discipline. This is either because they cannot be subjected to remaining a whole day in the same place, attentive and with their minds busy, or because they love to run about and play. Such children are ordinarily inclined to evil, and viciousness follows lack of discipline. For this reason, it is necessary to seek, with very great care, a remedy for their absence. Everything should be done to anticipate and to prevent it. It will be very useful to assign them some office in the class. This will give them a liking for school and will sometimes even cause them to become an example to the others. Much must be done to win them and to attract them, at times being firm with them and correcting them when they do wrong or absent themselves, but showing them much affection for the little good they do and rewarding them for little.

The third reason why students absent themselves is because they acquire a distaste for school. This may be due to the fact that they have a new teacher who is not yet sufficiently trained. Such teachers do not know how to conduct themselves in school. They at once resort to corrections, or they are too lax and have no order or silence in the classroom.

The remedy for absences of this sort is to leave a teacher neither alone in a classroom nor placed solely in charge until thoroughly trained by a teacher of great experience in the schools.

This is very important for the welfare both of the teachers and of the students. It is important in preventing frequent absences and various other disorders.

The remedy for teachers who are lax and who have no order in their classrooms will be for the Director or the Head Teacher to watch over them and require them to account for all that takes place in the classes. They will particularly be required to account for their actions when they have neglected to look after the absent or have been remiss in any of their duties, however small and of however little consequence it may appear.

The fourth reason why students absent themselves is that they have little affection for their teacher. This is due to the fact that the teacher is not pleasant and in almost every situation does not know how to win the students. This kind of teacher resorts only to severity and punishments, and consequently the children are unwilling to come to school.

The remedies for this sort of absence will be for the teachers to endeavor to be very pleasant and to acquire a polite, affable, and frank appearance, without, however, assuming an undignified or familiar manner. Let them do everything for all of their students to win them all to Our Lord Jesus Christ. They should all be convinced that authority is acquired and maintained in a school more by firmness, gravity, and silence than by blows and harshness, and that the principal cause of frequent absences is the frequency of the punishments.

Parents are the fifth principal reason for absence. Parents either neglect to send their children to school, or do not take much trouble to make them come or be assiduous. This difficulty is quite common among the poor, either because they are indifferent to school, persuaded that their children learn very little, or for some other trifling objection.

The means of remedying the negligence of parents, especially of the poor, is to speak to them and make them understand their obligation to have their children instructed. They should understand the wrong that they do to their children in not making them learn to read and write, and how much this can harm their children, since lack of this knowledge will leave the children incapable of any employment. Then they must be made to realize the harm that may be done their children by lack of instruction in those things which concern their salvation, with which the poor are often little concerned.

Secondly, since this class of poor are ordinarily those who receive alms, a list should be given to the parish priests of all those who do not come to school, their ages and their addresses. This is done in order that no alms be given their parents and that they may be urged and obliged to send their children to school. Thirdly, an effort must be made to attract the children of people like this and win them over by every possible means, which can often be done with success. Ordinarily, the children of the poor do as they wish. Their parents often take no care of them or even idolize them. What their children want they also want. Thus, it is enough that their children should want to come to school for them to be content to send them there.

When parents withdraw their children from school to make them work while they are too young and not yet sufficiently instructed, they must be made to understand that they harm them a great deal. To have their children earn a little, they will make them lose a very much greater advantage. It should be explained to them how important it is for an artisan to know how to read and write well. It should be emphasized that, however limited the child's intelligence, the child that knows how to read and write will be capable of anything.

Parents must be urged to send their children to school if not for the whole day at least for the entire afternoon. It will be necessary to watch very carefully over children of this sort and take care of them. To obviate the problem of having parents complain because their children learn only little or nothing and so wish to withdraw them from school, Directors or the Inspectors of Schools must watch with great care over all of the teachers under their direction. They must particularly watch those of lesser ability. They must see to it that they instruct as diligently as possible all of the students who are entrusted to them; that they neglect none and that they apply themselves equally to them all, even more to the more ignorant and more negligent; that they keep order in the schools and that the students do not absent themselves frequently. The freedom children have to be absent is often the cause of their learning nothing.

The sixth principal reason why students absent themselves frequently is either because the teachers are too complacent in bearing with those who are absent from school without permission or because they too readily give permission to be absent.

To provide a remedy for this problem, every teacher must be very exact in watching over those who go to visit the absent. Every teacher must make sure that these visitors go to the homes of all of the absentees, that they do not let themselves be deceived by false reasons, and that they afterward report to the teacher the reasons that have been given them. Secondly, the teacher who receives the absentees and excuses their absences is to require their parents to bring the children back, and to receive no student back in the school who has been absent without first knowing and investigating well the reason given for the absence.

The reasons ordinarily are that their parents needed them, or that they have been ill. Others are absent because they are delinquents.

For the first reason to be good and valid, the need must be great, and also be very rare. The Inspector or the teacher will not accept the second reason if the student has been seen outside the house or playing with other children. Every teacher will be sure that those who visit the homes of the absent see all the ill students and report on the state in which they find them.

As for the delinquents, the Inspector or the teacher will observe what has been said above in the article on students who must or must not be corrected. They will not correct them themselves, but will oblige the parents to correct them at home before permitting them to return to school.

Children who have been absent without permission under the pretext that their parents needed them must not be easily excused. It is ordinarily the same ones that are guilty of this fault. If they repeat it three or four times without troubling themselves about it, they must be sent home and not received at the school again until they as well as their parents are ready to ask permission for every absence from school.

When a student asks permission to be absent, teachers must always appear reluctant to grant permission. They are to investigate the reasons well, and when they find these good and necessary, they will always send the student to the Head Teacher to obtain the permission. The Head Teacher will, however, grant the permission only after great difficulty. The Head Teacher will never listen to a student who asks for a permission that has already been refused.

Absences for trivial reasons will be rare. This is a matter about which the teachers must be very careful. It is better to send students home than to permit them to absent themselves frequently, for this sets a very bad example. Three or four students will be found in every school who always ask permission to absent themselves. If it is granted, they will easily lead others to absent themselves without reason. It is better to send students of this sort home and to have fifty who are very assiduous than to have a hundred who are absent at every moment.

However, before sending students home for these or other reasons, the teacher will speak with their parents several times, and explain to them how important it is that their children come to school assiduously and how it is otherwise almost impossible for them to learn anything, since they forget in one day what they have learned in several. Students will not be sent away from school unless it appears that both they and their parents are not concerned about it and do not profit at all by all that it has been possible to say to them in this matter.

Finally, before sending away students on account of absences or for anything else, it is well to make use of the following means to remedy the situation: (1) deny the rewards for assiduity gained by a student who has been absent, even with permission; (2) do not promote the student to another level or to another lesson the next month even though the student knows how to read perfectly or is capable of being promoted; (3) make the student stand for several days in school or make use of some other penance that will embarrass the student, be unpleasant for the parents, and will incite the student to come punctually and thus will oblige the parents to force the child to be assiduous.[2]

Article 4:
Receiving and Excusing Absentees

The Director will appoint one teacher in each school to receive back to school the students who have been absent and to excuse their absences.

Students who have been absent may be received and their absences excused not later than 8:30 in the morning and not later than 2:00 in the afternoon. Teachers will notify students that all who have been absent must be at school before the teachers themselves arrive. Students must understand that if their absences have not been excused before the bell begins to ring at 8:30 and at 2:00, no matter what reasons they allege, they will be punished or sent away.

If parents make complaints when they bring back their children, the receiving teacher will be careful always to excuse the teacher, if it is of the teacher that complaints are made, giving whatever advice is judged necessary, and then carefully reporting later to the Director the complaints that have been made and the reason. The receiving teacher will be careful to finish with the parents in few words.

If the absence is the fault of the parents, the student will first enter school. The teacher who has received them will then speak with the parents in private to make them realize their fault and the wrong that they are doing their children in seeking such permissions for them or allowing them to be absent. The teacher will urge them to be more exact in making their children come diligently to school, and inform them that, if they fail to do so again for similar reasons, the children will not be taken back. This, in fact, must be done.

Students absent through their own fault must be reprimanded in the presence of the parent who brings them back. Later and in private, the parent will be given the necessary instructions for forestalling and preventing future absences of the child.

If the receiving teacher is not familiar with the conduct of the student and the reasons for the absence or is in doubt concerning them, this teacher will leave parent and student at the door and go to consult the classroom teacher. Then returning to speak with the parents and the student, the teacher will tell them what is considered appropriate.

When students who have absented themselves or who have been excused return to school, they will stand at the back of the classroom until the receiving teacher has spoken to the teacher of their class and the latter has instructed them to go to their seats or to the bench of the absentees.

Each time the receiving teacher has excused the absentees who have presented themselves, this teacher will tell each of their teachers which students have been brought back, what their parents have said, and in what manner and under what conditions the students have been received back, or will send someone to do so.[3]

7
Holidays

It is important that holidays and vacations should always be regulated in the same manner in all the schools. This is one of the things that will be of great use in maintaining good order.

There are four things to be considered in this chapter: (1) ordinary holidays; (2) extraordinary holidays and the occasions on which they may or may not be given; (3) vacation; and (4) the manner of indicating and making known holidays both to teachers and to students.

Article 1:
Ordinary Holidays

Ordinary holidays are those that are indicated below.

A whole holiday will be given every Thursday of each week in the year if there are no holy days of obligation during the week.

When there is a holy day of obligation in a week and if it falls on Monday, Tuesday, or Saturday, a half holiday will be given on Thursday afternoon. If it falls on Thursday or Friday, a half holiday will be given on Tuesday afternoon. If it falls on Wednesday, a half holiday will be given on Friday afternoon.

When there are two or more holy days of obligation in a week, there will be no holiday in that week.

On the day of the feast of Saint Nicholas, who is the Patron Saint of school children and on Ash Wednesday, a whole holiday will be given on that day instead of on the Thursday of that week. However, on each of these days, the students will come to school in the morning.

On the morning of each of these days, they will be taught their catechism from 8:00 until 9:00, at which time they will be taken to holy Mass in the church to which it is the custom to take them.

On Ash Wednesday, after holy Mass, they will receive the ashes. If there is an interval between the prayers in school and the time for holy Mass, students will be instructed by demonstration concerning what they should do and how they should approach the altar to receive the ashes. If there is no interval between the prayers and holy Mass, these instructions will be given during the last quarter of an hour of the catechism.

If the feast of Saint Nicholas falls on a Sunday, the celebration for the students will be transferred to the following Thursday, which will be observed as indicated above.

On the day of the feast of Saint Joseph, the Patron Saint of the Community [of the Brothers of the Christian Schools], a whole holiday will be given instead of on Thursday. When this feast falls on Sunday or in Holy Week, it will be celebrated on the day to which it is transferred by the Church.

Holiday will be given from Thursday in Holy Week inclusive to the following Wednesday, exclusive, on which day school will begin again. However, the students will be taken to the parish Mass on the two last-named feasts [Saint Joseph and Holy Thursday].

They will be taught their catechism on the days of the feast of the Transfiguration, of the Presentation, of the Visitation of the Blessed Virgin, and of the Exaltation of the Holy Cross.

On whatever day of the week these feasts come, a holiday will be given instead of on Thursday. No other holiday will be given during the week, unless one of the feasts comes on Sunday.

Article 2:
Extraordinary Holidays

No extraordinary holidays will be given without an evident and indispensable necessity. When the Director of a Community House thinks that it is necessary to give one, the Director will consult the Superior of the Institute before doing so, in case this necessity can be foreseen. If the necessity cannot be foreseen, the Director will inform the Superior afterward and will make known the reasons that required the granting of this holiday.

When it is necessary to give an extraordinary holiday, it will always be given instead of the regular weekly holiday. If there is a holy day in the week, the extraordinary holiday will be given only in the afternoon if that holiday calls only for the afternoon. If the holiday is prescribed for the morning, it will be given for the whole day.

The occasions on which extraordinary holidays will be given are the following.

First, extraordinary holidays will be given for fairs when they last only one day.

Second, extraordinary holidays will be given on the day of the burial of a teacher who has died in the Community in the town. If it is not possible to celebrate the funeral office either the next day or in the same week, a whole holiday will be given on the day of the burial instead of on Thursday. If it is possible to celebrate the office the next day, a whole holiday will also be given then. If the funeral office is celebrated in the same House on a day much later than that of the burial, or in another week, a whole holiday will be given on the day of the service.

Third, holiday will be given on the days on which some extraordinary ceremony is being celebrated in the town. This is provided that the ceremony is not bad, that it will not do the students harm to be there, and that it is not considered possible to prevent them from going.

Fourth, holiday will be given on the day of the feast of the Patron Saint of each of the parishes in which the schools are situated. This is also the case on certain days which, while they are neither days upon which it is necessary to refrain from servile work nor holy days of obligation, are nevertheless kept in the town or in the parish in which the House of the Institute is situated.

Fifth, holiday will also be given on the day of the octave of the Most Blessed Sacrament [Corpus Christi], even though there be a holy day in that week.

The occasions on which neither ordinary nor extraordinary holidays will be given are the following.

First, holidays may not be given on the Monday and Tuesday immediately preceding the first day of Lent. Furthermore, students will even be required to be more exact in their attendance at school on these days than on any other day in the year.

Second, holidays may not be given on Rogation Days[1] and on the feast of Saint Mark under the pretext of assisting at the processions.

Third, holidays many not be given on the feast of the Translation of the Relics of Saint Nicholas, even though this is one of the feasts of the Patron Saint of school children.

Fourth, holidays may not be given on the days of the feasts of the Patron Saints of the different trades nor on any one of them.

The time spent in school will not be diminished, unless for some evident and unavoidable necessity.

Article 3:
Vacation

This article comprises four items: (1) what concerns the vacation in itself; (2) the counsel that the teachers should give their students so that they may spend the vacation time well; (3) what is to be done in school on the last day before vacation; and (4) what is to be done on the day of the return to school.

Every year, school will be closed everywhere for one month. This is what is called vacation. Vacation will be given everywhere during the month of September. In all places, everyone will also return to school on October 1.

On the last day of school, nothing except the catechism will be taught from 1:30 until 3:00. The catechism lesson will be on the manner in which students should spend the time of their vacation. Among the counsels which teachers will give to students so that they may spend this vacation time well, the principal are: (1) not to fail to say each day the morning and evening prayers that are recited in the schools; (2) to assist at holy Mass daily with devotion and to say throughout holy Mass the prayers which are in the Manual of Exercises of Piety; (3) to assist at the holy Mass and vespers in their parish churches on Sundays and holy days of obligation; (4) to go to Confession and, for those who have already made their First Communion, to go to Holy Communion at least once during this time; (5) to go each day to some church to visit and adore the Blessed Sacrament for at least fifteen or thirty minutes; (6) to say the rosary every day, in order to acquire and preserve a devotion to the Blessed Virgin; (7) not to frequent bad company; (8) not to plunder gardens and vineyards, which would be thieving and a great sin; (9) not to go bathing;[2] and (10) not to play cards or dice for money.

At 3:00 o'clock, the prayers will be said. Following this, teachers will return their papers to the writers. This is done so that they may practice writing during the vacation, and teachers will even urge the students to do so. No rewards will be given at this time, but after the vacation and at the opening of school, unless the Director sees fit to do otherwise.

At the end of catechism, the teachers will notify all students to be in school after vacation on the appointed day as early as 7:30 in the morning. This is in order that they might assist at the Mass of the Holy Spirit, which will be celebrated for their intention.[3] On the day of their return and while they are assembling in school, they will be taught catechism from 8:00 until 9:00 o'clock. This will be after the prayers which are said for the opening of school.

At 9:00 o'clock, they will be taken to holy Mass, which will be celebrated for their intention, to invoke the assistance of the Holy Spirit.

The pastors of the parishes in which the schools are situated will be requested to say this special Mass or to have it said. Otherwise, it will be said at the expense of the Community.

Article 4:
Informing Teachers and Students of Holidays

On every Sunday at the end of the thanksgiving after Holy Communion, the Director of each Community House will announce to teachers the holy days of obligation that will occur during the coming week, the day on which there will be a holiday, and whether the holiday will be for the whole day or in the afternoon only.

If it happens that it is necessary to give some extraordinary holiday which was not foreseen on Sunday, the Director will give notice of it on the evening before or in the morning after the litany of the Holy Child Jesus or else in the afternoon immediately after the litany of Saint Joseph. If there is anything particular to be done in school during the week, the Director will follow the same procedure.

Teachers will announce in their own classrooms, at the end of school and immediately after evening prayers, the holidays and any other special events, above all, the feasts of the Church, that occur during the week. Teachers will take care to state these things in few words, to forget nothing, and to express themselves in such a manner that they can be understood by all students.

8

School Officers

There will be several officers in the school. These officers will be charged with several different functions which teachers cannot or ought not do themselves.[1]

These officers will be appointed by the teachers of each class on one of the first three school days after the vacation.

Each teacher will submit the names of those chosen as class officers to the Director or to the Head Teacher. The teacher will not have them begin to exercise their duties until they have been approved. If it later becomes necessary to change them or to change one of them, the nomination of another or others will be made in the same manner. These officers and their obligations will be discussed below.

The Reciters of Prayers

There will be two officers in each school to whom will be assigned the duty of reciting the prayers. One of them will recite the prayers in the morning; the other will recite the prayers in the afternoon. They will alternate between reciting morning and evening prayers.

The one who says the prayers in the morning during one week will say them in the afternoon during the following week. The other one will change in the corresponding way. They will recite all of the prayers that are said in school sedately, attentively, and decorously. They will recite all of the prayers in such a manner that they can be easily heard by all the students.

No students will be appointed to this office unless they know all of the prayers perfectly, recite them distinctly, and are reserved and well behaved, so as not to cause the distraction of the other students.

Two Reciters of Prayers will be appointed each month and will be chosen from among the class of writers. They may be continued in this office in case there are not others who can acquit themselves as well as they do of this duty, but for no other reason, for this appointment contributes much to making students recite the prayers well in private and to making them like to say their prayers at home with deliberation and attention.[2]

The Holy Water Bearer

There will be one student who will take an aspergillum[3] to holy Mass on every school day. On Sundays and holy days of obligation, this student will take the aspergillum to both Mass and vespers. In this way, students may take holy water on entering and on leaving the church. This officer and the Rosary Carrier will go first and will lead the others on the way to church. On entering the church, the Holy Water Bearer will stand near the holy water font and will remain there until all the students of all the classes have passed and have taken holy water. The Holy Water Bearer will do the same when the students leave the church. This student will be placed in such a manner that the students can easily take holy water from the aspergillum, which will be dipped from time to time in the font whenever the Bearer observes that there is no more holy water on it.

The aspergillum will be held straight out in front of its bearer, who under pain of punishment will not use it to sprinkle the others or to play with it.

For as long as the students are passing, the Holy Water Bearer will remain standing in a modest posture, with eyes lowered, without looking at any one of them as they are passing, and without turning. When all of the students have left the church and are not to go back to school, the Holy Water Bearer will return to the school with the Rosary Carrier and replace the aspergillum where it is usually kept. This student should be very pious and very well behaved and will not be replaced by another unless it is necessary.

The Rosary Carrier and Assistants

There will be one student chosen to carry the rosaries to the church every time the students are taken there. A teacher will count out the rosaries to this Carrier, who will take care to count the rosaries every day immediately after holy Mass or in the afternoon. If any of them are missing, the Rosary Carrier will notify the teacher who is responsible for counting them on the last school day of each week. There will be as many bundles of rosaries as there are rows in the church of two students in a row. If there is more than one row of two in a row, there will be one or more assistants to distribute the rosaries, one to each rank of two students in a row.

When the students are all kneeling in their places, this officer will take one or more bundles of rosaries to give to the assistant or assistants. Each one of them will go down a row between two students from beginning to end. Each will distribute the rosaries to those who do not know how to read, that is, to those who read only the charts of the alphabet and of the syllables.

As soon as holy Mass is finished, they will go in the same way, each down the assigned row to take back the rosaries from those to whom they were given at the beginning of holy Mass. The Rosary Carrier will then take the bundles from the assistants and add them to those already collected.

If the students do not return to the school after holy Mass, the Rosary Carrier will go with the Holy Water Bearer to take the rosaries back to the school and put them in their usual place.

It will also be the duty of this officer every day at the beginning of school, both morning and afternoon, to give the rosaries to those who are to be the first to say the rosary in school. This officer will be careful to remember those who were the last to say the rosary during the preceding session of school.

This class officer will notify the students who say the rosary in turn in the order of the benches, and will see that those who say the rosary in school say it with deliberation, piety, and decorum and that they do not talk and play. If any students are guilty of any of these things, the officer will at once inform the teacher.

If there are more than three classes in a school, there will be two or three students appointed to this office. They should be very sensible, very well behaved, and even very trustworthy, since they must be careful not to lose the rosaries.

The Rosary Carrier and the assistants will ordinarily be chosen from the class in which the rosary is said. If, however, there are not any in it who are capable, these officers will be chosen from another class.

The Bell Ringer

There will be in each school a student whose function will be to ring the bell for the beginning of school and of prayer exercises. At the beginning of school and at every hour this attendant will ring five separate strokes of the bell. On every half hour, five or six strokes of the bell will be tolled.

At the end of school, the bell will be rung and then also tolled five or six strokes. This will announce that it is the end of school and that the prayers are to begin.

Care must be taken to ring the bell exactly on time. About the time for a *Miserere* before the beginning of the prayers in the morning and before catechism in the afternoon, the Bell Ringer will toll two or three strokes to notify the students to put their books away, the Collectors to gather up all papers, and all to prepare themselves and be ready to begin the prayers without a moment's delay and as soon as the bell has ceased ringing. This officer should be very assiduous in attending school, careful, vigilant, exact, and very punctual in ringing the bell on time.

Monitors and Supervisors

There will be Monitors in all of the classes during the absences of the teachers but at no other times. The exception is in the classes of the writers. In those classes, there will be a Monitor during breakfast and the afternoon snack. The Monitor will supervise those who are repeating the prayers, the catechism, and the responses of holy Mass.

All the care and attention of the Monitor will be directed to observing everything that takes place in the classroom. The Monitor will do this without saying a single word no matter what happens and without leaving the assigned place. Monitors will not permit any student to speak to them or to approach them during the entire time that they are fulfilling their duties.

The Monitor will not threaten any student either by signs or otherwise no matter what the fault committed and will never use the ferule or anything whatsoever to strike the students.

The Monitor will always remain seated at the assigned place and will report faithfully to the teacher everything just as it has happened, without adding or concealing anything, noting those who keep silent and those who make the least noise, and above all, being careful to give a good example to the others. Students who have been appointed to this class office must be convinced that they have been put there not merely to watch all that takes place in the school, but even more important, they have been appointed to be the model for the others.

Teachers will examine carefully the things that the Monitor reports, in a low tone and privately, before determining whether or not to punish those who have been reported for having committed faults. In order to find out more easily whether the Monitor has told the truth, a teacher will ask privately the most trustworthy students who have witnessed the faults whether the matter took place in the manner and under the circumstances that the Monitor has declared. The teacher will punish the students who have committed the faults only in case the teacher finds that what the others say agrees with what the Monitor has reported.

Teachers will listen to complaints that are made against the Monitor, especially if those who make them are disinterested and if they are among the more sensible and more trustworthy students. Should the Monitor be found guilty, the punishment will be much more severe than for another student committing the same fault. Furthermore, this Monitor will at once be deprived of the office.

The Monitor must be very punctual and among the first to come to school. The Monitor must be vigilant, so as to observe all that takes place in the school. The Monitor must be neither frivolous nor a liar and must not be prone to partiality for anyone. In other words, students who have this office must be prepared to accuse their siblings, their friends, and their companions, that is to say, those with whom they associate as well as they are prepared to accuse others. Above all, the Monitor must not receive any gift from anyone. If detected in this fault, the Monitor will be very severely corrected and deprived of office.

Supervisors

There will be two students in each class appointed to watch the conduct of the Monitor while the latter is exercising the functions of that office. Their responsibility is to see whether students who hold the office of Monitor allow themselves to be corrupted by gifts; whether they demand anything from the others for not declaring their faults; whether they are always among the first to come to school; whether they speak when they should be silent; whether they leave their place; whether they see to it that no one else leaves their place; in short, whether they fulfill their duties with very great exactitude. It will be best if these Supervisors are not known to the Monitor. For this reason, they will not be appointed like the other class officers and will not even be called officers. These Supervisors will be among the most sensible, the most pious, and the most punctual students. They will be privately instructed to pay attention to the conduct of the Monitor, and will render an account of that conduct as soon as possible whenever anything extraordinary happens.

There will also be certain Monitors or Supervisors for the streets, especially for those in which many students live. They will watch how the students of the district to which they have been assigned behave when returning from school.

There will be Supervisors in each district or important street. They will watch everything that takes place and will at once notify the teacher of it in private.[4]

Distributors and Collectors of Papers

There will be in the class of the writers one or two students to distribute the papers to the writers at the beginning of the writing period, to take them again at the end of it, and then to put them back in the proper place.

If all students in the class are learning to write, there will be two charged with this function. If only some of the students in the class are learning to write and if they are not too numerous, there will be only one student assigned to this class office.

The Distributors and Collectors of Papers will be careful to place all the papers in the proper order, one upon another, in the same order as the students are seated to whom they belong. In this way, they can return all of the papers properly.

They will go from table to table, both to give the papers out and to take them back. If any students are absent, they will nevertheless leave the papers at their places. They must distribute and collect all of the papers promptly and silently.

If the teacher finds it useful, these officers will go to each writer a short time before collecting the papers to see what each has written. They will note whether students have written as much as they should have, whether the paper is rumpled, and the like. If they find that anyone has been remiss in anything, they will at once inform the teacher.

Collectors will make sure that all of the students dry what they have written and fold their papers before returning them.[5]

Sweepers

There will be one student in each classroom whose duty will be to sweep it and keep it clean and neat. This student will sweep the classroom once daily without fail at the end of the morning school session. If the students go to holy Mass, the Sweeper will return to the school for this purpose.

Before beginning to sweep, this student will put the benches near the wall, some on one side and some on the other. When there is need of it, the two Sweepers from the two adjoining classrooms will help one another to remove and replace the benches, but in nothing else.

After having removed the benches, the Sweeper will, if it is necessary, sprinkle the floor of the classroom. The student will then sweep the room and carry all of the rubbish in a basket to the designated place in the street. The Sweeper will then replace the broom, the basket, and the other things that have been used back in the place where they are ordinarily kept.

The teachers will see that the Sweepers always keep the classrooms of which they have charge very clean.

The Sweepers should not be slow, but very active, so that they do not take too much time in acquitting themselves of their duties.

They should be distinguished by a great care for neatness and cleanliness. They must, however, also be sensible and not given to quarreling or trifling.

The Doorkeeper

In each school, there will be only one entrance door. If there is more than one door, the others, which the Director will select, will be closed and always kept locked.

A student from one of the classrooms, ordinarily the one at the entrance, will be appointed to open and shut this entrance door each time that anyone enters the school. This student will be called the Doorkeeper.

The Doorkeeper will be placed near the door in order to open it promptly. The Doorkeeper will not leave the door open, and will always bolt it.

The Doorkeeper will allow no one to enter except teachers, students, and the priest of the parish in which the school is situated.

When someone knocks at the door of the school, the Doorkeeper will at once open it quietly, and with the least possible delay answer the person who is knocking. After having again bolted the door, the Doorkeeper will notify the teacher who has been designated as the one to speak with visitors.

While the teacher is speaking with someone, the Doorkeeper will leave the door sufficiently open for it to be possible to see from within the classroom both the teacher and the person with whom the teacher is speaking.

The Doorkeeper will guard the door from the time when it is first opened until the time when the students begin to leave the school. For this reason, this student must always be the first to arrive at school. The Doorkeeper will always keep silent and will never speak to any student who is entering the school or going out of it.

The Doorkeeper will be exact in reading in turn like the others, and as far as possible pay attention to and follow the lesson during all of the time when not busy at the door. Doorkeepers must be frequently changed, and care should be taken that they do not lose time for reading. This can be done by making the student read at the end of school or by having another act as Doorkeeper during the lesson.

This officer will also have charge of a piece of wood given to the students when they go outside, giving it to the one going out and taking care that no student goes out without it. In this way and as far as possible, no two will go out together for this reason. The Doorkeeper will put the item away every day after school, both morning and afternoon, and will let no student go out without it. The Doorkeeper will be chosen from among the most diligent and the most regular in attendance at school. The student should be sensible, reserved, well behaved, silent, and capable of edifying the people who come and knock at the door.

The Keeper of the School Key

The Keeper of the School Key will be at the door of the school punctually every day, mornings before 7:30 and afternoons before 1:00. This class officer will be forbidden to give the key to any other student without the permission of the teacher who is in charge of this school. When the students do not return to the school after holy Mass, the Keeper of the School Key will return with the Rosary Carrier, the Holy Water Bearer, and the Sweepers, and will see that the latter make no noise while they are sweeping. The Keeper of the School Key will not leave before the others do.

This student will also be responsible for everything in the school, and must take care that nothing is carried away. This class officer should be chosen from among those who are the most assiduous and who never miss school.

9

Construction and Uniformity of Schools and Furniture[1]

Room and Furniture

The schools should be arranged in such a manner that both the teachers and the students can easily fulfill their duties. The seats should be on the same level, whether low or high. The entrance door, insofar as possible, should be placed in such a manner that the students need not pass through another classroom in order to reach their own.

When school is held in a room which opens upon the street or upon a common courtyard, the windows must be at least seven feet above the ground, so that people passing are not able to see into the school.

It must also be so arranged that there are certain conveniences [lavatories] for the children. It would be bad for them to go out into the streets.

The classrooms must have good daylight and good air. For that reason, there must be, if possible, windows at both ends of each classroom for ventilation.

The classrooms should be at least eighteen or twenty feet square. At most, they should be twenty-five feet square. Classrooms that are very long or very narrow are inconvenient.

The small and medium-sized classrooms should be at least fifteen to eighteen feet square. The communicating door should be so situated that the teacher's chair can be placed against the wall opposite this door.

The benches of the students should be of different heights. That is, there should be benches which are eight, ten, twelve fourteen, and sixteen inches high. They should be from twelve to fifteen feet long, completely joined and fastened securely. The boards of each bench should be about an inch and a half thick and six inches wide. Each bench should have three sets of legs, each consisting of two uprights with a crossbar at the bottom. In each one of the lower classrooms, there should be two benches which are eight inches high for the smallest students; three benches which are ten inches high; and three benches which are twelve inches high for the medium-sized and larger students. The number of these benches can be diminished or increased according to the total number of the students.

In each large classroom, there should be a number of tables, depending on the number of the students, for writing exercises: two of the highest for the largest students and the other tables lower for the medium-sized and the smaller students. All of the tables should have benches of the same length. The highest tables should be two feet three inches high at the back and two feet one inch high at the front. This is done in order to give a slope to the table. The benches for these tables should be sixteen inches high. The lowest tables should be two feet high at the back and one foot ten inches high at the front. The benches for these tables should be fourteen inches high. The tops of the tables should be fifteen inches wide and at least an inch and a half thick. They should be nine, twelve, or fifteen feet in length, in proportion to the size of the classroom. Each table should be supported by three trestles or table supports. The top of each trestle should be as long as the table is wide, about three inches thick and five inches wide. The three uprights, which should be joined and fastened securely into the top, should each be two inches square and should open out toward the bottom. At the bottom, the spread should be of about fifteen inches. This will give solidity and balance to the trestle. Each support should be attached to the table with a large square-headed screw. The screw should be set in the table in such a manner that it is even with the surface, that it passes through the table and the trestle, and that it is fastened underneath with a bolt.

On the table, there will be as many leaden inkwells as necessary, each one to be used by two students.

If some teacher should later on find another manner of constructing these writing tables which would be easier and more solid, that teacher will propose this new manner to the Superior before making use of it.

Charts

The two charts of the alphabet and of the syllables will be arranged in the following manner. They will be the same in all the Community Houses of the Christian Schools [*See* Figures 6 and 7].

These charts will be at least two feet four inches long and one foot eight inches high, not including the border.

The letters and syllables will be placed one above another in columns, as illustrated by the models of the two charts.

Figure 6: Model of the Alphabet Chart (CL 24:221).

The chart of the alphabet will be divided into to parts, as shown on the model. The first part consists of the small letters; the second part consists of the capital letters. Each part will contain six lines. Each line will contain five letters, diphthongs, and letters joined together and therefore counted as one letter, for example, *ft, fi, fl*. Similarly for other combinations.

The table of small letters and the table of capital letters will be separated by a space of about three inches, so that there will be a space of about three inches between the last letter in each line in the first column and the first letter on the corresponding line in the second column. For instance, there should be a distance of three inches between the small *e*, which is the last letter on the line in the first column and the capital *A*, which is the first letter of the first line in the second column. The same should be true of all the other lines.

The first stroke of each letter in both parts should be at least an inch and two-thirds distant from the first stroke of the following one. The lines should be at least three inches distant one from another.

MODELE DE LA TABLE

DES SILLABES

me	ca	et	eux	ce	ga	nos
em	gl	jo	cho	of	cu	qui
œu	en	ei	l'hu	vu	go	one
n'y	ge	in	gue	ha	on	ſça
im	eu	xi	eun	ou	hé	pei
eſt	cé	el	gne	gu	j'i	nez
om	ex	ni	hau	co	ze	moy

Figure 7: Model of the Syllables Chart (CL 24:222).

The second chart, which is of syllables of two and three letters, should contain seven lines. Each line should contain seven syllables. The first three, the fifth, and the sixth syllables of each line should be syllables of two letters. The fourth and seventh lines should consist of syllables of three letters, all as is shown on the model. There must be at least two and two-thirds inches after each syllable, that is, between the end of one syllable and the beginning of the next. The lines should be about three inches apart.

MODELE
DU CHIFFRE FRANCOIS

Centaine de million	Dixaine de Million	Million	Centaine de Mille	Dixaine de Mille	Miille	Centaine	Dixaine	Nombre
								1.
							3.	2.
						5.	2.	3.
					6.	6.	5.	4.
				9.	8.	7.	6.	5.
			6.	3.	9.	8.	7.	6.
		6.	5.	6.	3.	9.	8.	7.
	2.	6.	3.	6.	1.	3.	9.	8.
I.	2.	3.	4.	5.	6.	7.	8.	9.
10.	11.	12.	13.	14.	15.	16.	17.	18.
19.	20.	35.	43.	51.	62.	73.	80.	93.
100.	1012.	10211.	1673167371.					

Figure 8: Model of the Chart of French [Arabic] Numerals (CL 24:224).

MODELE DU CHIFFRE ROMAIN

I. V. X. L. C. D. M.

I.	XIII.	XC.C.	I^c.	XXXV.
II.	XIV.	CC.	II^c.	XLX.
III.	XV.	CCC.	III^c.	LXIV.
IV.	XIX.	CCCC.	IV^c.	XCIX.
V.	XX.	D.	V^c.	IƆ.
VI.	XXX.	DC.	VI^c.	IƆC.
VII.	XL.	DCC.	VII^c.	IƆCC.
VIII.	L.	DCCC.	VIII^c.	DCCC.
IX.	LX.	DCCCC.	IX^c.	IƆCCCC.
X.	LXX.	M. CIƆ.	X^m.	II^m.
XI.	IIII^{xx}.	XX^{m}L^m.	LXX.	X^m.
XII.	IIII^{xx}X.	CLXIV^m.	MM.	

Figure 9: Model of the Chart of Roman Numerals (CL 24:225).

The chart of French and Roman numerals will be three feet eight inches in height and seven feet long. It will be divided into two panels.

In the first panel, a large sheet of paper will be pasted. On that paper, the French and Roman numerals will be printed [*See* Figures 8 and 9]. In the other panel, the chart of the vowels, the consonants, the punctuation marks, and the abbreviations will be pasted [*See* Figure 10].

Model des voyelles & consonnes

VOYELLES.

a, e, i, y, o, u

CONSONNES.

bé cé dé effe gé ache ca el eme ene

b   c   d   f   g   h   k   l   m   n

pé cu er effe té ve icci zede

p   q   r   s   t   v   x   z

PONUCTATIONS.

Point. Deux points: point & virgule; virgule,

interrogant?   admiratif!
Où eft Dieu?   O mon Dieu!

APOSTROPHE'

Il n'y a qu'un feul Dieu.

PARENTHESIS ( )

Donnez (dit J.C.) & on vous donnera.

LIAISON -

Y-a-t'il, eft-il, Trés-Saint.

ACCENT AIGU'

Aimé, loüé, prifé, amitié.

ACCENT GRAVE`

près, auprès, où, à, là.

CIRCONFLEXE^

vôtre, même, maître, être.

ë, ï, ü, avec deux points deffus.
vuë, ruë, aïez, haïr, feüil, deüil.

ABBREVIATIONS.

Deũ, āte, numquā, ej⁹, ut'iq, Doñs.

Figure 10: Model of the Chart of Vowels, Consonants,
Punctuation Marks, and the Abbreviations (CL 24:225-226).

In each classroom in which connected sentences are written there will be a large board, five feet in length and three feet in height, consisting of two panels. On each panel, two examples in arithmetic can be written. For examples in division, an entire panel will be required. This board should be attached to the wall in the most convenient place, the bottom about five feet above the floor and the top slanting forward. The two panels of this board are painted black with oil paint so that it will be possible to write examples upon them with chalk. The board should be made like this model [*See* Figure 11].

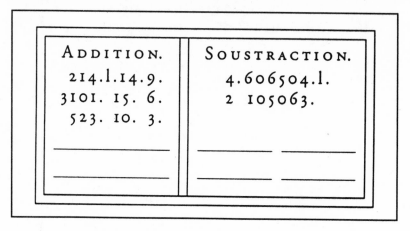

Figure 11: Model of the Chart of Addition and Subtraction (CL 24:227).

Other Materials

The chairs for the teachers in each classroom will measure twenty inches from the seat to the footstool. The footstool, which will be attached to the chair, will be twelve inches in height and eighteen inches from the seat to the top of the back. The chairs will have straw bottoms.

There will be a chest or cupboard in which to put away the papers and other things used by the teachers and students.

In each classroom, there will also be a picture of the Crucifix, of the Blessed Virgin, of Saint Joseph, of the holy Guardian Angels, and of the five rules mentioned in Article 5 of Chapter 2, [on Signs Used in Reference to Corrections], of Part Two. All of these will be pasted upon heavy backs or framed.

Finally, there will be in the classroom of the writers a little bell. This is the bell which will be rung for the school exercises.

The Twelve Virtues of a Good Teacher[2]

Seriousness — Gravitas, Dignity
Silence
Humility
Prudence
Wisdom
Patience
Restraint
Gentleness
Zeal
Watchfulness
Piety
and Generosity

APPENDIXES

Appendix A
Part Three:
Duties of the Inspector of Schools[1]

In every Community House of the Institute, there shall be an Inspector of Schools who shall supervise all of the schools that depend on that particular Community House. The Director shall be the Inspector. If there are three or four schools depending on the Community House of which this person is the Director, another teacher may be assigned to assist the Director in supervising these schools. The Director, however, actually exercises overall supervision of the schools. The teacher assisting the Director shall not do anything without the Director's order, and, furthermore, shall report to the Director everything that has been done or has taken place in the schools.

The Inspectors of Schools shall give as much time to one school as to any of the others for which they are responsible, not merely according to preferences, but as and whenever there is need for the Inspector's presence. The Inspector shall visit these schools one after another, following the order laid down by the Superior of the Institute.

The Inspector shall not be absent from the schools without an evident necessity. The Inspector, if also the Director, shall inform the Superior of the Institute of the length of any absences, together with the reasons and the necessity of the absences.

The Inspector shall remain in the same school from the beginning of classes in the morning until the end of the school day and shall take note of everything that occurs in all the classrooms. The Inspector shall take care that the rules and regulations of the school are faithfully observed, without any change or alteration.

The office of the Inspector of Schools consists mainly in two [sic] things: (1) to be vigilant over the schools, the teachers, and the students; (2) to place the students in their classrooms and assign the lessons they are to be taught; and (3) to promote the students from one lesson to another when they are capable of doing more advanced work.

1

The Vigilance of the Inspector of Schools

Article 1:
Matters Concerning School

The Inspector of Schools shall watch to be sure that a holy water font is placed at the entry of each school and that it always contains sufficient holy water.

The Inspector shall also see to it that there are four images in each classroom: a crucifix, a picture of the most Blessed Virgin, a picture of Saint Joseph, and a picture of Jesus in school; that every classroom also has a complete set of the "written orders"[2] to be used with the hand signal.

That there are enough rosaries in each school for the students who do not know how to read.

That there should be an aspergillum in each school so that the students may take holy water on entering and on leaving the church; that there is a basket in each classroom for the collection of the bread to be given to the poor during lunch and the afternoon snack.

That there are books for every lesson, with as many as necessary for the poor who have none of their own.

That there should also be enough writing paper for the impoverished writers who have none of their own; that each teacher should have all the books that are needed; that there are no other books in the school, no matter what the reason.

That in each writing class, there is a shelf or a cabinet, if there is no small closet, where all the writing papers, the registers, and the books used by the poor should be kept, all arranged in good order.

That between each pair of writers there is an inkwell set into the desk, and that these all have covers; that there is a piece of wood with a loop of string attached to it, big enough to fit over a child's arm; that when going to the lavatory, each child takes this piece of wood, so that there is only one student at a time [out of the room].

That there are as many brooms as there are classrooms, and that these brooms are replaced when necessary; that in schools located away from the Community House, there is a bucket, a sprinkling can, a rake, and a wastebasket for removing trash; that there is a register for each bench; that there is only one bundle of rods or one cat-o'-nine-tails for all the classes of a given school and that one teacher, appointed by the Director, is in charge of them; that everything is kept in its proper place, in good order, and very clean.

That all the benches are clean and safe, that is, in good condition and that minor repairs are taken care of promptly; that benches are carefully lined up, always in the same way; and that none is changed without the knowledge and permission of the Director.

That the classrooms are kept clean, and that there is on the floor no paper, no pieces of quill pens, no fruit pits, or anything else that might dirty or spoil the floor; that all the classrooms are swept daily and sprinkled with water during the sweeping.

That there is no dirt or caked mud on the floor of the classrooms, and floors are scrubbed from time to time; that the window panes are always kept clean.

Article 2:
Matters Concerning Teachers

The Inspector of Schools should pay attention to the following items concerning the teachers.

That those who teach in the school attached to the Community House go to their classrooms immediately after the rosary, and that on the way, they do not enter any other part of the residence without necessity and without permission.

That those who go to the schools apart from the Community House go directly to the door on leaving the chapel and do not stop anywhere; that they recite the rosary on their way and do not converse with each other.

That teachers ought to walk through the streets with great modesty, and by their external behavior edify everyone.

That they should approach no one in the streets nor enter any house under any pretext whatsoever; that if someone addresses them in the streets, the Head Teacher alone replies briefly to what has been suggested or requested, provided that a response is possible or necessary; if not, that the teacher gives a polite excuse.

That all begin the lesson and the exercises of the school day precisely at the appointed hour, without delaying a single instant; that in all classes the duration of each lesson is in proportion to the number of students.

That once the duration of each lesson has been established, no teacher either reduces or prolongs the prescribed time.

That no teacher undertake anything in class contrary to the regulations without an order from the Director; that teachers are always either seated at their desks or standing in front of them; that they never leave their place without an obvious necessity; that they must always keep an eye on their students, never leaving them out of sight.

That during class time, they make sure that the students read slowly and distinctly, neither too loud nor too soft, without any defective accent, and following the method and rules for reading.

That teachers always use the signal, never speaking aloud to the students during the time of the lesson itself; that they always follow in their own book and unfailingly correct all mistakes made during the lesson; that when the lesson is being given, teachers do not read from any book that is not a school book; that they make all the students read, skipping no one; and that all students should read approximately the same amount of text.

That the writing teachers are very careful to have their students hold their pens correctly and assume a proper posture, and that the teachers correct any mistakes made in writing; in a word, that they see to it that the students observe all the rules laid down in the regulations for writing.

That, depending on their age, their ability, the calling they will follow, and the length of time they can spend in school, the students should be taught to write either round hand or slanted hand; that teachers apply themselves with as much, or even more, affection to teaching the poor as to teaching the rich; and that they neglect no one and show no preference for anyone.

That the teachers do not have a particular affection for any student, that they never speak to a student in private, except very briefly and only concerning a past or foreseen absence; that they must never have any student sit next to them; that they take care to make new students learn their prayers; and that they are careful to perform all their duties very exactly.

That no teacher other than a teacher of writing does any writing during class, except to correct a student's work; that no teacher speak to another teacher in school, except to the one who holds the position of Inspector; that a teacher who has something to say or some question to make concerning the proper running of the school speak to the Director about it.

That teachers give the catechism lesson at the proper times, and on the topic set down for the week; that during catechism, teachers do not put forward anything which they have not found in duly approved and authorized books; and that they are never to judge whether something is a mortal or a venial sin.

That teachers never accept any gift from the students; and that if they take something away from a student because the student is playing with it or for some other reason, they give it back at the end of the school day; if they, however, judge that the object is useless or perhaps detrimental to the student, they give it to the Director; that they should never give anything to a student except as a reward and not out of special friendship or favor.

That the teachers do not become familiar or friendly with anyone, whatever the reason; that nobody is allowed to come to visit them at school; and that they speak only to the parents who bring their children back to school during the Director's absence; and that when they do so, they should speak very courteously and briefly.

That teachers allow no one to enter the school except the priest of the parish in which they are conducting the schools or some other person who has obtained the Director's permission to observe the school and its operations; that teachers leave their place only for the usual and ordinary necessities.

That they do not allow themselves to be carried away by impatience when reproving or correcting their students; that corrections with the rod are rare; that those with the ferule are not too frequent; and that nothing is done beyond the prescribed limits.

That teachers do not administer correction during prayers or catechism; that young, inexperienced teachers do not use the rod without having consulted with the Inspector or the one who replaces the Inspector; and that they not use the ferule too frequently.

That teachers are serious when they impose penances and that they give only those prescribed; that they take care that their students attend daily Mass with piety and modesty; that during Mass, the teachers should not have a book in their hands, but devote all their attention to watching over the student.

That those who teach in outside schools return to the Community House as soon as school is over without delay at the school or anywhere else; that they should proceed directly to the room where the spiritual exercises take place.

That when they return from school, the teachers give an account of the persons who may have come to the school or to the school door, of their reasons for coming, and of what they said and did, and that the teacher with whom they spoke reports on what it was that the visitors said.

The main things which the Inspector of Schools shall observe and take great care to prevent are: that the teachers never strike the students with their foot, hand, or a pointer; that the teachers never speak too loudly, except when very necessary and only outside the time for catechism, for the examination, and for the reflection; that teachers do not leave their places; that they follow in their own book what is being read by the students; and that they do nothing except their duties at all times; that they correct the students' writing at the time and with the method indicated; that they not place any student next to them; that no teacher speaks to another teacher, except to the one in charge of admitting absentees when such a child is brought back to class, or to the one in charge of speaking, when necessary, to outsiders; and that on both occasions, they should speak only as is necessary.

Furthermore, that teachers allow no one to enter the door of the school to speak with or to visit anyone, or leave the school to speak with anyone; that they do not accept anything from students, from parents, or from any other person for any reason or in any manner whatever; that they must not keep anything belonging to a student, even if it were only a pin.

Violations such as these are very fundamental and have very serious consequences. Hence, they must never be tolerated in the teachers, not even once. Teachers must never commit them, whatever pretext they may allege to justify their behavior.

Article 3:
Matters Concerning Students

The Inspector of Schools shall make sure that the students arrive before school starts, and that they do not miss school without permission and without a real and recognized necessity.

In the streets, students are to be modest, circumspect, and edifying. They should not crowd together either on coming to school or when returning home. None of them should loiter or shout in the streets. They should not gather in the street or before the school door when it is open. They must not fight either among themselves or with other children. They must not delay in the streets, not even to urinate. They must not attend to their necessities in the streets, either when coming to or on leaving school.

They are to enter the school building modestly and quietly and remain there in silence. They should always keep their eyes on their book and follow the lesson, reading along in a low voice what is being read aloud.

The Inspector shall also see to the following: that all students read during each lesson, and that all write during the writing period, doing so neither too quickly nor too slowly, and forming the letters properly; that, except when necessary, they do not speak to the teachers, and then only in a low voice and in few words; that they neither whisper to their companions nor look around from side to side.

That the students know the prayers and the catechism by heart, and even the responses for holy Mass, if they are capable of learning them; that they pray to God every morning and evening and cultivate devotion to the most Blessed Virgin and Saint Joseph; that they are modest and pious, and pray to God in church.

That if they pass a church on their way to school, they enter to pray to God and adore the Blessed Sacrament; that they go to confession from time to time, and even as often as possible; that, for this purpose, some priest be asked to be kind and volunteer to hear their confessions often.

That those who are old enough to receive Communion do so at least once a month; that they regularly attend their own parish church on Sundays and feasts, as well as the parish catechism lessons; that they behave very respectfully toward their parents, and they help them with great humility and concern.

That they courteously greet decent people, especially the clergy, religious, their teachers, and persons in authority.

That no student ever go to the lavatory without taking the piece of wood; that two or more should never be allowed to go at the same time; that these facilities are kept clean and decent.

That the children walk with their assigned companions on leaving school and not join up with others until they arrive home.

That the students keep away from bad companions, and that they very carefully avoid the company of girls; that they go with virtuous, reserved, and polite companions who can benefit them by their example and conversation; that all the student officers in each school and class perform their duties faithfully.

The vigilance that the Inspector of Schools must exercise over all these matters does not excuse the teachers from observing them and having their students observe them. All should cooperate in maintaining good order in their schools by acting together in a spirit of mutual dependence, by demonstrating a spirit of regularity, and by observing exactly all that has been prescribed for them and all that God expects of them.

2

Enrolling Students at the School

Article 1:
Who Shall Enroll Students and How to Do This

Only the Superior, or the Inspector of Schools in his absence and acting under his orders, shall enroll the students who present themselves for admission to the school.

The Director shall enroll students on the first school day in the week. If there are only two schools connected with a given Community House, the Director shall meet with the applicants for one school in the morning of the first school day and with those for the other school in the afternoon of that same day.

If there are three or four schools, the applicants for the third school shall be enrolled in the morning of the second school day. Those for the fourth school shall be enrolled in the afternoon of that same day.

Students shall be enrolled only on the day of the week and at the time appointed. Any who present themselves on other days or at other times shall be sent home and told to come back on the correct day and at the correct time, unless the Director happens to be present at the school when they arrive.

Those who are unable to come to the school on the day and at the time specified for registration, or those who find it very difficult to do so, may go to the Community House on Sunday. On that day, the Director shall enroll in the appropriate school all who present themselves.

When the Superior thus enrolls students at the Community House for schools other than the one attached to the Community residence, they shall be given a short note of admission to the school. On it shall be listed the name and surname of the student enrolled, the date of the enrollment, the classroom into which the student is assigned, the name of the father and mother, or the person with whom the student lives, their occupation, the street name and number and the room, as in the following examples:

> Jean-Baptiste Gribouval: age 6; residing with his father, Pierre Gribouval, a serge weaver, in a shop on Rue de la Couture; registered on October 19, 1706 for the school in Rue de Tillois; to be placed at the first line of the first reading chart.

> François Richard: age 12; living with his father, Simon Richard, a ticket collector, or with his mother, the widow Richard, a used-clothes dealer, or with his uncle, Jean Richard, a court registrar, in a surgeon's house on Rue de l'Oignon, in the second room from the front or back; registered in the school on May 1, 1706; to be placed in the sixth level of round hand writing.

Article 2:
Information Required When Enrolling Students

The Director shall not enroll any child in the school who is not brought by father or mother, by the person with whom the child lives, by some relative, or by some person of suitable age who comes in the name of the parents.

The Director shall obtain from the person who brings the student the child's name and surname; the names of the father and mother or of the person who is responsible for the child, and their occupation, address with the street name and number; the name of the parish to which the child belongs; the child's age, and whether the child has made first Communion and been confirmed.

The Director shall also inquire whether the child has ever been in school before and, if so, where and under whom; why the child left this school; whether it was for some misbehavior or because of having been punished; whether the child has ever attended one of the Christian Schools and, if so, for how long; whether the child was sent home therefrom, something the Director can verify by consulting the register; and whether the child's behavior is good.

If this is an older student, the Director shall ask what the parents expect the child to do later on; whether they hope to have the child learn a trade, and how soon; and the level of proficiency in reading and writing. The Director shall have the student read and spell something in French or in Latin, using a book which is not commonly known, in order to determine whether the student is not simply reciting something learned by heart. The Director should also ask about good and bad habits and whether there are any physical defects or illnesses, especially scrofula, skin itch, epilepsy,[1] or some other infirmity which might be communicable. This is something that must be carefully investigated. If there is some bodily ailment, the Director shall find out whether this will cause frequent absence.

The Director shall also ask how long it has been since the student went to confession, how frequently; and whether the student consorts with dissolute companions. The Director shall also ask whether the student sleeps alone or with someone else and, if so, with whom.

Article 3:
Information Required of Parents
for Students to Be Enrolled

When a student is admitted to the school, the students and the parents must have all the necessary books, including a prayer book if the student knows how to read; and if not, a rosary, so that the student can pray during holy Mass.

Students and parents must be told the following: that students must be assiduous in coming to school, and must never miss class without permission, and must be present every morning at 7:30 and every afternoon at 1:00.

That they must never miss the catechism lesson and High Mass on Sundays and feasts, without some major necessity and without permission; and that if they do, they will be sent home; that they are not to eat breakfast or the afternoon snack outside school, in order that they can be taught how to eat in a Christian and polite manner.

That students must never talk to anyone about what happened in school, either about themselves or about another student; that severe punishment will follow, if a student does carry tales back home or to other people.

That parents are not to listen to the complaints their children might make either about the teacher or about the teacher's way of acting; that when the students do complain, parents should take the trouble to come to talk to the teacher, in the absence of the children; and that the teacher will do all that is possible to satisfy them; that parents should send their little children to school in the winter as well as in the summer.

That students should wear clean clothes, and should not come to school if they are not suitably and cleanly dressed; that hair should be properly combed and free from vermin; that teachers insist on this of the students in their own class, especially those who are most lacking in cleanliness; that students never come to school barelegged or wearing only a shirt, and that if they do, they will be punished and sent back home.

That students are not to go swimming during summertime, this involving great risk to purity; that they are not to slide on the ice or throw snowballs in winter; that they not associate regularly with girls or with dissolute companions, even if merely to play with them.

That students are not sleep with their fathers or mothers or any of their sisters, or any person of the other sex; that, if the child does so, the parents should be urged to stop this; and that if necessary, the local parish priest should be advised, in order to take the necessary steps to set the matter right.

That parents neither give any money to their children nor allow them to have any, however little it may be; this usually being one of the main causes of misbehavior.

That, if a child attended another school, the parents should pay off any debt they owe to the teacher who previously taught their child, if they have not already done so entirely.

Article 4:
Those Who May or May Not Be Enrolled in the Schools

There are four categories of children whom people may bring to us for admission in our schools: those who have been in other schools; those who have never been in any school; those who had been in this school previously but who left in order to go to work, to remain idle, or to go to another school; and those who were expelled from this school.

Section 1: Those Who Have Never Been to School

No child shall be admitted who is not fully six years old unless, in some individual case, size and intelligence makes up for the lack of age. Little children shall not be admitted if they can come only during summertime, in good weather, or at a later hour than the others.

No children shall be admitted who are so retarded and of such a low intelligence that they cannot learn anything and might thus distract others or cause trouble in the school. No child shall be accepted if the child suffers from some communicable disease, such as scrofula, skin rash, or major epileptic seizures, no matter the reason. If it should happen that any student already in school contracts one of these infirmities, the Community House's doctor shall be asked to examine the child. If the malady is of this type and is curable, the child shall be sent home until the child recovers.

No student with wealthy parents should be allowed to come to the school beyond the first day without having the books needed for the lessons, or if in the writing class, without paper and an inkstand to do the writing. Neither shall any student be accepted who cannot come to school regularly, either because of some illness or for any other reason. Regular attendance means that the student shall not miss school more than twice a week, even for some good reason and with permission.

No student shall be accepted who is unwilling to attend church on Sundays and feasts with the teacher and the other students or to assist at the catechism lesson. Students who regularly do not attend shall be sent home.

No student shall be accepted who wishes to come in only for the recitation of the lesson or for writing and then be allowed to go home. A specific student can still be accepted if work or the fulfillment of some other obligation requires arrival at school later than the others; such a student must, however, come at a definitely arranged time; and no one shall be accepted who does not attend catechism and prayers. No student shall be allowed to come to school later than the others unless it is by reason of work. Those who enjoy this privilege of coming in later in the morning must still attend holy Mass with the other students.

A particular student might be allowed to enroll and come to school only in the afternoon, but no student shall be admitted who will attend only in the morning. No student can be enrolled who is expected to miss school occasionally to stay at home and watch over the house or the younger children.

Students can be admitted to the school who work at a trade that does not hinder or prove awkward for others, such as knitting or something similar. No students shall be admitted, no matter how old they are, unless they follow the same routine as the other students.

Section 2: Those Who Have Attended Other Schools

Students who have attended other schools shall be admitted only when the reasons why they left those schools are made known.

If students left the schools they were attending through an exaggerated liking for change, their parents should be made to understand how harmful this is to their children. They should make up their minds not to let their children change schools any more. They should be warned that, if the children subsequently leave our school, they will not be readmitted. If the children have left the other school merely because they have been corrected justly, the parents must be told that they should not listen to the children's complaints against the teacher. If they had been wholly innocent, they would not have been corrected. Parents should be willing to have teachers correct their children when they are at fault; otherwise, they should not send them to school. Students who have left a school because of having been badly taught or because in some way teachers were in the wrong, should be careful not to blame but rather to try to excuse teachers as far as possible.

If a child had been badly taught, for instance, made to write before knowing how to read, or made to read before knowing how to spell or even before knowing all the letters, the Inspector of Schools shall call the parents' attention to these deficiencies and indicate to them the remedies which must be applied. For instance, the child must first be taught the alphabet, to spell the syllables, and to read, before being made to write. What had been omitted in the previous instruction should be pointed out. Prudently, the Inspector of Schools should help the parents to understand the importance of this method, without which a student would never learn anything even if the child came to school for ten years.

A student of this kind, whose parents are unwilling to follow the system proposed to them, should not be accepted. If they cannot or will not listen to reason on this score, one might propose to them, as a last resort, a three-month trial period. They shall be shown that the foundation of reading depends on knowing the letters perfectly, knowing how to spell, and knowing how to read syllables distinctly. Without this, it is impossible for a child ever to read anything with understanding and not by rote.

Section 3: Those Who Have Left Our School by Choice

Students who have already attended our schools and who have left of their own volition or because of laxity and the over-credulity of their parents, and who try to come back, should be accepted only with great caution.

The reason for their departure shall be very carefully examined, and they are not to be readmitted too quickly. Without rejecting their request outright, the Director should leave the parents in suspense for a while. This will make them appreciate the favor they are asking. The parents should be told that, if children are doing well in our schools, they should not be withdrawn.

Students who leave our schools to go to another school should not be readmitted more than once. When readmitted, such students must be told that this is the last chance they will get; if they leave a second time, they will not be readmitted.

Section 4: Those Who Have Been Expelled

If a former student who had been expelled is brought in to be enrolled, the reason for the expulsion will be ascertained from the register. After reminding the parents of the serious reasons for the dismissal and after making them wait for some time, and if there is some hope of improvement, the Director may readmit the child with the warning, however, that if the behavior has not improved, expulsion will be final.

If there is little hope that the child will improve, which is most often the case, readmission should not be granted without a serious trial period. If the behavior is not corrected, the child should be expelled for good.

3

Seating the Students
and Regulating the Lessons

Article 1:
Seating and Placing the Students

After having admitted a student and ascertained the level of ability, in
the manner explained in the previous chapter, the Inspector of
Schools shall assign the student to the class, the lesson, and the seat
in the room.

The Inspector shall carefully place a newly enrolled student beside someone who will help the student learn to follow easily and
will not chatter with the newcomer. In all classrooms, there shall be
definite places assigned to each student for all the different lessons, in
such a way that all who are following a given lesson shall be grouped
in the same area within the room. This seating area shall be permanent, unless the lesson has to be transferred to another classroom.

Students in more advanced lessons shall be placed in the benches nearest the wall. Next to them, proceeding toward the middle of
the room, the other students shall be placed according to the order of
the lessons.

The Inspector of Schools shall see that the writing tables are
placed in full, clear light. The students who are reading from charts
shall be seated as indicated below, in the Article on the reading
charts.

Each particular student shall have a specific, assigned place.
None shall leave or change this place except at the direction or with
the permission of the Inspector of Schools.

The Inspector shall take care to assign the places in an orderly and prudent manner. Those whose parents do not take good care of them and who have lice are to be kept apart from those who are clean. A giddy and light-headed student should be placed between two students who are well behaved and serious. Trouble-makers should sit alone, or they should sit between two children whose piety is well recognized. A student inclined to be talkative should be placed between two silent and very attentive scholars, and so on.

When the students return to school after their vacation, the Inspector of Schools shall be sure to assign them to the various classes, to indicate which places in the rooms they should occupy, and to settle questions of order in the school. An appropriate number of students shall be assigned to each classroom.

Students shall be distributed among the various classes, not in view of the particular lesson they are following with all the students in a given lesson in one class, but in view of the total number of students. Thus, there shall only be a certain maximum number of children in each class. When there are too many students in one class, compared with any other classes in a school, the Inspector shall transfer some of the students to a higher or a lower class. The Inspector must make sure, however, that students who follow the same lesson are not put into two different classrooms unless it is absolutely impossible to do otherwise.

Each class should contain between fifty and sixty students. In schools where there are more than two classrooms, the number of students in the middle class can be greater than the number of students in either the higher or the lower class. In classes of students learning only writing or only reading from charts or from a spelling book, the number should not exceed fifty.

When the Inspector of Schools promotes students from one lesson to another, care shall be taken that one class does not contain too many students, in comparison to any others in the school, if there are more than two. If this happens or in case the Director, if the Inspector is not the Director, thinks such a measure advisable, the Inspector should reassign the students among the classes of that school.

Article 2:
Levels for Students Learning to Read

The Inspector of Schools shall divide into three levels the students in all lessons, except those who are reading from charts. The first level is for beginners; the second level is for those who have made some progress; and the third level is for the advanced and those who have mastered the material.

Beginners are so called, not because they have just recently begun a given lesson, for some may remain at this level for a considerable time, but because they do not know enough to be promoted to a higher level. The Inspector, therefore, shall place in the beginners' level of each lesson those who still make many mistakes.

The Inspector shall place in the middle level of each lesson only those who make one or two mistakes each time they read.

The Inspector shall promote to advanced and mastery level only those who read well and ordinarily never make a mistake. The Inspector shall, however, divide into only two levels the children who are reading *Les Règles de la Civilité chrétienne*. The first level shall be for those who sometimes make a mistake in reading; the second level, shall be for those who never make any mistakes.

The students who are reading the account books shall be divided into six levels, according to the gradation of account books. The account books of a superior level should be more difficult to read than those of the preceding lower level, as explained in Article 9 of Chapter [3], on Studies, of Part One.

The Inspector of Schools shall be sure to set aside a fixed and definitive place in the school for each level of a lesson, so that students in one level of a given lesson are not mixed up with those of another level in the same lesson; beginning readers, for example, with the more advanced level. All should be easily distinguished from one another by the places they occupy.

Nevertheless, those who are just learning to write shall be placed in the benches according to their height and not according to the level of writing they have attained. Students of about the same size should be in the same bench.

As far as possible, the Inspector shall try to place the writer so that a child who is just starting a particular level of writing is seated either beside one who has made some progress in that level or next to one who is in the immediately superior level. A student who finds it difficult to learn the proper strokes should be seated beside one who makes them easily. One who has trouble assuming the proper posture and holding the pen properly should be seated beside one who does both of these things well, and so forth. In this way, students may be of mutual assistance to one another.

Article 3:
Levels of Students Learning to Write Round Hand

The Inspector of Schools shall divide the writing students into eight different levels, distinguished by the various things that will be taught in each level.

The first level is for those who are just beginning to learn to write. The Inspector shall take care that these children apply themselves to sitting up straight, holding their pens properly, and making the straight and the circular strokes correctly.

The Inspector shall not promote to the second level any but those who hold their body and their pen correctly and who have learned to perform the straight and the circular movements easily. Students in this second level must learn how to form the five letters *c, o, i, f,* and *m*. They must write an entire page of each of these five letters, linked with one another, until they can give these letters their proper form and until they can write these five letters in large commercial characters.

The Inspector shall place in the third level only those who have a proper posture, who hold their pens correctly, and who have mastered the letters *c, o, i, f,* and *m*. The Inspector shall take care that the students of this level apply themselves to forming these letters well and to linking these letters properly when they should be connected.

The Inspector should also note whether the students write an entire page of each letter of the alphabet without omitting any and that they link only those letters which should be connected and not those which should not be connected. The students are to write an entire page of each letter until they can form and link them properly, with the letters properly positioned. The students should then learn how to form the three letters *o, i,* and *f* and the others which are derived from them, not forgetting to write a page of each letter.

The Inspector shall place in the fourth level of writing only those who can form, without exception, all the letters properly; who can link the letters clearly and properly; and who know the letters which are derived from *o, i,* and *f* and how they are derived from these three. The Inspector shall make sure that the students in this level apply themselves to give the letters the required position and evenness on the same line, to raise the upper loops, or heads of the letters above the body of the writing, and to keep the lower loops, or tails well below the line. Students of this level should write a line of each letter of the alphabet, one after another and all linked together.

In the fifth level, the Inspector shall place only those who, besides being able to form all the letters and link them properly, can write in straight lines, keep the letters evenly spaced, give them the same body height, and form the upper and lower loops with their proper dimensions, according to rule. The Inspector shall take care that the students in this level give the letters sufficient firmness and do not squeeze the letters too tightly together. The students should write boldly and with a certain lightness of touch, with letters properly spaced from each other, and the required distance between the lines. These students should always write the alphabet continuously and in its entirety on each line. If they experience some difficulty in forming certain letters, they should daily be made to write at the start of the lesson a few lines of these letters on the back of their paper, until they are able to form all letters perfectly.

The Inspector shall place in the sixth level only those who give all their letters the proper form, make the body of their letters equal in height, give the upper and lower loops the length proper to them according to the rule, and provide the required space between their lines. Finally, the writing of these students should be graceful and firm, showing some boldness and freedom of style.

The Inspector shall make sure that all students in the above-mentioned levels write the entire alphabet in sequence on the back of their paper at the beginning of each day's lesson. The students shall also write one page each time of dictation in large commercial characters. They shall write one line from their model every day for two weeks, and they shall write the entire model during the two following weeks.

Only the students who know how to write a connected text as mentioned above in large commercial characters shall be placed in the seventh level of writing. The Inspector shall take care that these students write in commercial hand in the morning and financial characters in the afternoon. They should copy their model immediately and continue to write the alphabet on the back of their paper.

The Inspector shall place in the eighth level only those who know how to write a connected text made up of financial characters, as indicated above. These students shall write in financial characters in the mornings, and slowly and carefully in small hand writing in the afternoons. Instead of writing the alphabet at the beginning of the lesson, they should write quickly in small hand on half of the reverse side of the paper. In the morning, they should copy something out of some good book; in the afternoon, they should copy handwritten material. After three months at this level, they shall themselves on the two days each week when writing and spelling are taught, write in legible, correctly spelled hand writing letters of their own, promissory notes, receipts, leases, workers' contracts, and other documents which might subsequently be useful. The Inspector shall also pay attention that the teachers carefully correct all the mistakes in pronunciation, writing, spelling, and punctuation.

Article 4:
Levels of Inclined Handwriting and Arithmetic

Section 1: Inclined Handwriting

The Inspector of Schools shall take care that no student begins to learn inclined hand writing before completing the second and third levels of round hand writing and prior to promotion to the fourth level. Exceptions can be made for the reasons suggested in Article 1 of Chapter 4, on Writing, in Part One.

A student shall not ordinarily begin to write inclined hand until promoted to the fourth level of round hand writing. Nonetheless, if the teacher and the Inspector of Schools think it wise to have the student learn the inclined hand style of writing, they shall have the student stop writing in round hand. The Inspector will set up five levels of inclined hand writing for those who have already begun to write in round hand.

The Inspector of Schools shall not put any student in the first level of inclined hand writing except for the reasons indicated in Chapter 4 of Part One. The student should have finished the third level of round hand and should know this type of writing reasonably well; the parents might want the student to learn inclined hand, or the student might tend to slope the letters a great deal anyway and cannot be made to break this habit. Finally, it might be desirable that the student, having finished every level of round hand writing, should learn both kinds of writing.

The Inspector of Schools shall make sure that the students on this level are taught the difference between the characteristics of round and inclined letters, the way of shaping and sloping the latter, and also their proper position. The Inspector should see that each student writes a line of each letter linked to each other.

The Inspector shall put into the second level only those who know how to form all the letters well, with no exceptions, and how to give them the proper slope and form. The Inspector shall make sure that these students pay attention to making all their letters the same height and that they space both the letters and the lines properly, in conformity with the rule for this. The students should be trained to give space to the letters, to move from one letter to the other with confidence, and to write the entire alphabet continuously as one line.

The Inspector shall promote to the third level only those who give their letters the proper form, position, slope, evenness, height, and space, including between the lines. Their writing should be open, graceful, and assured. The Inspector shall see to it that the students in this level write model texts in medium-sized characters. Those in the fifth level should do the same in the mornings, but they should write model texts in small hand in the afternoons.

In these first three levels of inclined hand writing, the Inspector shall observe and have others observe the same procedures as those mentioned regarding the sixth, seventh, and eighth levels of round hand writing.

If it happens that, for one of the reasons indicated in Article 1 of Chapter [4], on Writing, [in Part One], a student has to learn inclined hand writing without having begun to learn round hand writing, and if the student has only a year, that is eleven months, of schooling in which to do so, the Inspector of Schools shall determine the amount of time the student should spend in each level, as follows.

The student shall be kept in the first level for a month to learn the right body posture, the proper way to hold the pen, and the correct method of making the straight and the circular movements with ease. Secondly, the student shall be taught the alphabet for a six month period. During two months, the student shall write a page of each letter, with characters unlinked. During the next two months, the student shall write a line of each letter, linking the characters. During the last two months of the period, the entire alphabet will be written continuously in a line. Finally, in the last four months of the year, the student shall write model texts in medium-sized writing, in addition to the alphabet at the beginning of the writing lesson, as mentioned in a prior Article concerning those who write in the round hand style.

If a student has only six months to learn to write the inclined hand style, the Inspector shall schedule a program as follows. The student shall write the alphabet for three months, a single line of each letter linked, in the first two months, and the entire alphabet continuously on a line, in the third month. During the last three months, the Inspector shall have the student write model texts in medium-sized characters, and the alphabet at the beginning of each writing lesson.

The Inspector of Schools shall apportion the time, as indicated above, for the students who have only a short time in which to learn to write, in proportion to the amount of time available. The Inspector shall promote them if it is necessary at the end of the appointed time, whether or not they know all that they should in order to be promoted.

Section 2: Arithmetic

The Inspector of Schools shall divide the students who are learning arithmetic into five different levels. The first is for those who are capable of learning only addition. In the second, those who know addition well shall learn subtraction, how to prove their additions by subtraction, and how to prove their subtractions by addition. Only those who know addition and subtraction well, and how to prove both, should go on to the third level, where they will learn multiplication. The Inspector shall place in the fourth level only those students who are perfectly familiar with multiplication, and so are ready to learn division. The Inspector shall promote to the fifth level those who can perform all kinds of division easily and who will be able to learn the rule of three, the aliquot parts,[1] and fractions.

Article 5:
Determining How Long Lessons Should Last

Since the number of students is not always the same in every lesson but changes when students are promoted from one lesson to another, or when new ones come in or others leave, the time the teacher must spend in making the students read a given lesson cannot be regulated and uniform. It is the responsibility of the Director or of the Inspector of Schools to determine how long the children in each lesson and class should spend in reading.

The duration of each lesson should be determined in relation to the amount of time the instructor has for teaching reading, the number of students following each lesson, their ease or difficulty in reading each lesson, and the approximate number of lines each student should read.

The Director or the Inspector of Schools shall determine the duration of each lesson by adapting the timetable given below. This determination depends upon whether there are fewer, as many, or more students in each lesson than are indicated.

Twelve students can each easily read three times in half an hour the line found on the alphabet chart. Ten students can easily read three lines each on the syllable chart in half an hour. In the same time, eight students can readily spell out three lines apiece in the second spelling book. Ten students each can, again in half an hour, easily spell out and then read three lines in the second book.

If the above-mentioned students, numbering forty, are in the same class, the teachers ought to be able to have all of them read during the afternoon session. Because there is half an hour less of class time in the morning than in the afternoon, the teacher should have the students read for seven or eight minutes less in each lesson in the morning than is specified in the time allotted above.

It follows from what has been mentioned so far that, if instead of twelve students using the alphabet chart there are eighteen, they will have about three quarters of an hour to read from it. If they number fifteen, they will need about thirty-seven minutes. If there are only nine, they should be given about twenty-two minutes of reading time. The time for reading shall be increased or shortened in proportion to the number of students in the reading lesson. The same should be done in all the other lessons, whether in the same or different classrooms.

Twelve students using the third book can easily have sufficient time to read. The beginners can read eight lines each and the more proficient, twelve to fifteen lines each, in half an hour. The students who read from the book of Psalms can easily read six lines apiece if they are reading by syllables; those who read more fluently can each read ten lines in a [quarter of an hour].

Those students of the first and second levels who are reading *Les Règles de la Civilité chrétienne* can easily read eight lines each, and

those from the other levels, ten lines from a paper or document of ordinary size in a quarter of an hour.

Thus, if a writing class has fifty industrious students, twelve or
thirteen who only use the third reader, twelve or thirteen who also
read Latin, and twenty or twenty-five writers, of whom ten read from
the documents, these last ten shall have a quarter of an hour after
lunch to read documents and then an hour to read French. Those
dozen or so who read Latin shall do so for a quarter of an hour.
Those who read only from the third book shall read only Latin for
three quarters of an hour; then, those who read *Les Règles de la Civilité chrétienne* shall do so for a quarter of an hour. The ones who read
only French shall do so mornings from 8:45 until 9:00. The teacher
who has only half the number of writing students shall correct their
work only during this time. If all the students take writing, they shall
read Latin for three quarters of an hour and *Les Règles de la Civilité
chrétienne* for a quarter of an hour in the morning. After lunch, they
shall devote half an hour to reading contracts and the following hour
to reading French.

The Director or the Inspector of Schools shall see to it that the
teachers use all of the available time for reading and that on every occasion the teachers devote approximately the same length of time to
reading. Thus, if there are fewer students in a class than are required
to use the entire time devoted to reading, each student reading the required number of lines, the Inspector of Schools shall direct the
teacher to make each student read approximately as many additional
lines as needed to fill all of the time assigned to reading in that class.
There should be no wasted time in any class, nor should time be used
otherwise than as specified in the regulations.

If it should happen that a larger number of students must be
placed in a class than can be given a turn in the allotted reading period, each student reading the required number of lines, the Director or
the Inspector of Schools shall see to it that the students in each lesson
read fewer lines than specified for that lesson. This adjustment shall
be made in proportion to the number of students present, so that all
the students can read something, without using in this classroom more
time for reading than has been allocated for this particular subject.

4

Promoting Students
from One Lesson to Another

One of the most important things in a school is to promote the students from one lesson to another at the proper time. The Inspector of Schools shall pay much attention to this process. Promoting students shall be carried out with regularity and order. To achieve this, each teacher shall prepare the students for promotion according to what is indicated in Part One. The Inspector of Schools shall make these promotions with due preparation and care. The Inspector should make sure that the students fulfill the conditions and qualifications for promotion. Finally, these promotions shall be made at the time and in the manner that has been established.

Article 1:
What Is to Be Done Before Promoting Students

Toward the end of every month, the Inspector of Schools shall inform the teachers of the day on which they should examine the students who might be ready for promotion. The Inspector and the teachers shall then confer on those who should not be promoted because of inability, absenteeism, or lack of piety or modesty, because of laziness, negligence, or youthfulness, or, finally, because of the need to sustain the lesson and keep it in proper order.

The Inspector of Schools shall, however, take care not to let a student remain in the same lesson or in the same order of lesson, when the student is capable of doing more advanced work or is content to remain back. This case calls for diplomacy and concerted action among the teachers and may be accomplished either by use of rewards or by giving the student some class office. This does not apply, however, if the child is being held back because of absenteeism, negligence, laziness, or some other considerable fault. The Inspector of Schools can use these reasons as justification for the decision, should the occasion warrant it.

The Inspector of Schools, if the Inspector is also the Director, shall then set the deadline for the teachers to make their report, so that they can give it to the Inspector before the promotions are to take place. An Inspector who is not also the Director shall request the latter to fix the day. The Inspector, after receiving the reports from the teachers, shall ask them for further explanations and information needed to avoid mistakes in promotions.

The Inspector shall then inform the students in each school of the day on which the promotions will be made, so that all of them can be present, and shall warn them that any who are not present on the promotion day will not be promoted until the end of the following month.

In promoting students the Inspector of Schools shall neither be influenced by any personal considerations nor give weight to any extraneous influences. The Inspector shall not promote any students from one lesson or level to another unless they have the ability and fulfill all of the conditions laid down in the following Article. The Inspector shall also very carefully insist that the teachers not propose any students for promotion who are not quite capable of doing the required work.

The Inspector shall always follow the same procedure in making the promotions in all of the schools and classes, beginning every time with the same level and the same class, and always finishing with the same ones. In each school, the Inspector shall begin with the lowest class and end with the highest, and in each class, with the lowest lesson and at the level of the beginners in each lesson.

Article 2:
Requirements for Promotion

It is most important never to place any student in a lesson which the student is not yet capable of following; otherwise, the student will find it impossible to learn anything and will risk being kept in lifelong ignorance. Therefore, one should not take into consideration either age, size, or length of time a student has been in a lesson when promoting to a more advanced lesson, but only ability. Thus, for instance, a student must spell perfectly and read by syllables before learning to read fluently.

Smaller children, who are usually quick-witted and have good memories, do not always need to be promoted even when they could go on to more difficult work. It may not be good if they do not stay in school long enough. It is desirable, without displeasing the parents, to help extend their stay in school as much as possible. The two extremes must be avoided. It is not good to keep a student too long in the same lesson, for fear that the student and the parents may lose interest. However, for the reasons already given, it is not good either to advance too rapidly those who are very small, very young, or lack the necessary ability.

There are certain conditions and requirements for promoting or not promoting a student.

Those who lack modesty and piety or who show themselves lazy and neglectful in studying and in following the lesson shall be promoted only with great hesitancy; they shall be examined with greater rigor and exactness than the others. If in the succeeding month they fall back into their old faults, they shall not be promoted on the next occasion, no matter how capable they may be.

Those who have been absent for five full days during the month, even with permission, shall not be promoted to a higher lesson at the end of the month, even though they might be capable of doing the work.

Those who have been absent without permission for two full days during the month shall neither be promoted from one lesson to another nor from one level to another. Those who have been tardy six times during the month shall not be promoted.

No student shall be moved from one lesson to another unless the student has gone through the three levels of beginner, intermediate, and advanced, nor shall any student be moved to a higher lesson or level of a lesson without spending all the time prescribed in the lower one.

Students shall not be moved up from the alphabet chart unless they have been reading from it for at least two months. In other words, they should have read each line of it for at least a week, and the entire alphabet for the rest of the two months. They shall not be moved up from the syllable chart until they have read from it for at least a month.

Those who read from the spelling book shall not be promoted until they have spent at least five months on it, two months in each of the first two levels and one month in the third.

Those who are learning spelling from the first book shall not be promoted until they have spent at least three months on it, one month in each level of this lesson.

Those who spell and read from the second book shall not be promoted unless they have spent the same amount of time on it. Those who only read from the second book, and are not learning spelling, shall not be promoted unless they have spent an equal amount of time reading from it.

Those reading from the third book shall do so for at least six months, two months on each level, before they can be promoted to another lesson. Those who read Latin shall not read in phrases until they have read by syllables for at least two months. They shall not be promoted until they have been reading in phrases for at least four months, two months at the intermediate level and two months at the proficiency level.

Those who are reading from *Les Règles de la Civilité chrétienne* shall not be promoted from the first to the second level, unless they have been reading on the former level for at least two months. They shall then remain at the second level for as long as they continue coming to school. Those who read from the documents shall not be promoted from the first to the second level, unless they have spent at least three months reading on the former level. The same rule will also be followed in promoting students in the subsequent four levels. When they reach the last level, they shall remain there for as long as they continue coming to school.

Students shall not be promoted from the first level of writing, where they learn how to sit correctly, hold the pen properly, and make the straight and circular strokes, until they have spent at least a month in this level. Those in the second level of writing who write the five letters *c, o, i, f,* and *m* shall not be promoted until they have written these letters for at least three months.

Those who are in the third and fourth levels and who write the alphabet with linked characters, one page or one line of each letter, shall not be promoted until they have written them for at least six months, one page of each letter for four months and then a line of each letter for two months.

Those who write the alphabet entirely in linked characters on each line shall not be promoted until they have done this for three months. Those who write lines of large commercial characters shall not be promoted until they have done this for at least three months.

Those in the seventh level, who write in financial characters, shall not be promoted to writing small hand and rapid script until they have written at the sixth level for at least six months.

Those in the first and second levels of arithmetic, who are doing addition and subtraction, shall not be promoted until they have mastered both over a period of at least two months.

Those in the third level, who are doing multiplication, shall not be promoted until they have spent at least three months on this operation. Those in the fourth level, who are learning how to divide, shall not be promoted to doing the rule of three until they have spent at least four months doing simple division.

Article 4:[1]
Requirements for Promotion in Reading

Students who are learning the alphabet should not be set to reading a new line of letters until they know the first line very well. They must be able to pronounce the letters immediately, in any order, and without hesitation, as soon as the letter is pointed out to them. They shall not be assigned to reading the syllable chart until they can name all the letters of the alphabet, whatever they may be, promptly, and without hesitation.

Those who read from the syllable chart shall not go on to the spelling book until they can spell perfectly and fluently all the syllables found on the chart. The children who are spelling and reading, both in the syllable book and in other books of whatever kind, should be promoted from the first to the second level of spelling and reading only when they make very few mistakes, that is, one or two.

Those who are in the second level of spelling or reading in each book shall be promoted to the third level only when they ordinarily make no mistakes when reading, or when the mistakes they do make, if any, are very rare and occur only by surprise and not out of ignorance.

The students in the third level of spelling or reading, from whatever book it may be, shall be moved up to a higher level only if they can read the current lesson perfectly. Those who spell, for example, should not be promoted until they spell perfectly, without ever having to search for or to guess at the right syllable. Similarly, if they are reading syllables, they must not make two syllables sound like a single one. For two or three weeks, they should be accustomed to pronounce all of the syllables correctly, distinctly, and confidently. Finding no difficulty in so doing, they may begin to learn how to read with proper pauses.

Those who read in phrases, making the proper pauses, should not be advanced from the first to the second level until they no longer make any mistakes in punctuation, that is, they must pause where necessary, and not when they should not, and pause for the proper length of time. To be promoted out of the third level and so begin to read Latin, they must be able to read perfectly, distinctly, and intelligibly, and to know how to pronounce the words correctly.

Students who read Latin should usually be promoted from the first to the second level when they can distinguish and read the syllables correctly, usually without making any frequent mistakes. They should be advanced from the second to the third level when they are able to read in phrases without usually making any mistakes either with words or pauses. To be promoted from this lesson and to start writing, they must read perfectly and fluently.

Those who are reading from *Les Règles de la Civilité chrétienne* should be promoted to the second level when they ordinarily make no mistakes. Those who read from the account books must not be changed from one lesson to another unless they can read fluently from the account book they are using, without hesitation and without making any mistakes.

Article 5:
Requirements for Promotion in Writing

Section 1: From First to Second and Second to Third Levels

Those who are starting to learn to write and who are concentrating on assuming a correct posture, on holding the pen properly, and on making both the straight and circular strokes, shall not be promoted until they have the correct body posture, can hold their pen correctly, and can make these two movements easily. The Inspector of Schools, therefore, shall make them perform these movements, taking care that they sit properly and hold their pens correctly. Those who are beginning to write the letters *c, o, i, f,* and *m* shall not be promoted until they know how to give these letters their proper shape. The Inspector shall, for this purpose, go over their written work to see whether these letters usually have their correct shape and whether they do not show any of the faults mentioned below.

The *o* should lean neither to the left nor to the right. The strokes should be heavy or fine as required. The letter should neither be too wide nor too narrow, too round nor too flat, too long nor too short. It should not appear humpbacked. The fine strokes are not to be on the side and the heavy strokes underneath, but the heavy strokes are to be at the side and the light strokes at the top and at the bottom. The fine strokes should not be pointed at the top or bottom. The letter should be very slightly inclined to the left, and the upper part should be firmly closed and not left open.

The *i* should be inclined neither to the right nor to the left, but should be straight. The upper part should be made with a fine stroke, not crooked or stretched upward. This upstroke should be two pen tips wide. Its heel must be rounded and not crushed down, and not too high, only as long as one pen tip. The connecting stroke should be two pen tips wide and not rise too high, as though one wished to link the *i* with some other letter, as when joining *i* and *s*. The upstroke should be neither pointed nor too open, and be only one pen tip wide.

The *f* should neither lean too much to the right nor to the left, but should be inclined a little to the left, about the width of one pen tip. The head of the letter should not be flat, but rounded, and not wider than four pen tips. The *f* should begin with a square, heavy downstroke and not by a filled in loop. This full stroke should curve toward the inside of the *f* on the right where the body of the letter is, and should not flatten out as it goes to the left. The letter should be six pen tips wide and three pen tips high.

There should be two light upstrokes in the *f,* one at the top and the other at the bottom as it turns to the left. The crossbar should not be drawn vertically. It must neither cut the *f* in two nor be made with a heavy stroke of the pen. It should be a light stroke about two pen tips long.

With the *m,* the three legs or downstrokes should not be drawn one to the right and another to the left. They must all be drawn straight down, parallel to one another, of equal height, and from the same base. The upstrokes should not begin in the middle of the legs, but begin from the bottom. They should not join the middle of the following leg; rather, they should start from the bottom and immediately go up to the top of the next hump. The connecting links should not be rounded from right to left. They should neither be wavy nor concave, but rather, slightly convex. They should not be thick, but light, and the heel of the letter should not be crooked.

Section 2: From Third to Fourth Level

To deserve promotion from the third level of penmanship, where the students write one page of each letter of the alphabet, linked one to the other, to the fourth level, where they make a line of each letter, linked one to the other, the students should know how to give all the letters in the alphabet their proper form and how to link all the letters to one another in the proper manner. The first part of the *a,* which is round, should not be too wide and should have the same form as the *o.* The first part should flow into the downstroke of the *o* and should begin by an upstroke, as if one were about to make and *e* or a *c.* The upstroke and the downstroke of the second part should be separated by the width of a single pen tip, both at the top and at the bottom. This second part of the *a* should neither rise higher nor descend lower than the first part.

The head of the *b* should be like that of the *f.* It should be made straight and rounded out at the bottom, as if to make an *o.* The back stroke should rise as if one wanted to draw the straight part of the *b,* leaving a pen tip and a half between the upright stroke and the backstroke of the *b.* In the center, a space of three pen tips should separate the head and the bottom. The bottom round stroke should neither be too wide nor too pointed. It should not rise straight up, but should curve from right to left.

The head or top of the *c* should be like that of the *f,* and the light upstroke should be the same. It should be rounded off toward the left and must not be quite straight, ending with a fine connecting line.

The bottom of the *d* should be like an *o* in height and width. The upstroke should rise the distance of the full width of the letter, that is, the height of an *o,* and should not be completely straight, curving a little from left to right.

The *e* should be made like the *c,* except for the head. Its top should be like the first part of a broken *r,* beginning and ending with a light stroke. The letter should be round and not straight, leaning to the left by the width of a single pen tip, and not bent toward the right. The *f* should be made in the manner indicated in Section 1 above.

The first part of the *g* should be made like an *o.* The second part is the loop or tail. When making this loop and joining it with the first part, the heavy downstroke of the first part should blend in with the downstroke of the second part. This second part should begin about one forth the way up the body of the letter. Its point should protrude about the width of half a pen tip.

The first part of the *h* should be like an *l,* except the lower part, which should be made straight, without any hook or link, and finish in a square, heavy dot. The second part should begin in the middle of the first part. Its upstroke should begin a fourth of the way up the letter and move from bottom to top. It should be curved, as if one were trying to form a *p.* It should not be too flat, and its bulge should not extend more than its head. The extremity of the loop should reach the level of the first part, and it should descend some four pen tips below the body of the letter.

The *i* should be made in the manner indicated in Section 1 above.

The *l* should be like the first part of the *h,* except rounded at the bottom. This round part should be one pen tip wide and have a linking stroke, whose loop should be neither too wide, too inclined to the right, nor too flattened out.

The *m* should be made in the manner indicated in Section 1 above.

At the beginning of a word, an *n* should be made like an *m,* except that the *n* has only two down strokes, whereas the *m* has three. The first part of a terminal *n* should be made like an *i,* except that the final stroke should end in a square dot with no fine connecting line. The second part should begin at the middle of the *i,* finish like the second part of the *h,* and be equal in height to the first part.

The *o* should be made in the manner indicated in Section 1 above.

The *p* should begin by a back stroke of the pen, drawn downward and leaning to the left side. The bottom loop should be rounded like that of an *f*. The head should not be too flattened out, and it should begin by a light upstroke moving from right to left and returning from left to right. The second part should begin where the upper part touches the line as on the bottom of an *o*, not by a light upstroke, but by a heavy downstroke blended into the heavy stroke of the loop. It should end by a downstroke next to the head. It should be as tall as the head, neither higher nor lower. Between the top of the two parts, there should be no more than the space of one and a half pen tips. The tail should neither be too inclined to the left, nor too short. As a rule, it should not usually go beyond the head when it is very wide. The downstroke should not be over six pen tips wide, no matter how wide or how narrow the head is.

The first part of the *q* should be made like an *o*. The second part begins with a small dot. The downstroke should merge into the heavy downstroke of the *o*, like the second part of a *g*. It should extend below the body of the letter about one and a half times the height of the body. The tail should be drawn to the right, with the last part of the stroke thickened somewhat. There should not be any hook at the bottom.

The round *r* should be like the lower part of a *b* or *v*, and should have neither more nor less of an opening in its upper part. The connecting stroke should be like the upper part of the *i* or *v*. The top of the split *r* should begin by a light upstroke from left to right. At the end of this stroke, there should be a small loop, as found in the *e*. This is to be made without lifting pen from paper. The line should extend the width of one pen tip behind the second part, which should begin like the second part of a *c*. It should connect with the second upstroke at the head, curving toward the left and ending with an upward rising, connecting stroke, as when making a *c*.

The head of an initial *s* should be like the head of the *f*. Its body should be drawn a little to the right, and its second part curved toward the left. Its height should be twice that of normal letters, and its tail should be like that of the *f*. Its head should extend forward the width of two pen tips. It should neither be inclined to the right nor too much to the left. The bulge should neither stick out, compared with the head, nor should it lean like an *f*. The *s* found in the middle of a word should begin by an upstroke that rises from left to right. Its bulge should be drawn to the right, and its tail should curve to the left and be well rounded out. It should not be wider than an *o,* nor should it extend more than the width of one pen tip above the normal height of the letter.

The two parts of the *s* at the end of a word should be made like an *e.* At the top between the two parts, there should be a little loop, as on an *a.* The first part should extend below the second part by the width of half a pen tip. The second part should rise above the first by no more than the width of one pen tip. The little loop should be placed between the two parts. Its upstroke should join the upstroke of the second part at about the width of one pen tip higher than the top, and it should rise as high as the first part.

An initial *t* or one in the body of a word should be drawn straight and with no upstroke at the top. It should have a connecting stroke at the bottom like that of an *i.* Its upright shaft should be like that of an *f,* half again as high as the normal letters. This should extend just above the letter *o.* In this way, the *t* stands the width of two pen tips higher than the other letters. A final *t* should be made like a *j,* except that at the bottom one should make a small, straight upstroke.

The *u* should be formed like two *i*'s joined together and about as far apart from each other as the two down strokes of an *n,* that is, the width of two pen tips apart. The connecting stroke that joins the two downstrokes should extend from the bottom of the first downstroke to a third of the height of the second downstroke. An initial *u* should be made like the broken *r,* except that one must add the reverse of an *o.* It should be five pen tips wide and four pen tips high.

The *x* should be made like two *c*'s, one on the right and the other on the left. However, the head of the one which is reversed should be at the bottom; and the two downstrokes should blend into each other so that there seems to be only one downstroke. These downstrokes should not overlap each other. Neither of the two parts is to protrude beyond the other, either at the top or at the bottom.

The upper part of the *y* should be curved. It begins by an upstroke, going from left to right. Then it continues by a downstroke from left to right and terminates on the right with a rounded line, which then goes down to a square dot, something like the tail of a small *d,* which has only two high points. The first part of the *y* extends downward a little more to the left about the width of two pen tips. The second part begins by an upstroke like the tail of an *j,* but it is a little more inclined and thinner. It begins at about the middle of the first part and joins it at the bottom. In this manner, the two parts are joined together as far as the tail should be, only as high as one ordinary letter and as wide as an *m*. The *y* should not be too straight. Its width should be that of an *o*. The second part should neither extend higher nor descend lower than the first part. There should be an open space, the width of two pen tips, between the two parts. The line from top to bottom of this letter should not be too straight. Its tail should not go lower than two pen tips below the head. The tail of the letters *o*, *v*, and *y* extend below the body less than one and a half the body heights.

An initial *z* should begin like a broken *r*, by making a little line from top to bottom and from right to left, with a tail as wide as an *m* resembling an incomplete *o*. A *z* at the end or in the middle of a word begins with an *e* written backwards but unfinished, about two pen tips from the top. It should finish like an *s* in the middle of the body of a word, and should have none of the faults indicated above concerning such an *s*. The top loop should neither be too long nor separated from the first part. It should not be closed. The two parts should not be separated from each other. There should be only the space of one pen tip between the downstrokes both at the top and at the bottom.

Concerning the strokes, the Inspector of Schools shall not promote students in the third level unless they make these strokes neatly and not too heavily.

The Inspector shall also take care that the connections are properly placed. These linkings normally extend from the foot of one letter to the head of the next, except between *i* and *o*, and also the *e*, because its upper loop is linked from head to head with all sorts of adjoining letters. The *o* should not really be linked and is always connected to the next letter about two thirds of the way up, so that the link stroke joins only the beginning of the letter. One should make a preliminary link stroke that only lightly touches the *o*.

The Inspector of Schools shall not promote any students in this level unless they know the letters that are derived from *f* and *o*, and in what way they are so derived, and unless they can form these letters without any help.

Section 3: From Fourth and Upper Levels

The students in the fourth level of writing, who write a line of linked letters, shall not be promoted unless they know how to give the letters the required position and evenness. Thus, a student to be promoted should make the round hand characters precisely four pen tips wide.

The tails of the letters *g, p, q,* and *y* should extend one and a half times the width of ordinary letters below the body of the letters, that is, the width of six pen tips. The tails of the *f, h,* the capital *s,* and *z* should only extend the distance of the body of a letter below the line.

The heads of the *b, f, h, l,* and the capital *s* should rise only one body width over the body of the other letters.

The head of the small *t,* initial or middle, should rise only the width of one pen tip above the ordinary letters.

The bodies of all the letters should rest on the same line, and all lines should be straight. Except for the tails, no part of any letter should rise above or fall below the others.

The letters should neither be crooked nor leaning to the right, but should be straight. All of their bodies should be equal in height and width.

The students in the fifth level of writing, those who write all the different kinds of letters and make, as it were, only one word on the same line shall not be promoted to the sixth level where they write connected texts until they space their lines properly, not too spread, in such a way that the bodies of their letters are one and a half pen tips apart, except for split letters and the one immediately preceding them.

Between a downstroke and a curve, there should be the space of one and a half pen tips. However, between the *e, c, o,* and *y,* the space should be only one pen tip wide.

Words should be separated from each other by the width of an *m,* that is, eight pen tips. The distance between lines should be four times the height of ordinary letters.

Students in this level shall not be promoted as long as their lettering lacks firmness, confidence, and freedom. For this reason, the Inspector of Schools shall demand the following before students can enter the sixth level. They must make the downstrokes straight, leaning neither to right nor to left. Their *o*'s must neither be open nor split at the top. Their letters can be neither humpbacked nor pointed at either the top or the bottom. None of the letters may be slovenly, shaky, or cramped. The students should show that they can form the letters unhesitatingly and with freedom. They must give their letters a certain space and gracefulness, and each letter must flow easily on to the next.

Students in the sixth level of writing, who are writing passages in large commercial characters, should not be promoted to writing with financial characters until they can make the commercial letters with the same facility, boldness, and elegance required of students for promotion in the lower levels. They should show the same proficiency required of students in the preceding levels.

The Inspector of Schools shall prudently decide when the students who write with facility in a given level should be promoted. Those in the seventh level should go on to write with financial characters. Those in the eighth level should learn to write small hand.

Section 4: Promotion of Students Writing Inclined Hand

After they have learned how to write round hand, the students in the first level of inclined hand writing shall not be promoted to the second level until they know how to give all the letters their proper form. Their letters must not incline to the left more or less than required, that is, a distance of three pen tips. Students must know how to give them their proper placement, so that all the bodies of the letters stay on the same line, and all the lines remain straight, as in this example: *You do not know what we have prescribed.*

They must give the body of their letters the proper height and width: seven pen tips high and five pen tips wide. They must know how to make the connecting strokes properly, from the foot of the preceding letter to the middle of the following one, except in the case of a few letters like *x, y,* and *z.* The connecting strokes are made from the foot of the previous letter to the top of each of these.

What follows is how the characters in inclined hand should be formed, and what should be observed about each letter in deciding whether to promote those who are learning this type of writing.

All the curved lines should be ovals, not circles. The letters *a, c,* and *g,* and the head of the *f* and of the *g,* begin by a downstroke and not with an upstroke. The second part is to be made like a *t,* square at the top and rounded on the bottom.

The *e* begins with an upstroke and a loop.

The *d, o,* and final *f* also begin by an upstroke. The *o* by itself and the *u* end with a downstroke.

The body of the *b* should be a reverse *c,* beginning with an upstroke and finishing with a loop.

The *m*'s and *n*'s should be round on top and square on the bottom. All the upstrokes should lie between the two downstrokes. The four letters *i, l, t,* and *u* should be round on the bottom and square on top. The upright *r* should be square at the top and on the bottom. Its second stroke should start in the middle of the first, beginning with a light upstroke and ending with a downstroke which is curved on top.

The tails of these letters should be kept straight. The tails of *p* and *y* can be made either straight or curved.

The body of the *y* should be like a *v*, except that the first part should begin by a curving upstroke going from left to right.

Other details concerning the shape of the various letters in inclined hand writing, which are not mentioned here, are the same as those presented for writing round hand. However, the letters should be inclined and not straight.

To promote the students from the second to the third level, the Inspector of Schools should follow the same procedure mentioned with regard to promoting students from the fifth to the sixth levels of writing round hand. However, in inclined hand writing, the lines should be separated from each other by the height of the writing only.

To promote students from the third to the fourth level, the same things should be observed as when moving them from the sixth to the seventh levels in round hand. Those in the fourth level shall be promoted to the fifth, just as the ones in the seventh level of round hand are promoted to the eighth, for there is not as much difference in the size of the characters in inclined hand writing as there is in round hand writing.

Article 6:[2]
Requirements for Promotion in Arithmetic

Students shall not be promoted out of the first level of arithmetic, where they learn addition, and put in the second level unless they know thoroughly and can solve without any help all sorts of additions, no matter how difficult.

Those in the second level, where they learn subtraction, shall not be promoted unless they know how to make all kinds of subtractions very readily and without help and unless they know how to prove the additions by subtraction.

Those in the third level, where they learn multiplication, shall not be promoted to the fourth level until they can multiply all sorts of numbers without any help.

Those in the fourth level, where they learn simple division, shall not be promoted to the fifth unless they can solve without help and with ease problems in simple division of whatever difficulty and unless they can prove their divisions by multiplication and their multiplications by division.

Article 7:
How to Promote Advantageously

Students in all the lessons, except those who are learning the alphabet, shall not be promoted during the month, but only at the end of the month.

Those who are learning the alphabet and have one line of the alphabet for their lesson shall be promoted to a different line at the end of each week provided that they know well all the letters found in that line. They shall not be promoted from reading the alphabet in its entirety to reading the syllable chart until the end of the month.

If it happens, however, that a student has learned the whole alphabet chart at the beginning of a month, that student should be promoted to the syllable chart as soon as the alphabet chart is known perfectly. If the student knows the syllable chart at the end of the month, the student shall again be promoted.

The promotions from one lesson to another shall take place on the last two days of the month and on the first days of the following month, as designated by the Director and made known in each school by the Inspector.

Students in any lesson who have not been promoted at the end of the month shall be accepted for promotion at the end of the following month, if they are ready then. Those who have one line of the alphabet per lesson and who do not know all the letters of that line at the end of the week shall be accepted for promotion at the end of the following week, provided they know the line well by then.

On the designated day, the Inspector will test those who have been presented for promotion from the alphabet chart to reading by syllables. Each in turn will be required to read virtually the whole alphabet, the letters indicated at random. The Inspector will especially select the most difficult letters, those which resemble each other somewhat, in their shape, like *d, b, q, n,* and *u* or in their pronunciation, like *g* and *j,* and those which are linked together, like *et, fs, bf,* and *fb.*

To promote students who are reading the syllable chart, the Inspector will make them read the syllables, not in the order printed on the chart, but at random, especially focusing on the most difficult ones. The Inspector shall make the students read about half of the syllables on their chart and shall examine if they can read them all promptly and without hesitation. These children, in order to merit promotion, should all read separately, one after another.

In the classes where both spelling and reading take place, the Inspector of Schools shall make the students in each lesson and in each level of the lesson, read. Each will read individually something from the book being used, one after another, in a low voice, and from a part of the book they have not yet reached in case they have not finished reading it. The Inspector shall also make them read from a section of the book which they read a long time past and in which the reading and spelling are difficult. For instance, in the syllable book, the Inspector shall make them read syllables or words more difficult than those which they have already read. The Inspector shall require them to read these on the spot, without a chance to study them.

Students in each level of the lesson should read separately from those in another level. For instance, those in the first level, the beginners, should read separately from those in the second level, the average students, and so on.

Those who are learning spelling shall read at least three lines. Those who are reading in syllables shall also read at least three lines. Among those who are reading in phrases, those in the first and second level should read about four lines. Those in the third level should read at least six lines.

Students, in whatever level they are, should all read one after another according to the order of the benches. When they are reading for promotion, neither the Inspector nor the teacher shall correct any mistakes that the students make.

After all have been examined the Inspector shall write on the promotion list after the name of each to be promoted, the day in the fourth column and the month in the fifth column on which this student was promoted to a given lesson or level. New assignments will not be made until all have been examined.

The Inspector shall then call out the names of all of those to be promoted, and instruct them to bring on the next day the book they need, if they have been promoted from one lesson to another and not moved to a different class. They shall not be allowed to read in the lesson to which they are being promoted unless they themselves can bring everything needed.

The Inspector shall then distribute rewards to those who read the most fluently and who were found to be the most proficient. The Inspector will reward one in each level, if there are only a few students. The Inspector will reward two, if there are many students in this level.

Students of any lesson or level who have been examined three times for promotion and have not been promoted because of lack of ability, shall be assigned to a particular bench called the "Dunce's Bench" and placed in a conspicuous location in the classroom. On the wall behind it, there shall hang a sign reading: "Dunce's Bench." Students will remain seated there until capable of being promoted from this lesson or this level.

The Inspector of Schools shall promote the writing students from one lesson to a higher lesson. The Inspector shall examine them for this promotion during the regular writing lesson. The Inspector shall, first of all, have them all write during the first half-hour, during which period the Inspector shall examine their posture, the way in which they hold their pens, and the manner in which they make their movements, easy, awkward, relaxed, or careful.

For this purpose, the Inspector shall visit all of the writing students who are approaching the time for promotion and study them all, even write on a little slip of paper the faults that are noticed in their work regarding the points given above.

The Inspector shall examine all their writing, both what they have just written and all their papers from beginning to end. The Inspector shall examine whether what they have just written conforms to what they have written during the preceding fifteen days. If there is little conformity, they shall not be promoted. Then the Inspector will examine whether what they have just written and what they have written during the past fifteen days shows the proper qualifications to justify a promotion, as explained in the Article on the requirements for promotion. The Inspector of Schools shall promote only those whose work over the past fifteen days shows that they usually display what they should know and that they form the letters well enough to be promoted from the level of writing in which they are. The Inspector shall make sure that no student lacks the capacity for promotion, as discussed above in Article 5.

The Inspector shall also inform the teachers about the faults observed in each student and the reasons why each student was not promoted. The teacher shall take note and be careful that the student correct these faults prior to being presented for promotion at the end of the following month.

The Inspector shall give to each newly promoted student a writing model for the level to which the student is being promoted. The

Inspector shall take back from the student the model they used in the previous level.

When promoting students from any level in arithmetic, the Inspector shall examine in each copybook the problems they worked on by themselves and shall make them explain the reasons for the solutions to some of the more difficult problems. The Inspector shall write on the blackboard a problem from among the most difficult ones belonging to this level. The Inspector shall have the problem done publicly at the board by the student, and the student shall be required to give the proof that the solution is correct.

Appendix B
Extracts from the 1706 Manuscript
of *Conduite*

What follows is material that has been taken from the 1706 Manuscript of *Conduite*. Throughout the preceding text, note has been made each time there is a significant variation between the manuscript of 1706 and the printed edition of 1720. Therefore, what is provided here can help one better understand the evolution of the text as it was revised over the years by De La Salle and his first disciples.

Extract 1: *See* page 56 above; and CL 24:15-16

Article 3:
The Collection and Distribution for the Poor

During the breakfast and the afternoon snack, one of the students, who shall be the first in the bench which is at the front, shall have a basket before him for receiving bread for the poor. Any who shall have brought plenty of bread will be able to give some piece of it or what they have left after having had sufficient to eat. The teacher, however, shall see to it that they do not give so much of their bread that there is not enough left for themselves.

Teachers shall prompt them from time to time during the actual time of the breakfast, to that act of charity, either by some example or by some appealing reason, which will rouse them to this action out of goodness of heart and with affection for the love of God.

Teachers shall sometimes praise someone who has performed this action in a generous manner, for example, depriving oneself of the fruit one may have brought, or giving all of one's bread on a fast day in Lent; for example, once a week, or sometimes in passing on a Friday or a Saturday. This has to be rare, once at the most in a fortnight or in a week for the bigger students.

Those who have bread to give shall raise their hands showing the piece of bread which they have to give, so that the Almoner may see and go and receive it.

At the end of breakfast, some time before grace after meals, when the alms shall have all or nearly all been collected, the teacher shall take a piece of bread from the basket and, having made the sign of the cross, shall hold it in hand. Then all of the poor students shall stand up and remain standing without making any sign.

The teacher shall then go to all, one after the other, to distribute to them what is in the basket, according to their need.

If there is more or less bread in the basket than those who are poor can reasonably eat, the teacher shall inquire of the Director as to what shall be done on these occasions.

The teacher shall be careful to distribute alms given during breakfast and the afternoon snack only to those who are genuinely poor; and in order to ensure this, the teacher shall make enquiries and a roll shall be kept which shall have the approval of the Director or the Inspector of Schools.

A teacher shall not approve of it on the recommendation of the parents or on the fact that the student has not brought any bread, for several parents would be very pleased to be relieved of the responsibility of providing food for their children in order that it be given to them at school; and there are some that could easily be found who would not bring any bread for that reason.

Teachers shall make it an obligation upon those to whom alms have been distributed to pray to God particularly for their benefactors.

Extract 2: *See* page 77 above; and CL 24:51 and 231.

The Eighth Order or Level of Writing

The eighth order or level of writing shall include those students who practice writing financial characters in the morning and small hand in the afternoon.

Instead of copying the alphabet at the beginning of the lesson, the students on this level shall write in rapid small hand on half of the back of their paper at the beginning of each lesson. In the mornings, they shall copy passages from various good books which contain practical material adapted to their age. Every afternoon, they shall copy handwritten texts, also called documents, especially writs, promissory notes, receipts, worker's instructions, work agreements, leases, and notary contracts of various kinds. After they have spent three months copying such handwritten material, they shall, on the two days when arithmetic is taught, write material composed by themselves: personal letters, promissory notes, receipts, leases, worker's agreements, and other things which may later on prove useful to them.

Teachers shall see to it that students on this level are able to write things of this sort in a free and easy hand, very legibly, and properly spelled. The teachers shall correct the mistakes the students may have made not only in style but also in writing, spelling, and punctuation.

Extract 3: *See* page 111 above; and CL 24:232–233 and 109.

Article 6:
Those Who Attend the Catechism Lesson on Sundays and Feasts

Outsiders may be admitted to the catechism lessons on Sundays and feasts. This is permissible even though they do not attend the Christian Schools regularly on other days.

All these occasional students shall be received and admitted in the same way as the students who come to school regularly on other days. If they are young, under fifteen, they shall be brought in by their parents. If they are over fifteen, they may be accepted even if their parents are not with them. However, they shall not be admitted without being seriously examined.

For this purpose, the following should be done before they are definitely admitted. They should be made to come two or three times so that the teacher may speak with them, and instruct them concerning their duties and the rules they will have to follow when they do come to the catechism lesson. The teacher will instruct them about how they should behave at the lesson.

All of these occasional students shall be obliged to attend the catechism lessons assiduously. They shall be present from the beginning of the lesson and remain until the end. They must be very modest and attentive. They must not whisper or distract one another. They must not make any kind of trouble. They must observe the same posture, reserve, and attention that the other students are required to show.

They shall not be admitted to the catechism lesson unless it is obvious that they come to learn those truths which they are obliged to know and practice.

They shall not be obliged to assist either at vespers or at the concluding prayers with the regular students. It should be sufficient if they come to the catechism lesson regularly. When the prayer said at the end of the catechism lesson is over, the teachers shall allow them time to leave unless they are willing to remain. Teachers shall try to encourage them to choose to remain.

None of these occasional students permitted to follow the catechism lesson shall absent themselves without permission. If any of them are absent of their own accord, the teacher shall inquire why they failed to attend the lesson. If any one of these students is absent three times in succession without a good reason, especially without a permission for which the student could have asked in advance, or if any one of them disturbs the lesson or does not behave properly, or shows no disposition to change this way of acting, this student shall be dismissed and the name of this student removed from the register of students. This, however, should be done only after consultation with the Director.

A student who later asks to be readmitted should wait for two months before the request is granted. It should not be granted without serious safeguards, and only after the individual has given proof of a genuine change in attitude.

These occasional students shall not be obliged to answer questions as are the ordinary students. It should suffice that they pay attention. Care should be taken, however, to question some of them from time to time. This is especially the case for those who do not seem to be embarrassed at having to reply or for those who are even glad of an opportunity to do so.

Teachers shall strive to encourage these students to be punctual for class, attentive, and willing to answer questions in the course of the lessons. For this purpose, teachers shall make use of the most appropriate means and, from time to time, shall also give them some reward. This is especially the case for those who are eager to answer questions and make an effort to answer questions well.

Extract 4: *See* page 129 above; and CL 24:133 and 233.

Records or Registers

One thing that can contribute much to maintenance of order in the schools is that there be well-kept records or registers. There must be six kinds of Registers: (1) the Admissions Register; (2) the Register of Promotion in Lessons; (3) the Register of Levels of Lessons; (4) the Register of the Good and Bad Qualities of Students; (5) the Register of the Bench Leader; and (6) the Register of Home Visitations.

The first two Registers shall be for the use of the Inspector of Schools. The teacher shall make use of the next two, and the last two shall be held by the students.

Extract 5: *See* pages 129–132 above; and CL 24:233–235 and 133–137.

Article 1:
Admissions Register

The Admissions Registers are those containing the names of all the students accepted and admitted to the schools from the beginning to the end of the scholastic year.

All of these registers for all the years shall be written one after another in a large register book. The names of the students admitted in one year shall be separated from the names of those students admitted in another year.

At the beginning of each register the following title shall be inscribed: "Register of Students Accepted and Admitted to the Schools. . . ." After this, the month in which each student was admitted shall be inscribed in large letters. The month shall also be written at the beginning and above the names of the students admitted during that month.

In the margin, the day of the month when the student was admitted shall be written in abbreviated form. If several students were accepted on the same day, that day shall be marked in the margin only once, opposite the name of the first student enrolled on that day.

Each student's family name shall be likewise written in the margin next to the name in such a way that it can be easily found. If the student has been confirmed, a cross (+) shall be placed near the name. If the student has made first Communion, a *C* will be placed near the name.

At the end of the register, there shall be an alphabetical list of the names and surnames of all of the students in all of the Registers contained in this register book and a list for each scholastic year. After each surname, the page of the register where it can be found shall be added.

At the beginning of each index, there shall appear the title: "Index of the Names and Surnames of the Students Admitted in the Year. . . ."

The index for a scholastic year shall be drawn up only at the end of the year, when no more students will be accepted.

The Admissions Register itself shall contain the name and surname of each student accepted; the age; whether the student has been confirmed; whether the student has made first Communion, and how long it has been since the student last went to Communion; the names of the student's father and mother, or, if either is deceased, the name of the person whom the student is living; where the student lives, on which floor; the parish; to what class level the student was assigned; the reason why the student should not stay in school for the entire day, if any; the time at which the student should come to school, morning and evening; which day of the week the student may be excused from class; whether the student has already been in school, and for how long; whether the student was taught by a single master or by several; why the student left them; and whether the student has ever quit school altogether, and for how long.

After all of this information has been recorded, some blank space should be left to contain what may need to be added later. Examples of what might be added are: what is the child's character and disposition; whether the student has been confirmed; whether the student has gone to Communion since entering the school, with the date; whether the student attends school regularly, if not, why not; whether the student misses school often, how many times a month; whether the student is absent during winter; whether the student comes in late, if so, how often per week or month; whether the student is delinquent and whether the student learns easily; whether the student has been regularly promoted; whether the student knows the catechism and prayers; the child's good or bad traits of character; whether the student left the school, on which day, and why; the date on which the student was admitted, for the first, second, or third time; and whether the student dropped out a second time, on what date, and for what reason.

The Director shall write in the register whatever is thought proper to be added to the above list of remarks.

Model Register of Admissions

Register of Students Accepted and Admitted to the Schools
of the Community House of Reims in the Year 1706

Aug. 31   *Jean Mulot:* accepted on August 31, 1706; age 6;
Mulot   Confirmed two years ago; received Communion once
+ C   since last Easter; son of Joseph Mulot, wool comber;
           residing in the Rue de Contray, parish of Saint Etienne,
           at the sign of the Golden Cross, in a shop.

    He was placed in the third class of writing students, and in the
first of reading *la Civilité;* should come at 9:00 in the morning
and at 3:00 in the afternoon; spent two years in the school of M.
Caba in Saint Etienne Street, then eight months in that of M.
Ralot, one year in that of M. Huysbecq, and four months at that
of M. Mulot, the schoolmaster. He left these teachers because his
parents felt he would learn better elsewhere.

From what is written above, from what he has learned either by himself, by his own early experiences, or by the reports of the teachers,
especially from the **Register of Good and Bad Qualities** of their students, which they are to draw up at the end of the year, [the Director
adds the following]:

> He is light-headed; is absent about twice a month supposedly to
> help his mother. He applies himself fairly well; learns easily; has
> seldom failed to be promoted. He knows the catechism, but not
> the prayers. He is untruthful and greedy. His piety is very aver-
> age. He lacks modesty. He left school for three months during
> the winter. He left school for good on August 31, 1706, to study
> sculpture, or to be a footman, or to go to . . .

Extract 6: *See* pages 129–132 above; and CL 24:236–237 and 133–137.

Article 5:
Register of the Good and Bad Qualities
of Students

Toward the end of the scholastic year, in the last months of school before vacation starts, all teachers shall draw up a list in which they will
note the good and bad qualities of each student. This list should be
based upon their observations made during the year.

They shall record the name and surname of each student; how long the student has been in school; in what lesson and to what level in the class the student belongs; what degree of intelligence the student has; whether the student shows piety in church and during the prayers; whether the student is subject to any defects such as lying, cursing, stealing, impurity, gluttony, and so forth; whether the student shows good will, or resists correction; how the student should be handled; whether correction helps the student or not; whether the student has been assiduous in coming to school; whether the student misses school often or rarely, for some good reasons or without any, with or without permission; whether the student was punctual and arrived before the teacher; whether the student is diligent in school, and is so willingly; whether the student is apt to talk and play; whether the student learns easily; whether the student was regularly promoted at the usual times, or has been kept back, and whether this was due to the student's own fault or to dullness of mind; whether the student knows the catechism and the prayers well, or is ignorant of them; whether the student is obedient at school; whether the student is difficult to deal with, stubborn and apt to resist; whether the student is spoiled by the parents and whether they are unwilling to have their child punished and have at times complained about this; and whether the student has held any classroom responsibilities, and how they have been fulfilled.

Each teacher, at the end of the scholastic year, should give this completed register to the Director. On the first day of school following the vacation period, the Director shall give it to the teacher who will take over this class. If it is a different teacher from that of the previous year, the new teacher shall make use of this register for the first three months. In this way, the teacher shall get to know the students better and learn how to treat them. If it is the same teacher as the previous year, the Director shall keep the register. After the first three months of the new scholastic year, the teacher to whom the Director gave the register on the first day of school shall return it. The Director shall keep all these registers and shall compare those of previous years with those of the subsequent years, comparing those drawn up by different teachers who have taught this same class and these same students to see if their perceptions agree or differ, in whole or in part.

If some young teacher does not know how to draw up this register, the Director or the Inspector shall explain how to do it. If necessary, the Director or the Inspector shall do it.

Model Register of Behavior

Register of Students of the Fourth Class in the School in Rue Saint Placide for the Year 1706, Listing their Good and Bad Qualities.

François de Terieux: age 8½; has been coming to school for two years. He is in the third level of writing, since last July 1. He is fidgety. He has little piety and shows no self-control during prayers or in church unless he is carefully watched. This is due to light-headedness. His worst defect is lack of self-control. He shows fairly good will. He needs to be won over and prevailed upon to do well. Correction does him little good because he is thoughtless. He seldom misses school; he does so on occasion and without permission because of the bad example of some mischievous companions and because of his own fickleness of mind. He often comes in late. He applies himself more or less well. He often looks around and unless somebody is there to supervise him takes a rest while writing. Due to lack of application, he twice failed to be promoted from the second to the third level. He knows his prayers well and will submit to correction if the teacher has authority. If not, he can be mulish. However, he is not basically stubborn. Provided one tries to win him over, he will do what is wanted. He is spoiled by his parents, who do not like him to be corrected. He was not entrusted with any class responsibility because he is not very talented. He is alert. He would do his duty well, except that he often comes in late.

Lambert du Long: age 12½; has been coming to school for four years; has been in the seventh level of writing for the past six months, in the fifth level of writing registers and in the fourth level of arithmetic since last May 4. He is giddy and light-headed. He learns and remembers easily. He has little piety in church and during prayers, and seldom receives the sacraments. His main defect is pride; he feels it keenly when he is humiliated. Correction is sometimes useful for him. As a rule, he applies himself well, especially to catechism. In arithmetic and in writing, he has always been promoted at the regular times. He is submissive, if he finds a teacher who can control him. Otherwise, he is disobedient. His parents are not displeased when he is corrected. He was the reciter of prayers and the first student in the bench. He carried out his duties very well.

Extract 7: *See* pages 129–132 above; and CL 24:238 and 133–137.

Article 5:
Register of the First Student in the Bench

In each class, there shall be a register for each bench, containing the names and surnames of all of the students who sit on that bench.

One of the students from that bench shall sit in the first place, will be called the First Student in the Bench, and will be in charge of this register. The name of this student shall lead the list.

The names of the other students in the bench, in the order in which they are seated on the bench, shall follow the name of this student. These registers shall be made of a piece of cardboard covered with paper, and measuring six inches by four inches.

The names of the students shall also be written on small cards. The two ends of the cards should be strung through two cords running from top to bottom of the register. There should be two red strings on the two sides of each card, one to indicate those who were tardy and the other to indicate the absentees.

Both shall be marked by the First Student in the Bench, as stated in the article about the duties of this student. These registers shall be hung by a cord to a nail fixed in the wall, near the end of the bench where the students whose names it contains sit.

MODELE

ABSENTS   TARDS

Damien Rivasson

Lambert de Long

Martin Hacq

Jean-Bapte. La Chapelle

Nicholas du Four, etc.

Figure 12: Model Register of Daily Attendance (CL 24:238).

Extract 8: *See* pages 129–132 above; and CL 24:239 and 133–137.

Article 6:
Register of Home Visitations

In each class, there shall be a Register of Home Visitations for the use of those who visit the absent students. Each one shall contain the names of no more than fifteen or twenty students. Each such register shall contain the names of students who live in the same neighborhood and can be easily visited by the Visitors [of the absent students] for that neighborhood.

All Visitors shall have their own Register of Home Visitations. Each shall mark down every day those who are absent, as indicated in the article concerning the Visitors of Absent Students. These registers shall be made of a piece of cardboard which is folded in two, covered with white paper on the inside, and covered with parchment on the outside. The register should measure about six inches by two inches.

The names of the students shall be written on small cards. The two ends of these cards shall be laced into two cords running from top to bottom of the register. Along the side and at either end of the cards, there shall be a red string which can be drawn down, one on the left to indicate tardiness, and one on the right, absence.

MODELE					
o	Jean B. Lardier Rue de Tillois	o	André Gazin Rue St-Jacques		o
o	Nicole Ruvene Rue de Bourgrêle	o	Quentin Dubré Rue Maillet		o
o	Nicholas Le Becq Rue de la Coutre	o	Henry Guimbert A la Couture		o
o	Pierre Drotin Rue de Bourgresle	o	Jean Guimbert A la Couture		o
o	Joseph D'allure Rue Chativer	o	Thiéry Guimbert A la Couture		o
o	Nicholas Mulot Rue des Tapissiers	o	Pierre Henry Vieille Couture		o
o	Pierre Jobart Rue des deux Anges	o	Nicholas Muet Vieille Couture		o

Figure 13: Model Register of Home Visitations (CL 24:239).

Extract 9: *See* pages 135–137 above; and CL 24:140.

5
Introductory Remarks
on Corrections

The correction of students is one of the things which is of the greatest consequence in schools, and to which most attention must be given in order to carry it out fittingly and fruitfully, both for those who are corrected and for those who witness it.

It is for that reason that there are many things to be observed in the use of the corrections which might possibly be administered in the schools. We shall speak of these in the following articles.

Extract 10: *See* page 163 above; and CL 24:240 and 191.

Why Students Miss School

The fourth important reason why students miss school is because the Visitors of the Absent Students are not capable of fulfilling their duties, do not note the absentees exactly, do not call on the absentees every time they miss school, or let themselves be bribed by the parents or by the absentees themselves and so turn in false excuses.

To forestall this difficulty, the Inspector and each teacher should take great pains to choose carefully the students they appoint as Visitors of the Absent Students. Both Inspector and teachers should make sure that they possess all the qualities indicated in the article that deals with class officials. If later it is clear that they are not capable of doing their task or do not fulfill it properly, the teacher should change them. To motivate them to perform their duty faithfully, however, the Inspector and the teachers shall reward them every month, in proportion to their trustworthiness, and in such a way that they will be pleased and be encouraged to accomplish well a role of such importance.

Every day when school is in session teachers must carefully read the Registers of Home Visitations and of Daily Attendance, and insist that both be brought to them without fail at the time indicated in the rules for these functions. Teachers should read them to see if all the absentees are duly marked on both registers and verify that these tally with each other.

To oblige the Visitors to call at the absentees' houses without fail, teachers shall weigh carefully the reasons given for the absences reported by the Visitors of the Absent Students and see if these reasons are justified and coherent. From time to time, a teacher shall ask unexpected questions of the Visitors concerning the absences. In this way, the teacher will surprise them, see whether they say the right thing, and see whether what they say is in fact accurate.

To make sure that the Visitors have not allowed themselves to be bribed by the absentees or by their parents, the teacher shall forbid them under pain of correction to accept anything from these students or their parents.

Privately, the teacher shall inquire of students living in the neighborhood about whether they have not seen this absentee, whether they know why the student was missing, and whether they know what this absent student was doing. When the teacher has some doubt about the truth of the excuses which the Visitor has reported, the teacher shall send a reliable student to check on the missing student, and from time to time, to visit other absentees. The teacher shall do this even during school hours and when the Visitor does not know about it, to find out whether this messenger returns with the same reason for the absence that the Visitor gave. If the Inspector or the teacher ascertains that the Visitor has been so wanting as to agree to being bribed, they shall chastise the culprit as an example, instead of the absent student. If it happens again the offender shall be punished and deprived of office.

Extract 11: *See* page 164 above; and CL 24:241 and 196.

Article 4:
Punishment for Students Absent or Tardy Without Permission

When they return, students who were absent without permission shall take their place on the bench of "Negligent Students" in their classroom, a bench reserved for those who have been absent without permission and for those who are late-comers. They shall occupy this bench for twice the length of time that they have missed school. A student who has missed half a day shall remain for a full day on this bench; absentees will remain on the bench for a time proportionate to the time that they were absent. While they occupy this bench, they shall not follow the lesson with their companions. Another student shall make them read during breakfast and the afternoon snack. If they are in a writing class, they shall not write.

Late-comers shall also take their place on this bench every time that they come in late; they shall not be allowed to read. The Visitor of the Absent Students for their neighborhood shall after school inform their parents that they were not allowed to read because they had come in late.

A student who comes in late twice in a given week without having obtained permission shall be punished with the rod.

Those who have been absent ten times, that is, for five full days in a given month even with permission, shall not be promoted at the end of the month. They shall not be promoted even if they had permission to be absent or even if they are able to do the more advanced work.

Those who without permission failed to attend school for two full days, that is, four times in a given month, shall not be promoted to the next lesson at the end of the month. Nor shall those who have come late six times in a given month be promoted.

Extract 12: *See* page 170 above; and CL 24:204–205.

8

School Officers

There shall be several [student] officers in the school. These officers will be charged with several different functions which the teachers cannot or ought not do themselves. These officers shall be: (1) the Reciter of Prayers; (2) the one who says what the priest says in the responsories at holy Mass, and called for this reason the Mass Officer; (3) the Almoner; (4) the Holy Water Bearer; (5) the Rosary Carrier and assistants; (6) the Bell Ringer; (7) the Monitors and Supervisors; (8) the First Student in the Bench; (9) the Visitors of the Absent Students; (10) the Distributors and Collectors of Papers; (11) the Distributors and Collectors of Books; (12) the Sweepers; (13) the Doorkeeper; and (14) the Keeper of the School Key.

Extract 13: *See* page 171 above; and CL 24:242 and 206.

Article 2:
The Mass Officer

A student shall be appointed to fill the role of the priest in practicing the responses for holy Mass. These responses are practiced during breakfast on each Tuesday.

This exercise shall be carried out in the following manner. The student holding the role of priest shall always remain standing in the same place; the one who is to respond shall kneel as if serving Mass. The Mass Officer shall begin by saying, *In nomine Patris* . . . , *Introibo* . . . , and all that the priest says up to the point where the priest ascends the altar. The Mass Officer shall then say, *Kyrie eleison.* . . . The Mass Officer shall alternate these responses with the server. The Mass Officer shall alternate all of the rest which is found in the book which should be held in the Mass Officer's hand during this time.

At the end of each gospel, the Mass Officer shall make an inflection of voice on the final two or three words. When the words "Jesus," "Mary," or "*Oremus*" are said, both shall bow their heads. After the "*Sanctus*," the Mass Officer shall genuflect twice in succession and with dignity. This indicates to the server when to prepare to ring the bell for the consecration. At the *Agnus Dei* and the *Domine non sum dignus*, they shall strike their breast three times. After *Domine non sum dignus*, the Mass Officer shall present a small receptacle, one made for this purpose, as though about to receive the first ablutions. The Mass Officer shall then turn toward the server and put four fingers over this little vessel, as the priest does at the second ablution. In this manner, the Mass Officer lets the server know how to pour the water.

The first time that the responses for holy Mass are practiced, the Mass Officer shall shut the book after the last two orations. During the second time, the Mass Officer shall leave the book open. In this manner, the Mass Officer shall show the server that when the priest thus leaves the book open the server must carry it over to the other side.

The student who acts as Mass Officer should be well behaved, steady, self-controlled, and reserved. In this way, students who are practicing the responses for holy Mass will be edified and inspired.

If the teacher thinks it proper and proposes someone else to the Director or the Inspector, the student holding this office shall be changed monthly. The one who replaces the Mass Officer should likewise be well-behaved. This is a very important consideration for this role.

Extract 14: *See* page 171 above; and CL 24:243 and 206.

Article 3:
The Almoner

In each class, a student shall be appointed to gather the alms, that is, the bread to be given to the poor during the breakfast and the afternoon snack.

About halfway through both breakfast and the afternoon snack and again at the end, and after bowing to the teacher, this official shall take the basket destined for this purpose and pass it in front of the benches. The Almoner shall pass the basket first on one side of the class. The Almoner shall then pass it on the other side. This shall be done without saying a single word and while being very careful never to ask any food of any particular student.

When walking about the classroom during this task, the Almoner shall act with self-control and without noise. The Almoner shall be careful never to stare at anyone.

When the alms have all or nearly all been gathered and after again bowing to the teacher, the Almoner shall present the basket to the teacher to distribute the bread.

Teachers shall put in charge of this duty someone who is pious and shows affection for the poor, and, especially, not inclined to gluttony. Almoners shall not be permitted to give out any of the bread or anything else to anybody whatever, and especially they shall not be permitted to take something for themselves from what the basket contains. An Almoner who does either of these things shall be severely punished and immediately deprived of this position. This class officer should also be changed when the teacher thinks proper or necessary and has consulted the Director.

Extract 15: *See* page 175 above; and CL 24:244 and 213.

Article 8:
The First Student in the Bench

The first student in each bench shall be in charge of the Register of Daily Attendance for that bench. The student shall mark down those in the bench who are absent by drawing down the string belonging to the absentee. The student shall daily do this at 8:30 in the morning and again at 2:00 in the afternoon, and present the Register of Daily Attendance to the teacher as soon as it is completed. The teacher can, in this way, see who is absent and make sure that there are neither more nor less absentees than indicated.

In the lower classes where students do not yet know how to read, the First Student in the Bench shall be taught how to read the names in the register or learn them by heart. If there are no children able to read the names or learn them by heart and in proper order, the teacher shall read them, at least those that the First Student in the Bench cannot read. The teacher shall do this at the end of the school day, before morning prayer, and at the beginning of the afternoon snack. The teacher shall mark those who are absent by drawing down the strings in the register.

Students designated as First Student in the Bench should be among the most regular in attendance and among the most diligent. They should be among the best behaved and the most self-controlled. This role shall ordinarily be given to them as a reward for their assiduity, their good behavior, their self-control, and their ability. They shall not be changed unless the teacher judges it necessary either because of some fault they have committed or some other serious reason.

Extract 16: *See* page 175 above; and Cl 24:245–246 and 213.

Article 9:
The Visitors of the Absent Students

In each class, there shall be two or three students charged with seeing to the assiduous attendance of the students living in several streets of a given section of the town which have been assigned to them.

Each of these students shall have a record or register of the students living in the sector of which they have been put in charge. In this register, the names and surnames of the students and the name of the street on which they live shall be inscribed.

If in the lowest grades no child can be found to carry out this duty or if there are not enough students capable of this duty, the teacher, with the advice of the Director or the Inspector, shall choose some students from a higher class to assist with this task.

These Visitors of the Absent Students in the lower grades, who have been chosen from a higher one, shall go to the lower grade to mark down the absentees toward the end of school in the morning and during the afternoon snack. After greeting the teacher, they shall pull down the string markers of the absentees on the Register of Daily Attendance. They shall do this without saying a single word and shall then return to their own class at once.

When these Visitors have thus marked the absentees from the part of town assigned to them, they shall in turn present their Register of Daily Attendance to the teacher. The teacher shall take note of the absentees and then give the registers back to these Visitors.

Each of the Visitors shall on each occasion mark on the Register of Daily Attendance the absentees from their neighborhood, doing this by pulling down the marker. Each Visitor shall take care to go and visit each absentee after school. The teacher should not have to remind the Visitor to do this.

Each Visitor shall report to the teacher at the beginning of the next session what the Visitor found out at the home of each of the absentees; why the absentee was absent; to whom the Visitor spoke; and when the absentee would return to class.

From time to time, the Visitors shall call on the sick students from the area for which they have been given charge. They shall do this according to the instructions given them by the teacher and even on their own initiative. During the visit, they shall console the absentees and urge them to suffer their illness patiently for the love of God. They shall then inform the teacher of how the sick are, and whether they are getting any better.

The Visitors shall always speak to the parents of the absentee, to some other person old enough to know why the student is absent from school, or to one whose word can be trusted. They shall always speak to these persons very politely. They shall always extend their teacher's greetings to them.

A Visitor who learned that an absentee from their neighborhood is ill shall go to see the sick student, and earnestly ask to be allowed to do so, saying that they have come on behalf of the teacher who sent them to inquire from what the absentee is suffering and how the absentee is getting along.

The Visitors of the Absent Students shall be most careful not to let themselves be bribed either by the absentee or by the absentee's parents, not allowing themselves to be bribed to make false reports to the teacher about absences. The Visitors must never on any pretext whatsoever accept any present from students in their neighborhood or from their parents.

Each teacher shall be very careful about this. A Visitor who is found to have been bribed, shall be punished severely, instead of the absentee, and shall be deprived of this office unless a promise is made never to commit such a fault again. The Visitor who repeats this offense shall be permanently deprived of this position.

When a teacher has some doubts about the trustworthiness of a Visitor, that is, noticing that a certain student is often absent and that the reasons given are not very convincing, another student shall be sent secretly to the home of the absentee, even during school time, to discover more surely whether the reasons to be reported will correspond with those given by the Visitor.

It is important from time to time to give some recompense to those Visitors who fulfill their duties faithfully. This will encourage them to continue doing so. They should, as a rule, be rewarded monthly.

Visitors shall be chosen from among the students who are most loyal and most assiduous in coming to school. They should demonstrate good judgment, honesty, good behavior, no taint of falsehood, and the ability not to let themselves be influenced. They should also have much respect for the teacher and should show entire submission and docility of mind.

To demonstrate their affection and zeal for the school, they shall try to persuade the unruly students who easily and lightly miss school to come to class regularly. If they should happen on any children wandering the streets in idleness, not attending any school, they shall urge them to come to their school.

The teachers shall not change these officers during the whole school year unless, after consulting the Director, they feel this is necessary because they perceived that a Visitor is not fit for this position, or fulfills the role badly, and that there are other students much better qualified to serve.

Extract 17: *See* page 175 above; and CL 24:247 and 214.

Article 9:
The Distributor and Collector of Books

In every class, there shall be a certain number of the books used in each lesson which are to be loaned to the students too poor to buy any books. In each class, a student shall be assigned to distribute these books to those whom the teacher has designated. In each class, there shall be a list of those who have the use of these books. The Director or the Inspector of Schools will have identified those children they know are so poor that they cannot buy books. These books shall be loaned only to students in this category.

The Distributor of Books shall know the number of books available in each class for the use of poor students. In collecting them, the Distributor shall make sure that none are damaged and that the pages are not folded, not even on the corners. The Distributor must make sure that each student gives back the same book which that student was using. If any book is missing or if a student has ruined a book, this official shall inform the teacher as soon as the books have been put back where they belong.

The Distributor of Books shall also put away the papers, ferules, and books of the teachers, returning them to the teacher when needed. The Distributor of Books must be sure that none of these objects is lost or damaged.

Appendix C
The Training of New Teachers[1]

[This section on] the training of new teachers comprises two parts: (1) making new teachers lose the traits they have but should not have; and (2) making them acquire those traits that they lack, and which are very necessary for them.

The traits which must be corrected in new teachers are: (1) talking too much; (2) agitation; (3) thoughtlessness; (4) overeagerness; (5) harshness and severity; (6) impatience; (7) partiality; (8) torpor; (9) sluggishness; (10) slackness; (11) discouragement; (12) undue familiarity; (13) sentimentality and particular friendships; (14) inconstancy and fickleness; and (15) a distracted appearance, lack of concentration, or fixation on a single point.

Uprooting the Defects Found in New Teachers

Talking Too Much

A Supervisor training new teachers shall urge them not to talk at all for a predetermined length of time, not for any reason whatsoever, and not even when it might seem advisable and necessary. They should attempt this first for a quarter of an hour, later for half an hour, and finally for an hour or more according to what is judged appropriate. Thus, little by little, they will become accustomed to keeping silence. When a predetermined time has passed, the Supervisor should encourage them to again remain silent for a quarter of an hour or a half hour, as far as they are judged capable.

Second, when new teachers talk uselessly, the Supervisor must call their attention to this defect, without delay, perhaps right at the end of the class, pointing out the uselessness of the words and explaining at the same time what ought to have been done. An example of this defect would be personally to correct the mistakes by interrupting the students as they are reading.

Instead of speaking on such occasions, a teacher should give two clicks with the signal to oblige the student to repeat the word mispronounced. Perhaps the student might pronounce the word correctly; but if not, after one or two tries, the teacher should give one click of the signal to call the attention of the whole class, and then make a sign to one of those following the same lesson to read the word. This student would then read correctly the word that the first reader was not able to pronounce, and so on.

New teachers should not be compelled to keep silence in this way for a long period of time. That would only frustrate them and might even frighten them. Silence should be recommended only for a short time at first. Later they should be encouraged to continue doing so until school ends. They might be told that since they managed to refrain from speaking during the previous quarter of an hour, they can just as easily also continue doing the same for the next quarter of an hour. It might even be good to assign such practices as penances and have the teachers report at the end of class whether they have observed these penances faithfully, and how much it helped them. If the students have kept a more complete silence or if the teachers have spoken only rarely, one might suggest to them the following practices as actions which may remind them to be silent. Before speaking, they might: stand up at their place; make the sign of the cross; say a few words, such as "Jesus! Mary! Joseph!"; raise their hearts to God; or glance at the crucifix.

Agitation and Restlessness

Although it is not always recommended to be as stiff as a statue in school, foregoing both action and movement, neither is it good to be too fidgety or too flustered. The two extremes must be avoided. The one causes teachers not to be sufficiently vigilant and to lack firmness; the other robs them of all authority and brings down on them the contempt of students.

New teachers must learn to control a natural tendency to be hasty and too quick to react. To begin, they must be persuaded to sit quietly at their desk and remain seated without rising for a quarter of an hour at a time, or even for a half-hour.

New teachers must not go down among the students to administer the ferule, but they must stay in place and not move about so easily. They must not at every moment modify their expression, their posture, and their position, standing now on one foot, now on the other; constantly turning the head from side to side; unable to keep the same position for a moment. To help with this, the Supervisor should always, or as often as possible, be close to them and remind them when something undesirable is being done. The Supervisor should even give penances capable of making a teacher remember what should be done. The Supervisor should not permit beginning teachers to use the signal hastily or with gestures. If this does happen, they should be warned immediately.

Thoughtlessness

New teachers who are naturally thoughtless must keep very strict silence, and not be allowed to speak at all without a very great necessity. They must learn when it is really necessary to speak and when it is not. They must be constantly supervised, and corrected if they do anything in school which shows the least degree of thoughtlessness. They must not laugh. They themselves must not laugh, and they should not make the students laugh. They should not do anything in the least bit improper or ridiculous, or that can arouse the laughter of others. When they have acted thoughtlessly in class or have failed to act seriously, they should be given a severe penance. They must not allow any students to come up close to them.

All failings against seriousness must be called to their attention as soon as they are committed. This must be done every time something of this sort happens. The Supervisor must give a sign to let them know when they are doing something improper.

The Supervisor must insist that they remain seated on their chair at all times. They must not leave it for any reason whatever.

Harshness, Severity, and Impatience

New teachers must not administer correction frequently.[2] Instead, every effort must be made to convince them that it is not harshness and rigor that produce good order in a school. Good order is the result of constant vigilance, combined with circumspection and mildness. The Supervisor should keep watch over all of the corrections beginning teachers impose, and should take note of all the defects in their manner of making corrections. All these defects must be brought to their attention. Supervisors should accustom new teachers to assume an unruffled air, a calm countenance, and an exterior appearance which indicates a consistent and benevolent disposition.

The occasions when new teachers may administer corporal punishment shall, as far as possible, be set by the Supervisor, who should often illustrate for them how to do this with moderation, not permitting them to strike too hard with the ferule and fixing the number of strokes, which they must not exceed without permission. The Supervisor must not allow teachers to touch their students with their hands, to pull or push them rudely, or to punch them. Therefore, the Supervisor must insist that new teachers stay in their seats and not go down among the children to drag them out of their places, or the like. The Supervisor must never allow a teacher to give more than one correction with the ferule at a time to any given student.[3]

A Supervisor must never allow teachers to throw anything, such as the ferule, at the students, even if they do so with moderation. He must train them never to punish any student except after some moments of reflection and self-examination, and after having raised their hearts to God, and should impose on them some such practice as a penance when they have failed in this. New teachers must give an account to the Supervisor of all the corrections they have made, the reasons for them, and how they acted while administering them.

The Supervisor must invite teachers in training to keep complete silence and great self-control when they feel themselves moved by impatience, and should urge them to remain unruffled as long as they experience this emotion. There is no better means than this to bridle impatience. They should not keep within reach anything with which they might strike the students, not even the ferule or the rod.

Antipathy for Certain Students

The Supervisor shall inspire new teachers with perfect and disinterested charity for their neighbor, and encourage them to show even more exterior signs of friendship and affection for the poor than for the rich. The Supervisor must make new teachers realize how important their obligation is to love all of the children with equal charity and how important it is not to show preferences for certain students when they exteriorly display an aversion for others.

A Supervisor should encourage teachers to show more cordiality and affection in the future to those students for whom they have felt aversion than to the others. It is even sometimes good to oblige young teachers to take greater pains with those for whom they feel antipathy, to call on them to read more often, or to answer more often during the catechism lesson; to correct their writing exercises twice as often as those of the rest; to speak to them only in an affable and kind manner; to give them some reward, even if they did not fully deserve it; and to get close to them without emotional involvement even if they had some reason to feel like rebuffing them.

The Supervisor may even simulate the conduct that might provoke these reactions and invite the new teachers to overcome their feelings on such occasions. However, the objective for teachers in training is to learn to do what can be done in order to correct the defects of students either by punishing them or by urging them to do better.

Torpor and the Tendency to Discouragement

To overcome these attitudes all new teachers must be inspired to cultivate perfect charity for their students. The Supervisor should not call their attention to several defects and difficulties at one time, but mention only one or two at a time, suggesting the means to overcome these defects, urging them to do so, and encouraging them from time

260 ♦ *The Conduct of the Christian Schools*

to time. Certain precautions, which are not necessary with prudent people, need to be taken with persons with dispositions like these. The former need to be guided with gentleness and condescendence. Forcing them or putting too much pressure on them risks turning them away from their duty instead of bringing them to perform it well. The others do not let themselves be so readily discouraged.

Familiarity

To cure familiarity quickly, there is only one thing to be done: teachers in training must neither talk to the students nor allow the students to speak to them, the Supervisor being sure that these new teachers speak to their students only in cases of great necessity. They are not to speak from their place in the classroom. They are not to speak in a loud voice, and must never laugh with the students. They shall not give students anything out of favoritism nor make them do anything inspired by that same spirit. They should not tolerate the faults of students because of timidity or because of the familiarity they have contracted with them.

Teachers in training must not allow these students to speak to them, nor permit any student to ever do so without permission, respect, and reserve. Students must always address the teacher while they are standing, bareheaded, and must speak in a low voice. Teachers must never have a student come up to their seat to speak to them, nor shall they talk to the students at every opportunity and without gravity and restraint, as though speaking with a companion. The Supervisor must warn new teachers about all such defects; and whenever it is noticed that they fall into them, they shall be given means for avoiding them. For instance, they might punish with the ferule all those who talk to them without permission or from their places, or talk to them in a disrespectful manner. Or the teacher should send such students to the Supervisor to inspire them with salutary fear. Familiarity breeds contempt. Once a teacher is not respected by the students, whatever the teacher may say or do fails to impress them. All teaching and instruction then have little weight and produce no good effects. The students become insolent, and end up by making a joke of the teacher.

The Supervisor must pay great attention to this point; it is highly important. Nothing should be omitted to prevent such familiarity from happening to those who are being trained. To insure this, the Supervisor, if the Supervisor is also the Director, should impose suitable penances on those teachers who might show too much familiarity. A Supervisor who is not the Director shall inform the Director in cases like this.

A teacher can speak to students in a relaxed and friendly manner without being familiar with them and without allowing them to lose the respect they owe to the person with whom they converse.[4]

Sluggishness and Slackness

New teachers who are slow and sluggish must be carefully supervised and obliged, even by penances, to do their duty in school, that is, to supervise the students, maintain silence and order, make all of the students follow the lesson, and have all of them read as much as they are supposed to and as they need.

New teachers must begin all the school exercises precisely on time: the recitation of the prayers, the responses for holy Mass, the catechism, and the rosary which is said immediately after finishing morning prayer in school and after the blessing of the afternoon snack. Lessons should start immediately after finishing the thanksgiving in the morning and right after the school prayer in the afternoon, and so on.

The Supervisor must also see that the students recite all of their assigned lessons and that all have more than enough time to do this, rather than less. This can be achieved if the teacher makes each student read a little bit each time, and frequently. The Supervisor must make sure that teachers in training are not idle during school time, and shall insist that new teachers, especially during the lessons, constantly apply themselves to have the children read and follow.

Sentimentality and Particular Friendships

To prevent sentimentality and particular friendships the Supervisor shall make young teachers, even before assigning them to a class, realize that they must have a similar and equal charity for all of their students, just as they should have with regard to all the teachers. Teachers in training need to realize that they must never spoil certain students while neglecting others.

This, however, does not mean that we cannot and should not always prefer the poor to the rich, because they more closely resemble Our Lord Jesus Christ and because they belong to Christ more particularly than do the rich, since they are called brothers and sisters by Christ. Neither does this mean that we should not have a special love for those who by their piety, assiduity, faithfulness, docility, and punctuality in coming to school daily and on time, and by their other good qualities, make themselves especially recommendable. Ordinarily and before the entire group, however, no token of external affection should be given to some more than to others.

Therefore, the Supervisor shall never allow teachers in training to display more affection and benevolence toward some rather than others. Teachers should show all equally the same kind of affection, with the greater shown the poorest and those who possess no external advantages which might win the teachers' affection and friendship. If they do show more interest in poorer students, it should be to mortify themselves and overcome their inclinations, rather than to satisfy and content themselves.

New teachers must not keep their favorite students nearby, sharing confidences and secrets with them during school time. Neither should they place the cute, the nice-looking children, those who are quick witted, and those who are agreeable in appearance near to themselves. They must not speak to these children in private, except at the end of school and in their proper turn with the others, to encourage them to do their duty well. They must punish them if they deserve to be punished, and never tolerate in certain children what they would not be willing to put up with in others. The Supervisor should oblige them to act on such occasions in a way contrary to their likes and dislikes.

The Supervisor must make teachers realize that such particular friendships give rise to many serious problems, both for those who are thus cajoled and caressed and for those who are not. The former try to take advantage of this preference in order to do wrong; they later become insolent and lose all the respect and fear which they should feel for their teacher, and no longer pay any attention to the teacher. The others often grow jealous and conceive sentiments of hatred and aversion for their teacher and for the students who they think are favored more than themselves.

Lack of Concentration or Over-concentration

Although teachers should neither keep their eyes closed nor apply themselves to exterior recollection in school, as they would in the community room or in the chapel in the Community House, still they should make use of their eyes only to watch over and constantly supervise the students. The Supervisor must then take care that new teachers avoid both these extremes, avoiding any external appearance which on the one hand is too lax, too free, too flighty, or too giddy, or on the other, betrays so great a reserve or so continual a recollection they fail to watch over their students.

To remedy the first defect the Supervisor must oblige the trainees not to turn their heads too freely from side to side and not to observe and pay attention to what is going on in the other classes. To remedy the second defect, the Supervisor must make them keep their eyes on their students at all times, keeping all of them in sight without losing them from view for more than the time needed to say an "Our Father." They must also know what the children are doing. If someone were to ask what a certain student was doing, the teacher should be able to reply at once and say, "That student is doing this or that."

These new teachers must not keep their eyes fixed and staring at one spot, but should always be looking around the class. When they are thus looking about, they should put a finger or the tip of the signal on the book or on the line where the children are reading or some lines lower. In this way, they will not lose track of the lesson. They must not be so absorbed in reading in their book that they fail to be at least equally attentive to watching over and supervising the students. In a word, new teachers should try to do all of this as well as they can, with prudence, and with the experience which they will acquire over the years.

During the time of their training, and until they have become well accustomed to supervising children and at the same time having them read and follow the lesson, it would be good for teachers in training to read three or four times over the lesson for the morning or the afternoon, so that they have a fair idea of the contents of the text. This will make it easier for them not to lose the place so readily in the reading, and if they do, it will make it easier to find it again quickly.

Qualities Which New Teachers Must Acquire

The habits to be acquired are: (1) decisiveness; (2) authority and firmness; (3) reserve (i.e., serious, thoughtful, and modest behavior); (4) vigilance; (5) attention to oneself; (6) professionalism; (7) prudence; (8) winning manners; (9) zeal; and (10) facility in speaking and expressing oneself clearly and with order and in a way that the children one teaches can grasp.

Decisiveness, Authority, and Firmness[5]

In the novitiate, new teachers must often be given practice in teaching, and shown how to do all that is necessary in school. Once they have acquired a sufficiently clear idea of what a classroom is and before they are sent out to teach, they must learn to walk into the classroom with a deliberate and serious air, head held high, looking over all of the students with a self-assured manner, as though they had been teaching for thirty years. They should then do what is supposed to be done, i.e., kneel, bow to the crucifix, and then take their place on the teacher's seat. Any student who starts to talk to the teacher should be made to kneel down immediately without saying a word, the teacher going to the student's seat deliberately and in a dignified manner. Everything the teacher does should be done as self-assuredly as possible and as though the teacher had been teaching for a long time. A new teacher must not show any timidity.

During the first school days, a new teacher is not to be addressed by any student. If anything is to be said to the class, a teacher should first tell it in a low voice to one student, who will then repeat it aloud; however, this should happen rarely. All that the teacher does should be done in a resolute and easy manner, having one student tell the others whatever is to be done. When going to and during holy Mass, students who fail to do anything the teacher has told them to do must be punished very severely. New teachers must pay attention to the least thing that happens in school or in church; they must not even tolerate that a head should turn in church without reproving the child for it.

No corporal punishment should be inflicted during the first week, except for faults by students who have been previously warned. If it is necessary to use corporal punishment, a teacher should begin with the most troublesome children and with those whose punishment may inspire more fear in the others, such as the biggest ones, and not with the smallest or youngest.

To establish authority, teachers should not tolerate that any student speak to them out loud, without permission, or in a disrespectful manner; students must always address the teacher in a very low voice, with head bared, while standing, and in a serious manner. Teachers should not show much favoritism or partiality in general. They should speak little, and do so only with poise, assurance and firmness, and insist that their orders be carried out.

New teachers should not talk without prior consideration, in a confused manner, or by mumbling their words. They should not move about, not even when seated, and should not show any agitation. They should never laugh even when something really amusing happens. They should administer corrections only at their place; and if correction is needed, they should always begin with the biggest students. When things go wrong, they should keep an eye always on the bigger children, to correct them rather than the little ones.

When a big student wants to resist correction, a new teacher should not wait until the end of school to administer it, but should impose the correction in time for the offender to finish it and still have some time left over. The teacher should not let a culprit go without being corrected; and one who does not obey promptly should be punished for not obeying right away, even if it is only to get the ferule. Thus, the student will receive the ordinary correction which might not have been administered otherwise. If two or three students are to be punished, the teacher might tell them that the last one to get ready will be punished more severely than the others. If they are exact and prompt in getting ready, it might be good to pardon them, if the fault was not considerable and as a reward for their obedience.

When students cry out under the rod, the teacher should always continue to administer the punishment until they stop. The teacher should make them put their pants back on, then have them dispose themselves to go through the procedure all over again in preparation for another punishment, as though they had not already received it. Students must understand that the first correction was only to make them stop crying out. The way a teacher proceeds has much to do creating due authority.

Teachers should not give students a private hearing more than once a day, at most only once in the morning and once in the afternoon.

Firmness consists in making the students do what is wanted immediately and with no delay. A student who does not do right away what the teacher requires must be corrected until what is required is done, and done correctly. A repeated refusal will be followed by repeated punishment. The teacher must never give in to a student; the student should be obliged absolutely to carry out the teacher's commands.

The Supervisor must make young teachers being trained carry out everything they have undertaken. If need be, the Supervisor shall help them do this.

The Supervisor must not permit a teacher to overlook it when a student has resisted, but will oblige the teacher to do everything possible to constrain the delinquent, providing the new teacher with the means needed to do this successfully.

The Supervisor shall let the teachers exercise full authority in their duties, giving them to understand that they should act in all things as though the Supervisor was not present.

As far as possible, the Supervisor shall place a new teacher under another teacher who performs the duties of a teacher well.

A new teacher must act in such a way that children may always leave school satisfied. In this way, they may neither have anything to complain about to their parents nor have anything that might cause their parents pain.

When there is no order in a school, teachers must be very firm from the start, correcting with more frequency than if there was good order in the school. In the beginning, the teacher should give out some rewards to the students when they behave well. As a rule, the teacher should let no fault go by without a sanction, punishing those whose punishment will serve as an example to the others. These are usually the biggest and most unruly students.

A teacher should not intimidate the timid children, who rarely fall into faults or who do so without any malice.

A young teacher should carefully study the spirit, customs, and inclinations of the students, in this way becoming more likely to succeed in dealing with them in a manner likely to be acceptable. If children fail in some way, they should ordinarily be either warned about it or corrected at the very time and not at some later moment.

Promoting the Students' Spiritual Life

The students should be encouraged to piety, fear of God, and horror of sin. They should be exhorted to frequent the sacraments. Sufficient time should be given by the students to the examination of conscience and the reflections. Teachers should be trained and instructed in the proper manner of speaking to and of exhorting students.

Catechism should be taught on moral matters two or three times a week. Teachers should talk to the students in private, bring them to Confession and Communion every month, and be sure to provide them with good confessors.

Teachers should strongly recommend faithfulness to morning and night prayers, pious assistance at holy Mass, and frequent prayer during the day.

Manual of the Prefect of Boarding Students[6]

The Superior of the Institute shall entrust the supervision of the boarding students to one or several of the teachers, should several be needed. The Superior should entrust this to those who are judged most capable of this task.

The Prefect of the Boarding Students or the First Prefect, if there are more than one, shall, when the boarders are admitted, make an inventory of all that they bring for their own use: clothes, body linen, dishes, and so forth. This is done so as to return to students when they leave exactly what they brought in. The Prefect of the Boarding Students shall keep this inventory and any explanatory notes in a book especially designated for this purpose and will give a copy of it to the Superior of the Institute in order to give the Superior an account. When relieved of this duty by the Superior, the Prefect will give a copy of this inventory to the replacement.

The Prefect shall take care that all of the clothes and personal effects of the boarders are marked. In this manner, these things can be returned and accounted for at the time the students depart.

The Prefect shall likewise see that the boarders' clothes are well cared for and remain very clean and neat.

The Prefect shall have the boarders' dormitory swept, the beds properly made, and the bed straw changed as often as necessary. The Prefect shall remind the Superior of the Institute about this when the Prefect thinks a change is necessary and, in choosing to act, the Superior may provide for this need generously.

The Prefect shall provide the boarders with everything that they need, taking care that they do lack nothing in the way of nourishment when they are ill or indisposed. The Prefect shall and will ask the Superior for the needed authorization.

The Prefect shall especially make sure that there are no lice on the heads or bodies of the boarders, and shall inspect the heads of all of them weekly.

Every week the Prefect shall give an account of the boarders' behavior to the Superior or the Director. This is done after giving an account of the Prefect's own conduct. The Prefect shall often ask for their advice on how to act toward the boarders, both the group in general and certain ones in particular. The Prefect shall follow in detail the orders given by the Superior or the Director.

When the boarders are visited by their parents or by other persons, the Prefect, or one of them if there are several, or some other teacher as determined by the Superior, shall bring the boarders to the assigned place to see and to speak with their visitors. The teacher who accompanies them shall stay with them until the visitors leave.

Every morning and evening, and at the start of their principal actions, the Prefect shall have the boarders say slowly, in a moderate voice, and with piety, the usual prayers, and shall remind them to offer their actions to God and renew during the day this offering that they have made. The Prefect shall especially keep watch over their morals and seek to inspire them with love for virtue and hatred for vice, and should speak to them often about this and tell them impressive stories on the subject. Children are not capable of deep thoughts. They are more easily led and inspired to the practice of what is good by examples proposed to them, especially stories about young people like themselves, than they are by long-winded discourses.

The Prefect shall reprove the boarders for their defects and make them think with deep horror of them by using comparisons adapted to their mentality. The Prefect shall do this with so much charity and mildness that the boarders may be more touched by the thought of the faults that they have committed than by the thought of the pain that they might feel when they are reproached for their defects. When correcting them, the Prefect shall be careful not to do so with anger. If corporal punishment is called for, it should be obvious that the Prefect administers it with reason and with charity.

Prefects shall strive to be loved rather than feared. However, they shall not refrain from reproving the boarders for the faults which are done with malice. In this manner, the Prefect shall keep the boarders from getting into habits of this kind. A Prefect shall never show more affection for some than for others, and so prevent jealousy. An exception is when someone has acted especially well and thus served as an example to the rest. The Prefect shall at that time tell the boarders that anyone else who behaves similarly will also be equally cherished.

Among the boarders, the Prefect shall not tolerate gluttony, quarreling, jealousy, contempt for others, slander, lying, or tale bearing. These are, as it were, the roots of many other vices. Especially, the Prefect shall not put up with anything that leads to impurity.

During recreations, the Prefect shall neither leave any of the boarders alone nor leave a few separated from the rest. From time to time, the Prefect shall teach them a catechism lesson on Confession and Communion; in this way, they may learn the dispositions required to receive these sacraments properly. The Prefect shall do everything possible to get them to bring these dispositions to the reception of these sacraments.

Boarders shall have frequent opportunities to go to Confession. They cannot too early form the habit of doing so, and there is nothing more capable of preventing them from falling into serious sins.

Even though some among the boarders may not be old enough to receive absolution, the Prefect should still have them go to Confession. This will help to dispose and to accustom them to frequenting this sacrament. For this reason, the Prefect shall take care that no boarder, little or big, lets two weeks go by without going to Confession, provided the confessor judges this is appropriate, or goes to Communion without going to Confession.

The Prefect of the Boarding Students shall take considerable time, at least six months, to prepare those who are to make their First Holy Communion. With the advice of the Superior, the Prefect shall procure this advantage for those who are judged ready, on the basis of their piety and good conduct; the benefit they have derived from the instructions given them; the fact that they are at least twelve or thirteen years old; and their ability to preserve the grace of their First Holy Communion. If some of the boarders have not been Confirmed, the Prefect shall prepare them to receive the sacrament of Confirmation, if this can be arranged.

The Prefect shall teach the boarders how necessary it is to pray often, and shall teach them how to do so well. The Prefect shall take care that they faithfully perform this duty with piety.

The Prefect shall also remind them of the promises made at Baptism, and shall remind them of the renunciations they agreed to by the words of their godparents.

The Prefect shall inspire them with deep respect for the most Holy Sacrament of the Altar, and shall make them pay attention in church and during divine services, especially holy Mass. Boarders must understand that those who do not pray to God during this time are considered as having missed holy Mass; as such, they are obliged to confess this as though they had been absent entirely.

The Prefect shall inspire the boarders with a special devotion toward the most Blessed Virgin, Saint Joseph, their Guardian Angel, and their holy Patron, the Saint after whom they were named. The Prefect will have them read the summary of the lives of these Saints, or will relate it to them, thus making them look up to their holy Patrons. Those who are especially devout to these Patrons shall be given some reward.

Little by little, the Prefect shall inspire the boarders to practice piety. The Prefect shall carefully seek to preserve their baptismal innocence, and shall try to give them a high esteem for it and help them to understand its advantage.

Finally, the Prefect shall teach them reading, writing, arithmetic, and the rules of good manners. The Prefect shall especially teach them the rules found in *Les Règles de la Civilité chrétienne*, and must do this with much care to teach the boarders as nearly perfectly as possible.

One or several teachers shall be designated by the Superior to sleep in the boarders' dormitories and so to see that nothing improper happens there during the night. The Superior may change these teachers from time to time. This change is made at the end of morning prayer.

The Prefect of the Boarding Students, or Prefects if there are several, shall go to the dormitories to replace the teachers who have slept there. They are to insure that in rising and dressing the students are not guilty of any immodesty.

Once the boarders have left the dormitories, the Prefect shall have the windows opened, so that proper ventilation may take place. The Prefect shall also have these dormitories properly swept and see that this is done in silence. The Prefect shall faithfully see to it that the boarders observe the daily schedule prescribed for them.

Various Types of Community Houses in This Institute

To insure the full attainment of its end, this Institute shall include three sorts of Community Houses. In each of these, most of the exercises shall be different.

First, there shall be a Community House where those who offer themselves as candidates are trained and brought up in the spirit of this Institute.

Second, there shall be Community Houses in which live the teachers who conduct gratuitous schools.

Third, there may be Community Houses which are like seminaries, in which the teachers of this Institute spend some years training teachers for the parishes of small cities, towns, and villages in the country.

All Community Houses for schools conducted by the teachers of this Institute shall be in cities. In all of these, there shall be at least five teachers. Four will take care of the school, one of whom will be in charge of the Community House. The fifth, [usually referred to as a "serving Brother"], will take care of the temporal needs of the house and, if need be, replace a teacher who might fall ill or need a few days' rest.

However, there might still be Community Houses with only two teachers, but these shall be very few. Each such Community House shall be near some city where there is a complete Community House of the Institute. Community Houses of two members may also be occupied by teachers who, either old or infirm, need a place to rest and so may also reside in a house having only two teachers.

Notes

Foreword

1. *Cahiers lasalliens:* a collection of more than fifty scholarly studies on the life and work of John Baptist de La Salle, including many of his original writings. (Rome, Casa Generalizia).

Introduction

1. While the Brothers did not teach Latin grammar and composition, they did teach the reading of Latin after reading French had been mastered. This facilitated attendance at Church services.

2. For a thorough treatment of the use of the vernacular in eighteenth-century French schools, see the essays by Davis and Poutet, in *So Favored by Grace* (Lasallian Publications, 1991).

Preface

1. This third part is not included in the 1720 edition, from which this translation was made. However, it does appear in the 1706 ms. (Appendix A) and in the Avignon ms. (Appendix C).

Part One, Chapter 2

1. To the five decades which constitute a third part of the rosary and form a chaplet, the Brothers of the Christian Schools add a sixth decade in honor of the Immaculate Conception, for the needs of the Institute.

2. The 1706 ms. has here an *article 3,* on the collection and distribution of bread at breakfast in school. *See* Appendix B, Extract 1, pp. 235–236.

Part One, Chapter 3

1. The models of these two charts can be found at the end of Part Two, pp. 181–182.

2. The models of these charts are found at the end of Part Two, pp. 183–185.

Part One, Chapter 4

1. The 1706 ms. of *Conduite* has here an eighth level of students writing round hand, which is interesting in that it emphasizes the practicality of lessons in De La Salle's schools. See Appendix B, Extract 2, pp. 236–237.

Part One, Chapter 5

1. The *denier* was the smallest unit in the French monetary system. At the time of De La Salle the cost of living for a Brother was 200-250 *livres* per year. Twelve *deniers* equalled one *sol;* twenty *sols* equalled one *livre.*

Part One, Chapter 7

1. The hymn, "Come Holy Spirit," was said in school in Latin in the morning and in French in the afternoon.

2. The duration of this pause was to be about the length of time needed to recite the fifty-first psalm, which in Latin begins with the word, *Miserere* ("Have Mercy, O Lord!").

Part One, Chapter 8

1. Actually, this is found in Chapter 10.

2. In France it was the custom in many places for different families in a parish to make, in turn, an offering of small loaves of bread or rolls. This bread was blessed at high Mass and distributed to the faithful present.

Part One, Chapter 9

1. At this point in the 1706 ms. of *Conduite* an article 6 appears, on students who attend only for catechism, and that, on Sunday and feasts. *See* Appendix B, Extract 3, pp. 237–238.

Part One, Chapter 10

1. In the 1706 ms. of *Conduite,* the current Chapter 10 was Chapter 11. The 1706 ms. had a Chapter 10 which was entitled "Hymns." However, only the title appears; the rest of the page is blank. *See* CL 24:109.

Part Two, Chapter 1

1. A sabot is a wooden shoe, or a heavy leather shoe with a wooden sole, worn by peasants.

Part Two, Chapter 3

1. The Preface to Chapter 3 of the 1720 edition lists three kinds of registers, while the 1706 ms. lists six. *See* Appendix B, Extract 4, p. 239. The four registers found only in the 1706 ms. also appear in Appendix B: the Admissions Register, and the model, Extract 5, pp. 239–241; The Register of Good and Bad Qualities of Students, and the model, Extract 6, pp. 241–243; the Register of the First Student in the Bench, and the model Register of Attendance, Extract 7, p. 244; and the Register of Home Visitations, and the model Extract 8, p. 245.

2. No further mention is made of this Pocket Register.

3. An explanation of the terms used here appears in the Introduction to this text. *See* pp. 34–35.

Part Two, Chapter 5

1. These introductory remarks about correction are a significant change from what appeared in the 1706 ms. There, only two brief paragraphs introduced the observations about correction. That introduction is found in Appendix B, Extract 9, p. 246.

2. French has two forms of the pronoun "you" and its derived forms. Usually the singular, *"tu, toi, ton,"* is used for family, friends, closeness, familiarity, while the plural, *"vous, votre,"* shows respect, formality, separation.

3. Since all the teachers in the Christian schools at that time were Brothers, all would have made a novitiate upon entering the Institute.

Part Two, Chapter 6

1. In the original printed edition of 1720, there is an inconsistency in this Chapter in labelling "articles" and "sections." We have resolved this by labelling all parts "articles." See CL 24:180-196.

2. At this point in the 1706 ms. of *Conduite,* there is additional material on why children miss school. *See* Appendix B, Extract 10, pp. 246–247.

3. The 1706 ms. has here an "article 4," on punishing students who have been absent or tardy without permission. *See* Appendix B, Extract 11, pp. 247–248.

Part Two, Chapter 7

1. The Rogation Days are the three days before Ascension Thursday, on which processions of penance and supplication were widely held.

2. This of course refers to swimming in public, and probably nude.

3. It is customary in some Catholic areas to celebrate this Mass of the Holy Spirit to invoke divine inspiration at the opening of schools, parliaments, courts of justice, deliberative assemblies, and like activities.

Part Two, Chapter 8

1. The 1706 ms. has here a list of class officers. No listing appears at this point in the 1720 edition; however, all but five of these officers, the second, third, eighth, ninth, and eleventh, are retained and job descriptions as provided in this chapter. *See* Appendix B, Extract 12, p. 248.

2. The 1706 ms. has here the job descriptions of the Mass Officer and of the Almoner. *See* Appendix B, Extract 13, pp. 249–250, for the Mass Officer and Extract 14, p. 250, for the Almoner.

3. A short-handled brush or perforated globe holding a sponge and used for sprinkling holy water.

4. The 1706 ms. has here descriptions of the jobs of First Student in the Bench and of Visitors of the Absent Students. *See* Appendix B, Extract 15, p. 251, and Extract 16, pp. 251–253.

5. The 1706 ms. has here a description of the job of Distributor and Collector of Books. *See* Appendix B, Extract 17, p. 254.

Part Two, Chapter 9

1. This chapter does not exist in the 1706 ms. of *Conduite.*

2. This list is not in the 1706 ms.

Appendix A, Chapter 1

1. *See* CL 24:249-290. This is a translation of material found in the 1706 ms. of *Conduite*.

2. These were large pieces of paper or cardboard bearing some of the more important school maxims and rules, and posted on the walls. A teacher merely pointed to one or another when something was out of order.

Appendix A, Chapter 2

1. In seventeenth-century France epilepsy was considered a communicable disease.

Appendix A, Chapter 3

1. "Aliquot" identifies the number that is contained an exact number of times in something else; for example, a fraction and its percent equivalent, such as ⅛ and 12½%.

Appendix A, Chapter 4

1. There is no Article 3 in the 1706 ms. *See* CL 24:277.

2. This is entitled Section 6 in the 1706 ms. *See* CL 24:286.

Appendix C

1. This is a translation of a document found in the Departmental Archives of Vaucluse (Avignon), classified under "Brothers of the Christian Schools of Avignon," (H.1.2.3.). It is a simple copy book with no cover, about 46 by 36 centimeters, in 24 pages, plus a few lines. The entire manuscript is in good eighteenth-century calligraphy. In addition to the "Training of New Teachers," the document includes the "Manual for the Prefect of Boarding Students" and a listing of the "Various Types of Community Houses in This Institute." Although "Training of New Teachers" presents itself as Part Three of *Conduite*, it is neither found in the 1706 manuscript nor in the 1720 printed edition. The text here is a translation of the document as found on pages 305-319 of the 1951 French *édition critique* of *Conduite*.

2. The word "correction" in this text invariably refers to corporal punishment.

3. The following was scratched out in the original: "The Supervisor must not too readily permit them to correct students with the strap [cat-o'-nine-tails] or the rod. Above all, the Supervisor must insist that

such correction be done in the presence of the Inspector or the Supervisor, who must not allow that more than three strokes be given. These must neither be given too quickly nor with over-eagerness. Rather, they must be administered in the manner set down in the Rules." These lines were probably part of the original text but were suppressed some time in the eighteenth century.

4. This paragraph seems to be a later addition to the text.

5. The following does not correspond exactly with the items above, but seems rather to be a collection of various disparate recommendations.

6. This job description of the prefect of boarding students is not part of the original *Conduite*. However, the boarding school of Saint Yon (Rouen), which opened in 1705, and the continued involvement of the Brothers in boarding schools could easily be the inspiration for this manual.

Index

The Editors

Brother Richard Arnandez, FSC, was born in New Iberia, Louisiana. From 1933 to 1936, he taught in the boarding school of the De La Salle Christian Brothers in Passy-Froyennes, Belgium. He holds a bachelor's degree from Manhattan College and a *Licence ès Lettres* from the University of Lille, France. After a number of years as teacher and administrator, Brother Richard was appointed Visitor of the New Orleans-Santa Fe District. From 1969 to 1972 he served in Rome as Secretary General and Vice-Procurator General of the Institute. He is the author of several books and journal articles, and is a professional translator.

F. de La Fontainerie originally translated *The Conduct of the Schools of Jean-Baptiste de La Salle* as one of the McGraw-Hill Education Classics in 1935.

Brother Edward Everett, FSC, was born in Chicago in 1929 and entered the De La Salle Christian Brothers in 1946. He received his bachelor's and master's degrees from St. Mary's University of Minnesota and, in 1984, his doctorate in philosophy from Loyola University, Chicago. He has many years of experience in secondary and university teaching and administration, including three years in Belgium. Since 1994 he has been a member of the education department at Christ the Teacher Institute of Education in Nairobi, Kenya.

Brother William Mann, FSC, was born in New York in 1947 and entered the De La Salle Christian Brothers after graduating from Bishop Loughlin Memorial High School, Brooklyn. He earned a bachelor's degree from the Catholic University of America, master's degrees from the State University of New York at Stony Brook and from Salve Regina University, and, in 1990, a Doctor of Ministry degree from Colgate Rochester Divinity School. He taught at various schools in the Long Island-New England District before becoming its Assistant Visitor in 1979. From 1984 until 1990, he served as Director of Novices in the USA and Toronto Region, after which he assumed duties as Secretary of Formation for the entire congregation, residing in Rome. In 1996 he was named to serve as Visitor for the Long Island-New England district.